*f*P

THE CATERPILLAR DOESN'T KNOW

HOW PERSONAL CHANGE IS CREATING ORGANIZATIONAL CHANGE

KENNETH R. HEY
PETER D. MOORE

THE FREE PRESS

NEW YORK   LONDON   TORONTO   SYDNEY   SINGAPORE

THE FREE PRESS
A Division of Simon & Schuster Inc.
1230 Avenue of the Americas
New York, NY 10020

Designed by Michael Mendelsohn of MM Design 2000, Inc.

Manufactured in the United States of America

10 9 8 7 6 5 4 3 2 1

Hey, Kenneth R., 1944–
    The caterpillar doesn't know : how personal change is creating
organizational change / Kenneth R. Hey, Peter D. Moore.
        p.   cm.
    Includes bibliographical references and index.
    1. Organizational change.   2. Management.   3. Social change.
4. Consumers—Attitudes.   I. Moore, Peter D., 1943–   .   II. Title.
HD58.8.H494   1998
658.4'06—DC21
                                                              98–11999
                                                              CIP

ISBN 0–684–83429–4

*To Doris, for her "Lean on Me" support
and her "Blue Skies" disposition*
—KENNETH

*To Wendy, Sarah, Max and Jordan,
who continually inspire me to push water uphill*
—PETER

CONTENTS

PREFACE

RUNNING WATER IN A BUCKET

"Don't forget, most experts are using only half a brain." Our late partner, Ben Goodspeed, penned those words in his book *The Tao Jones Averages* (1983). In his text, he favored using both the left side of the brain (analytical) and the right side (intuitive) in order to create "whole brain" thought. He argued against "analexia," the tendency to accept as worthwhile only those areas that lend themselves to measurement, and he warned against "scientific fundamentalism," which depended upon specialists with narrower and narrower areas of expertise to attempt to describe a more and more complex and interrelated world. Citing Lao Tsu, the founder of Taoism, Goodspeed noted that using analysis and specialization to learn about a constantly changing world was like trying to understand running water by catching it in a bucket.

Goodspeed reported that the post–World War II world had given a huge boost to the rise of experts, specialists and charismatic leaders—all of whom, while advancing their own special areas of interest, had robbed us of our own confidence. Writing in the early 1980s, he saw that some of these experts were experiencing difficulties. He added that society's excessive dependence was changing and that individual abilities and responsibilities were regaining appeal, thus threatening the dominance of doctors, lawyers, politicians, professors and others who carefully controlled their special knowledge. "As we gain more self-confidence, we are coming to rely more on our own ability to sense reality directly," Goodspeed wrote, "and conversely, we are less likely to blindly follow the experts who claim to have all the answers." To a certain extent, our book is the story of how that subtle shift in perspective, when accelerated by unanticipated changes in the social, political and institutional milieu, redirected individuals away first from the leaders

and then from the institutions that dominated postwar America—and
how that shift eventually restructured the relationships between individuals and institutions.

A BOOK ABOUT CHANGE: "MORE, BETTER, FASTER" MEETS "ENOUGH IS ENOUGH"

We have organized the content of this book into three parts. Part I, "The
Pursuit of Wealth," outlines the success of post–World War II institutions but describes new realities that threaten their continued viability.
Organizations have a problem: Their time as a successful caterpillar has
dwindled. Part II, "The Pursuit of Meaning," outlines why old organizations have a problem: Individuals have undertaken deep personal
changes, and they do not relate to organizations, services and products
that do not harmonize with their new attitudes and values. Part III, "Sustainable Relationships," adds that some organizations are undertaking a
reassessment process to transform what they have been and also are creating a more viable organization—one that values and develops enduring relationships with employees and customers.

Chapters within each part develop the story of a changed and
changing society arising from changed and changing individuals. To
make connections clearer between what is happening and how leaders
need to alter their perspectives, each chapter concludes with a Critical
Insight which highlights a new way of looking at society's evolving
realities.

To offer an overview, Chapter 1 outlines the organizational problem. A disconnect between leaders and "followers" has created a battle
for control over which perspective—the old or the new—will be in
place in the years ahead. In the first Critical Insight section, we observe
that institutional leaders need to recognize the difference between tactical restructuring, which they have been trying at great expense and with
fewer and fewer favorable results, and strategic restructuring, which
involves a much more thoroughgoing assessment of what has taken
place in society, and how institutions must realign with the new consumer, employee and citizen.

Chapter 2 retraces the success of post–World War II institutions, most of which have had as their primary organizing principle the advancement and spread of wealth. Their success over several decades has now become a problem because institutional leaders, who rose to prominence within these communities of wealth, are not grasping the significance of the personal changes under way. The second chapter's Critical Insight draws a clear distinction between cyclical and secular changes in the economy.

Chapter 3 describes how the communities of wealth started losing their impact in "a world out of control." Starting in the middle 1980s, everywhere individuals looked they saw institutional breakdowns and leadership failures. As you reach this portion of the book, you should sense that consumers, employees and citizens could not have continued acting as if nothing had changed. They needed to see things differently. This chapter's Critical Insight identifies Magic Eye, a children's visual game that requires using a new way of focusing on an image in order to grasp a deeper and more lucid meaning than at first is seen, as a metaphor to help leaders understand the deeper meaning behind society's seeming chaos.

Part II starts with Chapter 4 and shares with you both the ways in which individuals responded to the world out of control and how they reassessed their personal priorities as a result. This personal reorientation altered markets, jobs, politics and personal relationships. For the Critical Insight section, we note that women have led this personal revolution and that their actions have served as leading indicators for those broad societal changes.

Chapter 5 looks at the consequences of the personal revolution on the communities of wealth. We examine what kinds of groups and organizations individuals have founded on their own and ultimately conclude that something we call "the communities of meaning" are displacing the old wealth-driven organizations. We suggest that institutions will need to rethink the way they set goals, provide incentives and establish relationships in the years ahead, in order to accommodate the employees' and consumers' new interests. The personal-reassessment process that is motivating this search for a new institutional relationship also stands behind a new definition of "the pursuit of happiness," the subject of this chapter's Critical Insight.

Part III opens with Chapter 6, which looks at how institutions have so far responded to these massive personal changes. Some have ignored them, others have revealed an interest in piecemeal adjustments, and a few have even undergone significant change. In the Critical Insight section, we offer two metaphors—natural horsemanship and fly-fishing—which, if properly understood, can guide those who seek to make real changes in their own organizations.

The world out of control and the resulting personal reassessment shredded the old social contract. In Chapter 7, we look at companies that are leading the effort to create a new and rewarding relationship between employees and the workplace. Because of the need for a new social contract, companies must shift from the old metaphoric model of a "lean machine" to a new, more effective metaphor, that of a "vital organism." That shift is the subject of this chapter's Critical Insight.

While companies need to restructure the employee–employer relationship, they also need to rethink their understanding of, and relationship to, the marketplace. The personal changes that are affecting employee needs and interests are also affecting consumers, creating a new market reality. The fundamentals of this new market reality receive attention in Chapter 8, and the connected Critical Insight section discusses the way in which what we call "context" marketing has created some interesting and different connections to consumers.

As you, the patient reader, finally reach Chapter 9, we hope you will feel optimistic about the potential for real change as we look at the ways in which institutions are responding overall to the new employee/consumer, and we highlight some actions that have worked for some companies so far. When undertaking a strategic restructuring, each organization must start with its own unique parameters, and therefore, no single answer or theory will work, and we offer none here. Strategic restructuring is a process, not an established set of goals, and the process requires letting go and opening up. Because of that requirement, leaders who themselves have passed through the personal-reassessment process will best be able to acknowledge the need for such a process at the institutional level. That topic—personal transformation—constitutes our final Critical Insight section.

Our observations tell us that the "more, better, faster" mentality that drove the communities of wealth through decades of success has now run headlong into a personal reassessment that insists "Enough is enough." Only this explanation answers real business questions about why, in the seventh year of the recent economic recovery, price increases were nearly impossible to try, and why voluntary employee turnover rates increased despite offers of higher salaries. We hope you will realize that individuals who drive American culture have changed, and that the changes are not temporary.

Companies have spent huge amounts of money reorganizing, reinventing, reengineering and TQMing themselves into a corner. *Any* theory applied to *all* companies usually falls short of its promise. We do not offer yet another single answer. We do, however, suggest that the needed strategic restructuring must take into account the personal revolution that has changed American society. Recognition of a changed individual should underlie the entire process of changing the organization. For that reason, leaders need to think of consumers and employees as the same people in different roles and must work to develop an organization that brings those two elements into harmony.

ACKNOWLEDGMENTS

This book covers a wide array of subjects and gathers information from an equally wide array of resources. It seeks to bring that spread of material into a context that is both readable and usable. Such a task lies well beyond our authorial abilities, and for that reason we have many people to thank for their insights, contributions and support.

Inferential Focus is a collaborative enterprise, a unique combination of personalities, interests, capabilities and preparation. Likewise, this book is a collaboration, involving as it does all four principal partners. While just two of our names appear on the cover, the work is equally that of Charlie Hess and Joe Kelly. Also, none of these ideas would have reached printed form without the diligence and skill of still another partner, Fran Insinga. Throughout the project, IF staff—Mila Brojan, Michele Fischetti, Risa Hess and Gene Brojan—offered their time and energy to see that materials were put together and delivered on time. Despite our often changing demeanor, they managed to maintain a sense of humor throughout.

At Inferential Focus we are fortunate to have clients who enjoy discussing the topics we raise, and as a result we have benefited from their observations and insights as well. Over the years, we have enjoyed open and enlightening conversations with leaders at American Express, AIG, AT&T, Bankers Trust, Cigna Insurance, ED&F Man, Fidelity Investments, GE Capital, KeyCorp, Leo Burnett, Merrill Lynch, MetLife, J.P. Morgan, NationsBank, PepsiCo, Philip Morris and the White House. All of that personal contact certainly made the content of this book better, and we feel fortunate indeed to have been allowed to engage these many talented people in conversations that eventually affected this book's scope and focus. However, several individuals contributed directly to the content by reading and commenting on it and by offering observations that found their way into the text. Specifically, we would like to thank Ron Askenas, Harry Beckwith, Arthur Einstein, Jan Klug, Geoff Moore and Jim Oates.

Our agent, Jim Levine, stayed with the project from start to finish, making invaluable contributions in the book's early stages and offering useful suggestions as the text emerged. He also kept the project moving on the bureaucratic side, freeing us to concentrate on our work.

Even with a unique collaborative process, diligent staff, involved clients and persevering agent, we would still have fallen short of a complete text without wonderful editorial assistance—first from Curtis Hartman, who brought order to the chaos of a rough copy, and then from Free Press's Bob Wallace, who saw the work through to its present form. Editing is such a delicate contribution that often its final effect is overlooked; readers rarely are aware that an editor's fine touches have throughout been hidden within the lines they learn from and enjoy. Such seeming reader oversight in this instance merely verifies editing quality.

Offering special thanks to all who had a direct impact on the text misses a less obvious but perhaps even more important contribution: that of moral and personal support. We both had that in abundance. Wendy, Sarah, Max and Jordan Moore and Doris Von Glahn stood behind us at every moment and also accepted additional duties in order to free our time to see this project through. We are both fortunate and thankful for their understanding and patience.

A book is a strange undertaking, one that starts with a deceptively simple idea captured in passing and grows into a mind- and time-consuming project around which one's entire life seems to revolve. And then it's *over.* In between our idea and the finished product, we were fortunate to have the support and backing of the best colleagues, clients, professionals, friends and family anyone could hope for.

PROLOGUE

INTO THE COCOON

As president of Electronic Data Services (EDS) from 1979 to 1986, Mort Meyerson made a lot of money—for himself, his employees, and his investors. He loved the game, and he loved winning. To succeed in such a commanding way, he had to drive employees through 80-hour weeks and push clients through grueling negotiations. He punished competitors, squeezed profits from the operations and increased shareholder value. In short, he worked the system, played to win, pushed the envelope, pursued excellence and realized all the other clichés that commentators often used to describe a successful leader at that time.

In 1986, when General Motors bought EDS, Meyerson, satisfied with his work, left the company. But in the six-year interim before returning to the fray in order to run Perot Systems, he reached some startling conclusions about what he had done. For example, he learned that while he had indeed made people wealthy, he had also made them miserable. (After he left, they told him so.) He also realized that while he had exacted huge sums of money from customers, he had also insulted their intelligence. (They, too, told him so.) These new perspectives moved him to rethink what he had done. In moments of reflection, he wondered: "In order to be rich, do I have to make people miserable? In order to run a successful company, do I have to beat up on the customers?"

Despite his successes, he ultimately admitted that the answer to both questions was "no." Upon reflection, he could see that the implied tradeoffs—misery for wealth, insulting relationships for success—were starting to tilt more forcefully toward the negatives, that employees and customers alike were resenting the tradeoffs, and that eventually the business would suffer. The profits that resulted from the old way of operating would decline, the best employees (the ones who produced the most) would find a better place to work, and the customers who paid handsomely for what those employees did would drift away. "If our company were entered in a 100-yard dash," he later mused, "we were beginning the race from 50 yards behind the starting line." The corporate culture he had created, the one that seemed to succeed so well by historical standards, was killing the company's vibrancy.

As these reflections suggest, during his personal hiatus between running EDS and returning to run Perot Systems, Meyerson changed. He rethought his views on relationships, on work and money and on what employees and customers want and need. During this period of reassessment, he cast aside old attitudes and practices, and focused on developing new ones which matched his new perspective. Every morning, Meyerson walked to a mirror and said to himself: "You don't get it. . . . You're like a highly specialized trained beast that evolved during one period, and now you can't adjust to the new environment." Rather than fade into extinction, as his beast metaphor implied, Meyerson envisioned himself as a caterpillar spinning a cocoon, prepared to change, all the while not knowing in what way or how. Letting go of so much control, over even personal matters, frightened the once-confident, sure-minded leader. Meyerson reminded himself of what Tony Athos once said: "The caterpillar doesn't know that he'll come out as a butterfly. All he knows is that he's alone, it's dark, and it's a little scary."

After Meyerson himself had changed, he realized that institutions, to be successful in a world filled with changing individuals like him, must also change. They, too, must pass through a period of reflection and reassessment. In short, they must transform themselves. "Organizations must change radically," Meyerson later told an interviewer. "We are at the beginning of a revolutionary time in business. Not just an evolutionary time. Not a year-to-year change. A fundamental revolution. Many companies that have enjoyed decades of fabulous success will find themselves out of business in the next five years if they don't make revolutionary changes."

In 1992, Meyerson became CEO of Perot Systems, and in just six months realized that his new company was repeating the same bad practices of EDS—practices that he now knew to be ineffective in the long term. Intuitively, he knew that such an approach would result in the same 50-yard disadvantage that EDS had created for itself. Slowly, he implemented changes that would avoid such a competitive disadvantage, and he first targeted the obstacle that has always prevented companies from successfully making fundamental changes: the compensation system.

As constituted at Perot, that system included incentives which encouraged employees to do anything that benefited the bottom line. "The emphasis on profit-and-loss to the exclusion of other values was creating a culture of destructive contention," he told a journalist. It encouraged employees to take actions that were good for them and the company in the short term but "weren't in the company's long-term interest." To be successful in this bottom-line, winner-take-all atmosphere, "You had to be tougher, smarter, sharper. You had to prove that you could make money. You had to prove that you could win at negotiations [with customers] every time." In other words, to be successful in this type of compensation program, an employee had to undermine the very relationships that ultimately would help the company succeed in the long term. "[At the time] it never occurred to me that winning big could be a negative thing." After his personal reassessment, he knew that the old definition of "winning" had side effects and consequences heretofore ignored in the name of short-term gain.

While Meyerson recognized the need to reassess both Perot Systems' fundamental goals and its policies for realizing those goals, he did not want to *impose* those changes on the organization. He wanted ideas and solutions to emerge from within the company. He would serve as motivator and facilitator, but not as dictator. In pursuit of this approach, Meyerson scheduled company-wide seminars to allow employees and leaders to wrestle with what they were really trying to do and to learn how to disagree without tearing each other apart (as the old competitive culture had encouraged). They met to learn how to enter into agreements with customers as partners, not as dominated clients, and to discuss how individuals could initiate their own personal reassessments that might create better ways to lead. He convened other gatherings to discuss, develop and then draft the values that the company should adopt, and behavioral styles which the employees wanted to accept. Meyerson and all employees were, in short, discovering the company's new basis for strategic planning and operations. They were beginning a strategic restructuring of the organization.

EMERGING FROM THE COCOON

The institutional reassessment that Meyerson initiated transformed Perot Systems; indeed, it created a new corporate culture. It changed the compensation package to fit the new values that the company embodied. It reworked the employee evaluation system, installing a new 360-degree review approach that gathered information not only on the employee's financial performance but on his or her attitude, energy, sociability and growth, and it acquired this information not just from bosses but also from peers, subordinates and customers. These ratings from all sides of the employee's activities affected bonuses and other compensation. Profit moved down the list of principal salary determinants.

Meyerson was particularly gratified: "We started to behave like a company whose people not only focused on day-to-day business and economic performance, but also concerned themselves with the well-being of the people and their teams, and the concerns of the customer. We were becoming a company where the larger issues of life were as important as the demands of a profit-or-loss performance—a human organization."

Even though the reassessment's resulting procedures and value seemed extreme at the time, they nonetheless proved effective, helping the company to avoid the potential 50-yard disadvantage that bothered Meyerson. In 1996, when Meyerson stepped aside as CEO, Perot Systems had increased its revenues 90 percent during the prior year. At the end of 1997, when he left Perot Systems to reflect and think about his next project, he left behind a company that had reverted back to old management models, still resisting significant change. While he had moved forward, Perot Systems had stepped backward.

In Meyerson's mind, the transformation from the old bottom-line-only perspective to the "human organization" perspective is part of a larger historical shift that affects all aspects of business. "There's a much larger calling in business today than was allowed by the old definitions of winning and losing," he later commented. "One hundred years from now, we'll know we were on the right track if there are more organizations where people are doing great work for their customers and creating value for their shareholders. And raising their children, nurturing their families, and taking an interest in their communities. And feeling proud of the contributions they make. These are the things you can't measure when winning and losing are the only financial metrics."

Why did this highly successful leader, guiding a highly successful company, reach a point where radical change—a strategic restructuring—was the only answer? What changed in the world around him, and what change of perspective did he undergo that urged him to focus on restructuring his company? What changes were taking place in society so that the company's new procedures worked so successfully in the marketplace?

This book answers these questions, and tries to help you to understand the very forces for change that Meyerson intuitively recognized and acted upon. According to our observations, Meyerson's reassessment exemplifies the personal transformation that forward-looking leaders themselves must undergo before they can lead the organizational transformations necessary for companies to forge sustainable relationships with employees and customers. The reassessment process that leads to such a transformation has been under way for several years among individuals in our society. Leaders need to see those changes in their employees and customers, recognize the power of those changes, and put themselves into the process.

We intend this book to be a catalyst for this kind of transformation. We want to alter the way you look at what is taking place around you, to bring a new context to the overload of information you face and to encourage you to rethink your perspective on what is the best course of action for your organization in the years ahead. By showing you how others are addressing this new business environment, we hope to give you a basis on which to act, as well.

We realize that this is no small order, but we also know that our intelligence methodology, which we describe in the Appendix, is as rigorous as it is unique. As a result, we feel comfortable in encouraging you to initiate a reassessment process. As you read through this book, we hope you will become so engaged by the methodology, as well as the content, that you will begin to apply our discipline to observations you make herein as well. We would like this book to help you *rethink your perspective on* what is taking place around you *by altering the way you look at* what is taking place around you. If we can succeed in this, we feel that you will understand the transformation process better than Meyerson's caterpillar does its own—and even become comfortable with what that means for you.

PART I

The Pursuit
of Wealth

T he harder America's business and political leaders try to link with citizens, consumers, and employees, the less connected they become. The more aggressively politicians try to guide citizen opinion, the more distant they seem. The more value business leaders add to their stock and the more costs they cut from their operations, the more alienated their employees become. The louder marketers yell and the less they charge, the more isolated from American consumers they appear to be.

Leaders are clinging to ineffective tactics, even in the face of new cultural realities, simply because these tactics have worked so well for so long. For more than 50 years, experience-proven actions have helped expand America's economic fortunes—but that very longevity has led many leaders to conclude mistakenly that the success would continue indefinitely. When critical problems started to surface, leaders misinterpreted the signals, misunderstood the implications and prescribed the wrong actions.

While leaders were making decisions based upon one view of society, Americans were experiencing a very different reality.

Unlike most leaders who viewed contemporary market and political problems as temporary aberrations, individuals in general were experiencing a world completely out of control. Americans soon realized that their leaders "just didn't get it" and that their institutions were incapable of halting the spreading chaos. In time, Americans disconnected (some emotionally and others physically) from the old institutions, creating a cultural division that promises to keep leaders distant, isolated and eventually ineffective.

Confronted with citizens, consumers and employees who no longer operate the same as before, leaders do not need another operations manual telling them "how to" make their institutions work more efficiently. They do not need another journal article explaining motivations, margins and economic survival. They need *a new perspective on what is taking place in society,* because if they continue to misunderstand what Americans are doing, they will continue to misinterpret their behavior and consequently to misapply institutional resources. In short, leaders, before they take any further contrary actions, need a new, broader and more accurate perspective on what is happening in contemporary American society.

CHAPTER 1

CHANGE AND THE BATTLE FOR CONTROL

IN THE INFORMATION AGE, INFORMATION IS A NUISANCE

I'll believe it when I see it" intones the empiricist when confronted with new evidence. What the reluctant observer really means, however, is "I'll see it when I believe it." Breaking old beliefs and seeing real change can be extraordinarily uncomfortable for some people, yet in periods of significant change, like the present, this resistance to seeing can be a costly liability. In fact, both seeing real change and understanding its implications are absolutely essential to organizational survival.

In *Only the Paranoid Survive* (1996), Andrew S. Grove, president and CEO of Intel, admitted that identifying crucial moments of change has become extremely difficult for today's leaders. His own experience in the computer-memory business—in the 1980s, his once-dominant company lost its market to the Japanese—taught him that most companies reach a "strategic inflection point . . . a time in the life of a business when its fundamentals are about to change. That change can mean an opportunity to rise to new heights. But it may just as likely signal the beginning of the end." With either growth or stagnation as alternative results, identifying real problems and responding effectively become essential. Grove added: "The ability to recognize that the winds have shifted and to take appropriate action before you wreck your boat is crucial to the future of an enterprise." Curiously enough, following his yachting metaphor, one would expect the boat's captain to see the new situation first and call for corrective action. Yet, according to Grove, "the leader is often the last of all to know." But if the last person to know is also the person organizations depend upon for leadership, how can one lead from behind?

With the disparity between the need to lead and the ability to see real change causing organizational problems, many have resorted to resources that give them a feeling of comfort and control ("the warmth of the herd," as one observer has called it). In recent times, this comfort has come from studies, surveys, polls, focus groups, and other research sources and devices that offer numerically precise conclusions—hard-edged answers to seemingly intractable problems. However, while these approaches may indeed give a warm feeling of control, such numerical distillations of behavior actually represent a step away from actual experience. In essence, because direct observations during periods of change are fraught with complexities requiring time and thought, many leaders have opted for techniques which, in effect, remove them even farther from the very direct experience that can save them at their inflection points.

Rather than analyze the impact of change downward into smaller and smaller units, as traditional research tends to do, executives could use a larger context. They need information—but they also need a reliable context for that information. One of the ironies of the so-called information age is that information *itself* is becoming a nuisance. So much information pours into everyone's daily lives that it crowds out time to think about any of it in depth. Information-begets-reaction begets more information, and yet another reaction. Many leaders who have confronted this overload have responded by narrowing their fields of vision, pushing aside anything reflexively deemed irrelevant and focusing all energies on what seems like a controllable segment of the overall enterprise. In short, they feel comfortable seeing what they believe. They allow limited information to guide them, rather than piecing together a new context that can shape the huge amount of information into an overall picture. Such a new context, which we describe in this book, organizes and arranges significant changes, like pieces of a mosaic, into a larger picture. This context, in turn, gives leaders a vantage point from which to view the flow of events and make effective decisions.

Those who lead with limited understanding of what is changing in society stand in stark contrast to those who have recognized that something has changed and are looking for the new societal, management and economic context. In a way, the two sides are opponents in a battle for control.

The battle for control in American society pits individuals who are moving through a personal reassessment process and forging a new social order as they go against public and private institutions (and their leaders) which are trying to sustain a weakening societal order. The outcome of this struggle will affect how marketers present their products and services to consumers, how organizations recruit and retain employees and how politicians gain and sustain voter confidence. The bald reality of this struggle, however, is that individuals are changing, no matter what the leaders prefer. The sooner that leaders recognize this oncoming tidal wave of social change and take appropriate action, the greater the surge of competitive advantage they will enjoy.

WHAT HAS CHANGED

After World War II, Americans and their institutions launched a joint effort to expand the country's wealth. Businesses sought growth and rising profits, public institutions supported institutional and individual efforts to increase the country's standard of living, and individuals acceded to the general theme of expanding wealth. The unanimity of the quest eliminated any real challenges to the shared social objectives—focusing energy on bringing more people into the quest (social change), and expanding the ability of all institutions to realize that wealth objective (technology and capital investment).

The effort was not small. "We had a grand vision," explained Robert J. Samuelson, in *The Good Life and Its Discontents* (1995). "We didn't merely expect things to get better. We expected all social problems to be solved. We expected business cycles, economic insecurity, poverty, and racism to end. We expected almost limitless personal freedom and self-fulfillment. For those who couldn't live life to its fullest (as a result of old age, disability, or bad luck), we expected a generous social safety net to guarantee decent lives." The massive and unified effort actually realized many of the objectives sought and made genuine progress on others.

Business practices in this period were simple and direct. Incentives that furthered the individual's wealth brought favorable responses from employees, and product-linked images that expressed an enhanced standard of living caught consumers' eyes. As a result, expanding benefits, fewer work hours, rising compensation, and other personnel reforms yielded employee loyalty, while omnipresent advertisements, distribution power, brand-exploiting imagery and other marketing practices brought consumer loyalty. With most everyone accepting the general movement toward greater wealth, these interactions worked smoothly together. "Success" came to equal "financial success" and the "pursuit of wealth," and "power" meant the ability to affect financial outcomes. The homogeneous focus on expanding the standard of living and spreading the pursuit of wealth survived several recessions, widespread social unrest, political corruption, and international change.

In the late 1980s, this economic juggernaut ran into what for a shorthand reference we have called "a world out of control," a period when those leaders and institutions charged with sustaining social, economic and organizational stability as well as social security seemed especially ineffective, and even seemed at times to cause the breakdown of the structure they were supposed to sustain. The 1985 *Challenger* shuttle disaster, which killed professional astronauts and a school teacher alike, triggered the concern about American institutions. Astronauts knew about risks, but the message that NASA sent when it sought a "regular" citizen to fly in the shuttle was that the government agency had eliminated most of the risk. The tragedy seemed to trigger a unique response: If white-coated NASA scientists with all of their expertise and experience could not protect an innocent school teacher, then what else was in danger?

Americans soon learned that they were *all* in danger. Los Angeles freeway shootings, street-corner drive-by shootings, pit-bull dog maulings, unusually forceful hurricanes and floods and earthquakes all gave the feeling that not only street crime but Nature had gotten out of control. In addition, Iran–Contra hearings, the savings-and-loan debacle, religious leaders lacking scruples, celebrity athletes without self-control, and a congressional check-kiting scandal combined to reveal that the country's leaders had apparently lost their moral compass. The scourges of drugs, AIDS, teen violence, and teen pregnancy added to the feeling that institutions created to sustain control were no longer up to the task.

These and other events, especially when crowded together as they were over just a few years, worried victims and observers alike. Collectively, they undermined trust in and support for the old institutional structure. How could an individual remain loyal to a government that allowed the savings-and-loan debacle to extract $500 billion from the taxpayers' pockets? How could a country based on the rule of law have so many corrupt leaders, whether they were heading Wall Street companies, religious institutions, or the U.S. Congress? How could a society that called itself civilized educate and nurture individuals who could sit atop buildings next to Los Angeles freeways and shoot randomly at drivers, or intentionally kill hapless children just because the kids were standing on a street corner at what proved to be the wrong time? How could political discussions among American citizens reach the point where a few individuals could plant a bomb in a public building, hoping to kill everyone inside, yet feel justified in the action? How could a country with such an advanced scientific community with the best research facilities and the greatest wealth on earth not halt the AIDS epidemic? Where does a citizen develop the mind-set to mail bombs to innocent victims? How can individuals protect themselves from strangers who kidnap children from their homes and leave their corpses buried in the woods? How could leaders so casually decide that social-security systems in place for decades should dwindle, that pension plans developed over decades should no longer be the institution's responsibility, and that insurance and health costs, which seemed themselves out of control, could be eased only by passing costs along to the neediest individuals?

These types of thoughts arose because individuals felt that they, too, were becoming victims, specifically of someone else's decisions, and that the institutional structure created to insulate them from these types of problems was both inept and culpable. The structure and its leaders seemed to take care of themselves, often leaving individuals to their own devices—whether they were Hurricane Hugo victims waiting for help that did not come, or embattled citizens watching their property taxes rise 50 percent, their insurance costs more than double, or their health-care quality decline. Individuals felt that institutions had abandoned them and that they were left to their own best devices.

In the midst of this highly destabilized environment, American corporate leaders decided to respond decisively to "globalization" and started downsizing and reengineering. The effect was to further the perception that leaders and their institutions were interested only in advancing their own best interests, even at the cost of making matters worse for individuals. The changes that ensued from this social upheaval broke apart the post–World War II shared focus on expanding and spreading wealth.

Americans faced this new world by disconnecting from these ineffectual institutions and undertaking a complete reassessment of their own priorities, needs and interests. At the end of this extended reassessment process, they discovered that much of what had worked for them in the past would not work any longer. What they had valued they no longer did, and what they had once pursued wholeheartedly they now found bothersome. Many products and services which formerly sparked consumer interest—women's fashions, drop dead vacations, brand-name consumer products—lost their appeal. Starting a job to build a career to validate self-worth and increase personal wealth lost its hold on individuals. Surprising to many managers, employees started saying "no" to job transfers because they were inconvenient and began rejecting lucrative offers to become managers because the positions demanded too much of their time and energy. Much of what worked so well in the post–World War II era now seemed tarnished or wasteful. Individuals had changed.

The battle for control developed because leaders failed to grasp how significant these changes were for employees and consumers. Having focused on their competitive problems (i.e., globalization), they incorrectly assumed that all of the "anger" they saw "out there" resulted from downsizing, not from the reassessment process that individuals had undertaken. Individuals' thinking had changed—and this meant that, whether as citizens, employees or consumers, their *behavior* was in the process of changing also. But leaders stubbornly continued to direct operations, manage employees and guide marketing as if globalization and technological innovation had created this discomfort. Yes, their organizational drive to efficiency was a necessary response to globalization and technological change, but it was insufficient to connect with the new employee–consumer–citizen. While linking with these management abstractions, they were actually disconnecting from the new social realities unfolding before them. The leaders' obsession with productivity overlooked both where employees were headed and what consumers needed.

SIGNIFICANT CHANGES EVERYWHERE

Part of the "noise" that keeps leaders from understanding what is taking place involves, ironically, talk about change. Certainly, many people counsel that nothing has really changed, but far more people counsel that many things are changing. The problem with so many commentaries about change, however, is that they just add more information noise without placing that information in context.

Nearly everyone acknowledges that changes are taking place, but theory usually overrides observations, leading to a battle of opinions that results in stalemate. Essentially, the battle for control is a battle of opinions—or, more specifically, a battle of mind-sets and mentalities. The old mentality, which developed out of post–World War II experience, is confronting a new mentality which emerged out of the changing realities of the past decade. When responding to difficult times, the old mentality resorts to past practices: work longer hours, increase advertising, create more brand-name "buzz," cut costs. None of these approaches connects with an individual passing through a personal reassessment process, and it actually encourages a disconnect (a separation from the organization) for those who have finished the process. Confusion over specifics about what these personal changes mean, and the impact they are having, comes from not only the lack of insights about change, but also from everyone talking so much about change.

Some descriptions of change hint at alterations so huge that effective responses seem impossible. Robert Heilbroner's *Visions of the Future* (1995), William Strauss and Neil Howe's *The Fourth Turning* (1997), James Taylor and Watts Wacker's *The 500-Year Delta* (1997), and Hugh De Santis's *Beyond Progress* (1996) outline "epochal" changes that encompass centuries of development and involve decades of transition. While their sense of something substantial taking place may be accurate, the size of the changes they outline defy a leader's ability to undertake reasonable responses.

Meanwhile, books and articles everywhere describe changes in politics, governments, scientific discoveries, health and other large areas of concern. These changes fight for attention with the daily barrage of "news" about changes in world, national and local events, fashion and style, pop culture, consumer gadgets or any other example from a ceaseless barrage of "what's important now." With so much change noise constantly assaulting the senses, some leaders miss fundamental changes. Most leaders have taken refuge in two areas of change that fit easily with their already existing opinions about what is important.

Globalization, a concept that has stood for everything from transnational manufacturing and marketing to the blend of politics and business on an international scale, has become one of the most facilely adopted concepts of change. For all the talk, however, leaders have boiled down globalization to two things for American businesses: new competition and new markets. Because past "best practices" still yield favorable results in the battle for markets against new competition, leaders have been comfortable with globalization, and for that reason have concentrated their energies on it. Focusing on efficiency became the simplest way to react to new competition and new markets, and that meant cutting costs. Dismissing large numbers of people and forcing cost reductions have given leaders a renewed sense that, even in a world out of control, they *are* in control. Oddly enough, as time goes by and leaders exhort employees to work harder, or entice consumers to spend more, they are finding it harder and harder to trigger the right response. Moreover, they are running out of theories to blame for this shortcoming.

A second area of change that leaders easily acknowledge is technology. They note that changes in technology, and particularly digital technology, have already pushed aside traditional methods in agriculture, manufacturing, and even services, and are moving toward human intelligence itself. Nicholas Negroponte, in *Being Digital* (1995), even suggests that we must stop thinking in terms of things (or atoms) and start thinking in terms of bits and bytes (or electronic impulses). Individuals must change to fit technology more easily. Information-centered cybernetic theorists are even suggesting a change in American consciousness.

Again, business leaders have found technological change quite compatible with their derived concepts of managerial change. After all, technology—which one historian called "the lever of riches"—creates greater productivity, which historically has yielded ever greater profits. In short, technological change has advanced the post–World War II objective of expanding wealth. Again, oddly enough, as time passes these very successes seem to have less and less impact on individuals as they express greater and greater dismay with their work, their leisure time and the "spoils" that advancing technology once promised.

As leaders worry about these problems and seek ever-more-innovative tactics to address them, they have created a huge market for management consultants. In their assertively titled book *The Witch Doctors* (1996), an examination of the plethora of management theories and their gurus, John Micklethwait and Adrian Wooldridge note that "even if [consulting advice] is not all 'bullshit,' then enough of it is to disqualify the rest." Noting that American firms spend roughly $15 billion a year on "outside advice," they advance the critical perspective that the management gurus "are . . . the witch doctors of our age, playing on business people's anxieties in order to sell snake oil." For all the talk, the authors assert, the real problem is not that new ideas are accepted and deployed, but that "these ideas contradict each other. The real problem with management theory is that it is pulling institutions and individuals in conflicting directions." Said another way, institutions lack an overall context for looking at change, and therefore willy-nilly grab the latest "answers" to specific problems, often creating thereby contradictory efforts within their organizations.

Our observations tell us that much of the disparity between management's focus on globalization and technology on the one hand, and the consultant's fix on tactical problems within the organization on the other, occurs because the organization lacks an overall context for what is taking place in society. Consequently, planning new-market and human-resource strategies without first looking at the new context that individuals have developed for themselves is nothing more than mental aerobics.

ANOMALIES AND CHANGE

Recognizing change in individuals requires a close examination of their behavior. Surveys and opinion polls ask people what they think, then assume a connection between those answers and subsequent actions. That is a huge assumption, especially in periods of substantial change. A more reliable approach eliminates this surmise and goes straight to individual actions. Studying individual behavior requires studying events—things that actually happen, rather than posited events.

Studying actual events yields a sense of the expected flow of routine societal events. That is, an observer discerns a pattern of behavior and, if nothing changes, can anticipate certain types of responses to certain types of stimuli or events in the future. In this flow of routine events, *anomalous actions* are the first signals of change. An event which at first glance contradicts what would have been anticipated could be a sign that the dynamics of that social situation are changing. If more of these anomalies surface, then the challenge becomes diagnosing what must have changed so that what seemed, at first glance, like an anomaly is not an anomaly at all, but rather the first event in a new pattern. Sometimes anomalies are just that. But often they are red flags highlighting a change. When they grow in number and become more pronounced, then more significant changes have indeed taken place.

The following anomalies all took place between 1994 and 1997. These anomalies are all signals of individual changes so widespread and so pronounced that they imply significant societal changes as well.

1. By lowering their advertising budget, Marshalls department stores increased sales. In marketing theory, just the reverse should be true. "The greater the 'noise,'" the standard theory says, "the greater the response." Marshalls' experience hinted at a new type of consumer response to commercial messages.

2. Procter & Gamble decreased its hair-care product line by 50 percent and thus increased its market share from 31 percent to 36 percent. Another counterintuitive example that contradicted traditional marketing theory, the P&G change and response offered an insight into how consumers were behaving.

3. Interest rates declined, and housing sales declined. The great power of the Federal Reserve has been to "control" the economy through manipulation of short-term interest rates. In the past, this manipulation has worked. In 1996, the manipulation did not work, indicating a change not only in the relationship between interest rates and consumer behavior but also between an institution (in this case the Federal Reserve) and the economy.

4. In 1996, the number of people paying off their credit-card accounts monthly increased, and the number of people behind in their monthly payments increased. Historically, these statistics have moved in opposite directions, serving as reliable indicators of a weaker or stronger economy. However, movement in the same direction suggests that the links between individuals and the economy are changing, and that the changes vary considerably across economic groups.

5. In 1995, the fourth year of the cyclical recovery, while reporting an average 11 percent annual profits, American businesses laid off roughly as many workers as they did during the 1990–1991 recession. The link between corporate financial health and individual financial welfare had been steady since World War II. This change suggested a disconnect between individuals and institutions, a

disconnect that has had an impact well beyond the employee–employer relationship.

6. In the sixth year of the recent economic recovery, personal bankruptcies rose, reaching 1.2 million filers in 1996, the most in any year in history. As with the disconnect between individuals and institutions, this anomaly suggests a personal and financial disconnect between some consumers and financial institutions, and between individuals and the general economy.

7. By large margins, California voters in the 1996 election passed politically contradictory referenda, one that (a) accepted marijuana use for medicinal purposes, and another that (b) rejected the use of affirmative action to balance institutional access to all races. Those who financed the campaigns in support of their referenda came from completely opposite ends of the political spectrum, the left favoring the marijuana issue and opposing the affirmative-action referendum, and the right favoring the affirmative-action referendum and opposing the marijuana issue. Still, voters passed both measures, signaling that the traditional left–right scale that most commentators and political parties use does not accurately reflect the way individuals think about issues today.

8. A senior executive at a major advertising firm, when offered the top position (one he had long sought, and had been groomed to perform), turned it down. A flood of these types of examples highlight a change in attitude about work and its place in an individual's life.

9. In the third year of the recent recovery, women's apparel prices dropped 4 percent, the steepest decline ever. This confirmed that consumers were approaching the retail market differently because they had reset their personal priorities.

10. In the fifth year of the same recovery, demand drove used-car prices higher, while the lack of demand drove new-car prices (via promotions and rebates) lower. This anomaly indicates that individuals relate differently to products and services they buy, and that this altered relationship is different from the one that had been in place since World War II.

These types of anomalies say quite forcefully that individuals have changed. They also reveal that institutions have not changed. The historical irony is that the leaders of most institutions, because they have responded to globalization and technology, *think* they have changed, and further believe that individuals must catch up with *them*. From their slanted perspective, leaders see these anomalies as simply that, and cling to the idea that the world moves ahead as it always has—with the lone exceptions of globalization and technological change. For them, seeing still follows believing, and they believe the same things they have always believed—so, consequently, they still see things the way they have always seen them.

STARTING THE BATTLE FOR CONTROL

Historian Richard Maxwell Brown, in his book *No Duty to Retreat* (1991), discussed how the American frontier experience altered the British legal tradition of encouraging everyone to flee danger and avoid confrontations. In place of this tradition, Americans developed the concept that any threat should be met head-on, with violence if necessary. Brown noted the gunslinger showdown on a dusty Main Street as the mental model for Americans confronting trouble. That seeming moral obligation became embedded in American perspectives on conflicts, and remains so today, Brown insisted, even though world tensions from the Cold War have vanished and military threats in the world have dwindled. He could well have added that American leaders also adhere to the stand-pat-and-fight mind-set.

Robert J. Samuelson, in *The Good Life and Its Discontents,* recognized this same mentality and suggested it gained widespread approval because of World War II experiences. The allies' ability to overcome an organized and brutal enemy became a metaphor for American "can do" thinking. No problem for the American would be too big or too difficult. Harder work, more discipline, better organization, grueling schedules, hardened leadership, huge rewards, and outsized optimism would always bring desired results.

These traits, as practiced in the contemporary world, have started to cause problems. The more individuals change and anomalies surface, the more companies stick to their best (past) practices and concentrate on their former strengths. For example, in the early 1980s, the more individuals turned to the personal computer to expand their capabilities, the more IBM insisted that its future would always remain in mainframe computers. Only late in the game, at a considerable loss of prestige and market share, did the company shift to personal computers and service. Similarly, as individuals turned to the Internet because it granted them greater control and more effective access to the resources they needed, Microsoft fought to restrict customer range and freedom. The company created operating software to hold onto the customer, and it developed a proprietary "closed architecture" on-line network that housed the customer in a closed architectural environment. But the runaway success of the open-ended Internet and of access providers undermined Microsoft's strategy. Not until losing time denying that his company had lost control of its market did CEO Bill Gates change course, at last responding to the Internet reality and bending company products to accept the "open architecture" approach.

Efficiency became a 1990s management obsession as public and private institutional heads sought to reduce process times and costs in order to do the same thing faster, cheaper and, with luck, better. But even that practice has demonstrated its vulnerabilities in the new reality. General Motors, for example, certainly learned the price of succeeding in the drive toward efficiency. In 1994, having adopted a "just-in-time" delivery system, GM started reducing its staff size. Productivity numbers did indeed respond favorably, but more-concentrated job responsibilities made remaining workers even more crucial to company operations. At GM's giant Buick City complex, remaining workers responded negatively to added production pressures that forced them into overtime schedules, including 12-hour days and six-day weeks. When workers requested additional employees to ease the pressure, GM executives refused. Tempers flared, and the United Auto Workers' 11,500 plant workers went on strike. Because of the new downsized, highly efficient system, Buick City workers made torque converters for

85 percent of all GM automatic transmissions, and trucks delivered these converters "just in time" for utilization. Within a week the strike had shut down 28 of GM's 29 North American assembly plants. In another four days, GM capitulated and agreed to hire another 1,000 hourly workers. The lesson that General Motors should have learned was simple: Downsizing severs links with employees, and risks institutional implosion.

For some companies, the answer to the labor-risk problem that GM experienced has been additional technology. In 1993, for example, U.S. companies invested in excess of $592 billion on capital improvements. However, just $120 billion of that went into new-factory construction. The remainder went into upgrading the efficiency of existing facilities, which they hoped would add productivity without adding workers— that is, they played the technology card. By pursuing the goal of lowering production costs to lower prices, U.S. business leaders are playing the low-cost provider game, a contest that only puts them in direct competition with other efficiency-driven companies, and results in pressure on everyone's margins. Another round of efficiency-driven tactics lowers the price again, and then someone else's efficiency efforts lower the price even more. That is a game of diminishing margins, always demanding another tactic to increase efficiency in order to sustain some profit. Cost-cutting leads to downsizing leads to expanded overtime leads to mergers and acquisitions leads to something else. Leaders fighting this battle for market control are using old-style techniques in a new and different business environment. Like the great theories of change that lack context, this strategy does not take into account how individuals have changed, and what they as employees and consumers need. Leaders are looking around the globe for inspiration while missing significant personal changes in their own markets and organizations.

GM and IBM are not alone. Kellogg's, Ford Motor Company, and Connecticut Mutual Life Insurance have fought the battle for control on the reactionary side. Throughout 1995 and 1996, Kellogg's watched its market share slide while executives insisted that lower prices, better promotions and stronger market presence—techniques from the old style of marketing—would regain lost market share. They were wrong. After a 19 percent reduction in prices, the branded cereal products continued to *lose* market share.

In a similar vein, Ford insisted that its redesigned 1996 Taurus automobile, which had been the best-selling car in the country for the previous three years, would win customer approval even with its price increase and would need no market boost from rebates or special financing. Ford thought it knew its customers, and it felt they would pay the higher price. Ford was wrong. After first-quarter sales declines, Ford offered $500 rebates through 1996, and launched their 1997 model with a $1,000 rebate.

Connecticut Mutual executives offered early-retirement buyout packages to all its 1,650 home-office employees because they were confident that the overwhelming majority of their workers were loyal and wanted to stay. When 1,200 employees accepted the offer, executives realized how disconnected the work force had become from the company. Many other company executives continue to fight a two-front battle for control over an institution that needs to change, but against employees and consumers who already have changed.

Leaders weaned on post–World War II thinking—hold to your singular vision, never deviate, never back down—are ill-equipped for what lies ahead. The social environment that nurtured these values is fading into history, and something entirely different is taking its place. American institutions are having difficulties making the proper adjustments to these new realities precisely because their leaders are still clinging to the old "can do" mentality, and they are creating a battle for control which is turning out to be precisely the wrong approach at exactly the wrong time.

OPTING OUT OF THE BATTLE FOR CONTROL

The more that companies try to gain control over their financial capital by downsizing and rightsizing, the more they lose contact with their employees and customers. The more they rely on "tried and true" research techniques to guide marketing decisions, the more surprised they are when those decisions fail to produce anticipated outcomes. The harder they try to leverage the strength of marketing tools like advertising, product-line extensions, trade promotions and giveaways, the harder it becomes to realize that these tactics no longer have the same impact they once did.

What Intel's Andrew Grove learned about competing in the new marketplace was that everything, including what Intel made and how it marketed, had to change when the company was confronting a strategic inflection point. What formerly worked no longer did, and what formerly proved profitable would soon no longer be so. A similar lesson—this time related to employee relations—was waiting for yet another executive to grasp. Mort Meyerson, the successful executive who pushed EDS and Perot Systems to new levels of profitability, came to that realization. He knew that what had been successful was actually causing troubles and pain. He soon realized simply: "Everything I thought I knew about leadership is wrong." He went to Perot Systems and revamped the way the company related to its employees and its customers, and those changes quickly resulted in increased employee retention and loyalty, which in turn led to gains in customer retention and loyalty and, ultimately, to a better bottom line.

Grove and Meyerson chose to opt out of the battle for control. They recognized the changed environment and let go of past practices, models, and assumptions—the very ones that had made them and their companies successful but also the very ones that would keep their companies from connecting with changed and changing markets and employees in the future. They realized that because markets and individuals had changed in significant ways, they needed to understand and respond effectively to those changes.

Most American institutional leaders have two problems, related to the spreading social revolution, that they have not recognized: a systemic structure inappropriate to both new employees and new consumers, and a lifetime of experience that is pointing them in the wrong direction. They continue to use *tactical* responses to tweak the old system, and deny the need to undertake the *strategic* restructuring that is necessary. The longer they hesitate, the less advantage will they realize in the market when they finally do change. Without grasping the new context, leaders can only plow ahead doing what they have learned in the old environment. In essence, they continue with their tactical restructuring when they should be undertaking a strategic one.

CRITICAL INSIGHT:
Tactical Versus Strategic Restructuring

In 1993, Michael Hammer and James Champy wrote *Reengineering the Corporation,* which offered a direct approach to making operations more efficient. This book led to a multibillion-dollar consulting practice designed to help corporations and their leaders reduce costs and restructure their way of doing things.

The piece of reengineering that captured the most attention and caused the greatest public discussion called for reducing the company employee base, a tactic labeled variously as "downsizing" and "rightsizing." In 1991, before Hammer and Champy's book and in the middle of a recession, American corporations did what they had always done (reduced their labor force), this time cutting 555,292 jobs. Historically, when a recovery started, companies would rehire most of those workers. This time, they did not rehire most laid-off workers, and in 1994, in the midst of a fairly vibrant recovery but after the Hammer and Champy book championed a permanent reduction of staff, American corporations shed another 516,069 jobs.

While downsizing their employees, company executives also reduced business costs. In 1980, for example, 95 percent of U.S. employers offered some kind of health insurance. By 1996, that number had fallen to 80 percent. Right through the recovery, employers lowered the number of holidays that workers could take, cut break time during work days and lowered sickness- and accident-insurance coverage. Throughout the recovery, American workers' salaries remained essentially stagnant, increasing just 2.7 percent between 1994 and 1995 (the peak of the recovery), the lowest yearly increase since the deep recession of 1981–1982.

These necessary tactics, typically used when a slower economy pressures lowered margins and squeezed profits, were simply extended into the economic recovery. Management acted as if the economy had entered into a permanent recession. Much of the savings, of course, went straight to the bottom line, pleasing many Wall Street investors. When AT&T announced huge layoffs, its stock spurted upward; and when Mobil Oil announced huge profits, its stock price jumped. Then, in the next week, when the same company announced layoffs, its stock price took still another leap upward.

Much of the downsizing project, however, was illusory. Stocks did rise (although, between 1987 and 1997, stocks seemed to rise no matter what), but other results were less positive. Fewer than half the firms that downsized managed to increase profits, according to an American Management Association study. Of those companies that did manage to raise profits after layoffs, the positive results did not reach the balance sheet for three years. Worse, companies that downsized had more stress-related disability claims after the reductions than did companies that had avoided downsizing. Also, long-term disability leave demands rose above historical averages after layoffs.

Companies seemed to be insisting that their workers were disposable, and this implied another unintended message: Customers are disposable as well. When employee retention declines, so does customer retention; and when companies forcefully cut loose employees, they also cut loose customers. Frederick F. Reichheld, in *The Loyalty Effect* (1996), explained that "the typical Fortune 500 company has real annual growth of 2½ percent. If it retains 5 percent more of its customers each year, real growth will triple to 7½ percent." The curious aspect to this perspective is that senior executives believe that customers and employees are two separate areas of the company, and that they should receive separate treatment and have different priorities. Our observations suggest they are wrong, and First Tennessee Bank proved that point. When the company restructured its operations to let employees take control over their work schedules, the company doubled the length of time its average employee stayed in a job. That change also increased customer retention by 7 percent, which went straight to the bottom line in the form of a 55 percent profit gain in two years. In essence, retaining employees helps retain customers, a phenomenon which invigorates profits.

Pressure from Wall Street to meet or beat "the numbers" has encouraged many leaders to focus on quick-fix tactical maneuvers to keep their numbers moving upward. For the purpose of jump-starting some favorable "numbers," firing employees and cutting costs for a quick stock-price jump seems easier than reworking employee relations to keep customers. Consequently, tactical restructuring tools like reengineering, total quality management, quality control, work teams and core competencies became extremely popular. When those lost their appeal, other theories like "organizational agility," "value engineering," and "business transformation" surfaced to take their place. They all produced better short-term numbers, but they did so at the cost of long-term customer and employee loyalty. Focusing on efficiencies required looking inward for change, something that completely ignored what was taking place outside the company. Even "outsourcing," a tactic of finding outside resources to do jobs that once took place internally, was an inward look at cost reductions. While many leaders spoke extensively about competitive pressures, that glib and often misused term hardly rationalized the extensive expenditure of resources, time, and energy that all of these different tactical efforts consumed.

Tactical restructuring has become necessary, but it is no longer sufficient. Sufficiency now rests with strategic restructuring—a complete rethinking of the company's objectives, organizational structure, operations and relationships in order to reconnect effectively with customers and employees. We discuss examples later in this book. Successful strategic restructuring has ultimately altered the flow of information, creating an outside-in and bottom-up organizational model. That is, the changes touch the employees at the client-contact point first and then spread throughout the organization.

By 1996, Hammer and Champy were pulling back from their reengineering enthusiasm and suggesting that they had misperceived the situation. Specifically, Hammer explained, "I wasn't smart enough about [the people side of the equation]. I was reflecting my engineering background and was insufficiently appreciative of the human dimension.

I've learned that's critical." Perhaps attitude changes in his own market helped him realize the errors of his way. In 1996, Bain & Company, a Boston consulting firm, asked 1,000 companies to rate various management tools, and reengineering failed to rise above average in all five categories of interest (financials, market share, competitiveness, growth and teamwork). In 1994, reengineering had led four of the five categories.

Not only was the "human dimension" misjudged in the rush to reengineer, but the entire focus of the company was in the wrong direction. Looking inward for efficiency was so much navel-gazing while the world outside was changing beyond recognition. While executives focused on saving another several thousand dollars, consumers were changing in ways that made the efficiency drive insufficient to sustain long-term relationships and threatened millions (and even billions) of dollars in business. Peter Drucker, Clark Professor of Social Science at Claremont Graduate School in California, observed that all great change in business has come from outside the firm, not inside, yet leaders continue to study their own best practices, refine their own competencies and streamline their own operations.

Strategically rethinking the company starts with letting go of all past models, assumptions and practices. Leaders should realize that what worked so well on the other side of the massive changes that individuals have made has now become ineffective. Next, the company must undertake its own strategic reassessment, first rethinking its purposes, objectives, methods and relationships, then reworking its priorities, and finally resetting its operations and marketing to fit the new model. This part of the process, unique to each institution, requires that its own resources and relationships—leaders, employees, customers— be integral to the process. Management theories can add very little to this part of the process. Ultimately, this outside-in reassessment process leads to new foundations that help management to establish priorities and reset objectives. The cumulative effect of all this then leads the company forward.

The reason why strategic restructuring is necessary is that the world outside the company has changed extensively, and the firm must integrate those new attitudes, beliefs and priorities into its own outlook, processes and market approaches. The reason why most companies are still fighting a battle for control, seeking to retain the old assumptions, models and practices, is that those tactics worked so well for so long, including for America's current generation of leaders, who rose to their present positions using those tactics. For these reasons, we now turn to the post–World War II era as a way to understand its hold on current American leaders. We need to look quite closely at the success that these "communities of wealth" enjoyed.

CHAPTER 2

THE COMMUNITIES
OF WEALTH

When historian David M. Potter completed the manuscript for his most successful book on the American character, he titled it *People of Plenty* (1954). Writing in the early 1950s, Potter recognized that the availability of abundant resources, matched with the uncanny knack of Americans to turn those natural resources into wealth and prosperity, had contributed "in the most fundamental way to the shaping of the American culture and the American character."

Through much of American history, abundance and wealth had nurtured and reinforced certain personal traits which Potter saw as basic to the American character: a sense of optimism, belief in opportunity and progress, desire for personal independence, recognition of change, and an acceptance of hard work and delayed gratification. These values guided individual behavior and brought affluence to the country. They also lay the foundation for a strong middle class, which itself guided American business and national politics.

In essence, "middle-class values" became synonymous with "American values." America's dedication to middle-class values became so strong that late in the Great Depression a Gallup Poll revealed that fully 88 percent thought of themselves as middle-class. Yet only 30 percent of American families actually qualified for middle-class status in terms of household income. Their values helped Americans defeat economic and military enemies and drove them to redirect their postwar energies to expanding standards of living and to creating growth.

In the five decades that followed World War II, American institutions and their leaders followed a steady course: expand and grow the

institutions, and raise everyone's standard of living. Industrial production, personal employment, national politics, advertising, home-building,
product development and seemingly everything America grew or made
changed in conformity with this course of action. Suburban homes,
multicar families, televisions, toaster ovens, designer clothes, widespread
credit, social activism, pop music, movies and more all added impetus
to the drive to create wealth. By any measure, the public and private
institutions that manufactured and facilitated these wealth-expanding
opportunities—what we prefer to call the "communities of wealth"—
were incredibly successful.

Communities of wealth are institutions whose primary appeal to
participants is their ability to expand wealth. While the country's economic system had always stood for the creation of wealth, what made
post–World War II more dedicated to this proposition was the Depression that had preceded the war. Denial increased desire, and the postwar
quest for greater wealth attracted a broad spectrum of American society.
For that reason, these are "communities." Employees, consumers and
citizens—all the different roles of Americans in the working society—
shared this common objective. For that reason, sacrificing now for
greater rewards later made sense to all who participated.

The problem with the success of these communities of wealth, however, is that they were so successful that American business and political leaders underestimated the pact of new realities when they surfaced,
realities that would eventually undermine and discredit those same
leaders. In the early 1990s, when older institutions struggled to remain
viable and when leaders embraced management and financial engineering tactics to sustain them, the context that had buttressed those institutions started to change. The abundant success that many of the country's
leaders rode to the top ultimately kept them from grasping the scope
and implications of significant changes as they unfolded before them.
They were unable to grow their institutions and raise the employees'
standard of living. They were failing to realize the implicit promise
between individuals and institutions that had marked the postwar economy. Some leaders tried to divert attention from this shortcoming
by trying various cost-cutting measures, and others tried to shift their

historical responsibility from that of the wider institution to that of the stockholder. In each example, they were admitting they were losing control of the once-successful communities of wealth. To understand why success deflected the attention of sophisticated leaders away from new social and economic realities, it is necessary to examine more closely how that past success was achieved.

ORIGINS OF THE PURSUIT OF WEALTH

In the early years of the Depression, few Americans thought the economic malaise would last more than a few months—at worst maybe a year. America's economic history seemingly lent credence to the belief that progress, development and growth were consequences of the American character, and many believed that character would, in no time, overcome economic adversity. When the crisis stretched through the 1930s and into the 1940s, Americans wavered in their dedication to the values that had created so much growth. This waffling belief in America's mission and ability prompted President Franklin D. Roosevelt to shift the discussion: "We have nothing to fear," he argued, "but fear itself."

Fear or no fear, American productivity and economic expansion did not revive again until the war years. World War II, when it came, brought back to life the "people of plenty." They had a mission. Flying under the banner of the great "Arsenal for Democracy," American manufacturers created weapons and armaments at a frantic pace. In 1939, America manufactured 2,000 military planes. Five years later it welded and pounded together more than 100,000. In fact, in 1944, America produced nearly half of all the arms created in the world at that time.

The work week rose from 38 to 47 hours, with massive increases in overtime. Incomes and standards of living rose, as well. Between 1939 and 1945, per capita income climbed from $1,231 to $2,390, and purchases of consumer goods more than doubled. Even in the midst of this spending spree, Americans had enough additional money to push personal savings from $2.6 billion in 1939 to $29.6 billion over the same six years. Military success against sizable odds, matched with the domestic economy's resurgence, gave Americans the feeling that they could do anything, make anything happen—indeed, turn difficulties into triumphs.

When the war ended, American production was riding high, but some worried aloud that the Depression would return. The decade-long economic crisis had seriously challenged the American character, and many citizens wondered if the war effort, which had simply overwhelmed economic weakness with its manufacturing demands, was a temporary stimulant that masked fundamental troubles. If so, they wondered, would those troubles return when the war stimulant dwindled? Fortunately, that did not happen, partly because Americans started spending, and partly because American institutions converted their war-machine productivity into consumer-satisfying productivity.

The transition went quite well. Between 1947 and 1959, the percentage of American families earning less than $3,000 dropped from 46 to 20, while the percentage earning between $7,000 and $10,000 jumped in the same time frame from 5 percent to 20 percent. In the 13 years following 1947, the great push of American productivity and growth increased the average real income of Americans by as much as it had increased over the previous half century. From the other extreme, in 1935 roughly half of all Americans were living in poverty, but by 1960 that number had declined to less than 20 percent.

The postwar economic expansion narrowed the American Dream to a dual concept of growth and expanding personal wealth. Institutions that facilitated this explosion in growth became communities of wealth, enabling institutions that expanded the country's standard of living and added to its wealth. These institutions won citizen and employee loyalty because they effectively provided the growth and wealth objectives. The coalescing of individual and institutional objectives pushed growth figures higher. Between 1945 and 1960, America's Gross National Product rose by 250 percent.

Before the Depression, Americans believed that the individual was responsible for his or her own financial well-being. The powerful suggestion that individuals carried their own destiny in their hands had endured World War I, the rise of corporate and urban America, and even the first years of the Depression. Consequently, in the early years of the

Depression, most Americans blamed themselves for whatever hard luck befell them as a result of the declining economy. However, the depth and breadth of the Great Depression and the immensity of World War II made that individuality seem naive. These huge events proved that larger, impersonal forces and ever-larger economies were making it nearly impossible for the individual to survive isolated from larger institutions. As a result, Americans turned easily to large corporate structures, institutions that could bring security to the individual.

American military might prevailed because public and private enterprises joined hands, and that alliance for success lasted beyond the war. Depression-era government had created the Social Security system and other programs to assist Americans in need and to create the sense that individuals did not face these huge impersonal forces alone. One congressional bill in particular, the Servicemen's Readjustment Act of 1944, carried the World War II brand of economic dynamism into the postwar period. Michael J. Bennett, author of *When Dreams Came True* (1996), a study of the so-called G.I. Bill, called it "a Marshall Plan for America" and the catalyst that "made modern America." In 1945, some 22,000 veterans used the G.I. Bill, but by 1947 that number had sky-rocketed to 2 million. In 1948 alone, 1.4 million World War II soldiers signed guaranteed loans to buy houses, while roughly 45,000 used the money to buy farms and farm equipment, and another 94,000 deployed the money to buy or start businesses. The other roughly 8 million veterans who took advantage of the government-backed loan system used the money to pay for an education.

These types of actions reignited American optimism, and that optimism sparked a new social and economic dynamism. In the first year of peace, 2.2 million couples married, more than twice the number of any prewar year and a record that stood for decades. But the country was not ready for this huge increase in the number of potential households. In 1948, for example, roughly 2 million married couples were living with relatives, suggesting a dire need for housing and an equally dire need for financing plans to pay for that housing.

The postwar housing and financial boom furthered the joint efforts of public and private institutions to enhance the country's standard of living. Public institutions essentially financed the housing boom that followed World War II. The New Deal's Federal Housing Authority and the postwar Veterans Administration backed veteran loans to buy houses. Because the government backed home loans, mandatory down payments for houses dropped from nearly 67 percent of the sale price before the Depression to just 10 percent after the war. That same government backing lowered interest rates between 2 and 3 points, and when the tax breaks for interest payments were added, the housing market enjoyed a huge public-sector boost.

In 1944 the nation's builders sold 100,000 houses, but just two years later they sold a million, and in 1950 they built 1.7 million houses, a record that lasted well into the 1980s. The combination of government financing and a building boom impacted American lives substantially. At the end of the war, 40 percent of Americans owned their own houses; by 1980 that percentage had risen to 60 percent.

The postwar housing boom gave birth to the "suburb," a land beyond city boundaries where homeowners worked tiny plots of land, grilled hamburgers in the backyard, and commuted miles to work. Most of the postwar housing boom took place in the farmland surrounding America's cities. In fact, between 1950 and 1960, contractors built 13 million homes, 11 million of them in the suburbs. For many white-collar employees, the American Dream existed outside the densely populated cities. By 1955, more than 4,000 families a day were leaving the cities for the suburban beyond, which became known as the "crabgrass frontier." That level of migration matched the mass immigration from Europe at its peak earlier in the century.

The suburban rush put greater distances between homeowners and their places of work and expanded the distances between home and basic services. In response, suburban Americans came to depend heavily on private automobiles. In the 15 years after the war, Americans increased the number of cars on the road by 133 percent, making General Motors a key player in the U.S. economy. GM employed more than 130,000 white-collar employees, and its blue-collar contingent grew annually. GM soon had profits in excess of $1 billion, a figure that AT&T also matched because all of those suburban homes had telephones.

According to GM head (and President Eisenhower's Secretary of Defense) Charles "Engine Charlie" Wilson, "What's good for General Motors' business is good for America." The pursuit of wealth was becoming so pervasive that Wilson's point, while politically awkward, was easy enough to understand and accept.

In postwar America, large institutions made large changes. The giants of World War II—government and industry—became giants in postwar America. The war's "can do" attitude converted easily into an optimism that gave energy to the country's economy. Individuals and institutions—once seen as antithetical—were now intertwined in a joint effort to expand wealth. For the individual, success in war meant staying alive, which usually meant depending on fellow fighting men; success in postwar America meant raising one's standard of living—which soon meant working for a corporation.

INDIVIDUALS AND THE COMMUNITIES OF WEALTH

In the years that followed, the newly married, home-owning, securely employed veterans retreated to their new bedrooms and shared in the birthing of a demographic bulge. They produced 30 million babies in the 1940s, and another 41 million in the 1950s. During the 1940s, school enrollment had increased by a sizable 1 million students. During the 1950s, enrollment jumped by 10 million. This population protuberance, later dubbed "the baby boom," would force changes in everything from education to pop culture (rock and roll, blue jeans, Hula Hoops, T-shirts), all with a stimulating impact on the economy.

While this boom affected spending habits of the average family, it also influenced the spending habits of the government that needed to build the infrastructure to service the "boomers." In 1957, shortly after the Soviet Union launched the Sputnik satellite on October 4, a panicked Congress passed the National Defense Education Act in order to advance educational levels of the young. This law made access to tuition funds easier, and consequently boosted college enrollment. From 1963 to 1973, that enrollment doubled, representing a $10 billion increase in tuition dollars rolling through the economy. In 1956, President Dwight D. Eisenhower had pushed the Interstate Highway Act through Congress, which budgeted $32 billion to build 41,000 miles of dual-lane expressways, coast-to-coast. Although the rationale of the Highway Act was to facilitate troop and materiel movement around the country during wartime, the huge project in practice advanced interstate commerce instead.

More than commerce traveled easily throughout the country. Corporations, having spread their operations from coast to coast, moved employees around to different facilities with increasing frequency. Businesses were offering lifelong employment in return for loyalty and obedience, which meant that when they needed to move personnel, those people simply picked up stakes and left. Because an expanding standard of living was an ideal that both employee and employer shared, the familial or housing difficulties that these frequent moves caused did not appear problematic. The American military routinely transferred soldiers, and its wartime successor, the American corporation, did the same with its own "troops." Moving-van companies of the 1950s revealed that 40 percent of their overall business derived from corporations transferring white-collar workers from one city to another.

Seeing such mobility, critics carped about compliant "organization men"—those who acceded to company rules and plans without hesitation, surrendering their individuality to corporate conformity just to get ahead. However, such loyalty did bring greater wealth, and the unhesitating followers soon enjoyed fast-rising standards of living and not much later watched their children receive superior educations from better and better schools. In fact, employees in general at these large enterprises shared a focus on careers as a positive contribution to one's overall, lifetime accomplishments. Careers figured prominently in individual and family decisions about where to live, how to behave and what to dream about. Americans shared the perception that working hard and sacrificing immediate gratification for work would bring benefits later—financial security, a satisfactory level of affluence, and a comfortable retirement.

People *liked* being at work. Forty percent of Americans preferred working to being at home, according to one mid-1950s survey. That appeal carried across the family, as increasing numbers of women started reporting for work. Female employment increased 400 percent between 1940 and 1960, and during the 1950s rose four times faster than male employment. Once at work, men and women cooperated as a team, because teams could accomplish more, and doing more meant getting more in return. They further trusted that helping to nourish the company's bottom line ultimately meant growing their own personal bottom line.

Company bottom lines did, indeed, grow. Between 1937 and 1958, for example, Dow Chemical Company grew by 750 percent. IBM's net earnings rose from $11 million in 1945 to $250 million in 1960 and on to $3.4 billion in 1980. Between 1959 and 1977, ITT bought and acquired its way from $765 million in annual sales to $28 billion. This steady growth in production and profits returned Americans to their basic beliefs that progress was inevitable, and that during their time, at least, progress would mean personal financial growth as well.

The work was worth it. Companies flourished, and the rewards they offered their hardworking employees brought back an all-around belief in the future of one and all. Individuals made sacrifices in their personal lives to enhance their position at work (long hours, dedicated participation, willingness to transfer locations). They made those sacrifices because they believed that their future would be better as a result. Indeed, welcome advancements and fair pay increases did follow. By 1960, family income had doubled from the already high level of the war-based 1945 economy.

Postwar institutions created security, optimism and a new sense of well-being. In the mid-1950s, what these institutions offered became, for many, an assumed fact of economic life. American employees planned their lives while counting on the belief that overall economic growth would lead to personal financial growth, which in turn would ultimately lead to greater happiness. The sense that the communities of wealth were the beginning point for a quest for material contentedness reassured one

Princeton senior thus: "In fifteen years," he confidently projected, "I look forward to a constant level of happiness."

This focus on the pursuit of happiness as a derivative of a pursuit of wealth changed America's economy. Whereas industrial America developed the country's infrastructure and won a war, postwar America used that industrial base to make consumers happy. In the process of playing to the consumer's wants, America in 1956 became a "postindustrial" society, employing more white-collar than blue-collar workers.

The constant level of happiness that the Princeton senior anticipated depended not only upon an ever-expanding standard of living, but also upon an increasing availability of credit. When consumer wants exceeded their financial capabilities, and when the acquisition of goods and services implied a rising standard of living, conflicts developed. But credit eased those conflicts. Short-term credit leaped from $8.4 billion in 1946 to $45.6 billion in 1958; and by 1975, consumers held $167 billion in personal debt (excluding mortgages). Within another 10 years, that number rose to $517 billion. Overall, between 1965 and 1985, consumer debt as a percentage of disposable income averaged 15 percent, moving to a record high of 19 percent in 1988.

Spending money came easier and easier to consumers as businesses made buying simpler and more fun. First, local mom-and-pop stores gave way to strip malls, and eventually to area shopping centers. Next, developers covered their shopping centers, adding air-conditioning and lavish interior decorations to create regional malls. Such malls evolved into regional centers enclosing everything from movie houses and restaurants to banks and massive food courts, amusement areas, and adult education centers. As shopping areas evolved, Americans changed interests as well. Consumers first envisioned shopping as a necessity—but that view soon lost ground to shopping as an expression of the good life. It even became a statement about the relative success one enjoyed within the communities of wealth. These changing consumer attitudes supported the growth of consumer brands as symbols of an achieved standard of living, thus creating a synergy between wants and images that helped advertising become *the* modern American medium.

In *People of Plenty,* Potter identified advertising as *the* "institution of abundance." Advertising presented the consumer with items to buy—and, when successful, it actually provoked the need to spend. Advertising "as an institution of social control," Potter thought, was "comparable to the school and the church in the extent of its indulgence upon society." Events proved Potter correct. Between 1945 and 1960, advertisers increased their annual ad budgets by a whopping 400 percent. In 1970, advertisers spent $19.5 billion, while the entire country spent $17.6 billion on higher education.

Advertising, the institution of abundance, and Americans, the consumers of abundance, met in the living rooms of America's new houses—via television. These employees, homeowners and consumers sat before the new broadcast medium and watched advertisers sell their wares. Television (or "sell-o-vision," as one wag dubbed it) brought advertising and entertainment together in order to bring seller and buyer together.

The shared exuberance of suburban consumers, TV entertainers and branded advertisers helped the television industry grow rapidly. In a way, television's postwar rise paralleled the country's rising standard of living. In 1946, just 8,000 households owned television sets. By 1950, 5 million households owned a TV set, and by 1959, 44 million American homes had televisions. Not only did Americans buy TVs, they used their new entertainment instruments a lot. When the 1950s ended, the average American family was watching television six hours per night, seven days a week. To extend viewing hours, American consumers quickly assimilated into their evening rituals ready-to-eat meals called "TV Dinners," frozen concoctions to be heated and then eaten while watching the evening fare. With this sort of consumer interest, the number of local television stations rose from 69 to 586 in the 10 years following 1949.

As a result, national television networks became broadcast versions of the communities of wealth. On their airwaves, companies pitched everything, including toothpaste, automobiles, cigarettes and clothes. Programs like *The U.S. Steel Hour, Kraft Music Hall, General Electric Theater, Hallmark Hall of Fame* and *The Camel News Caravan* brought advertiser and program together to blur the distinction between product and entertainment.

Connecting viewers with advertisers worked effectively. When *Kraft Music Hall* advertised a new recipe and offered it for free, the company received 500,000 requests. When Hazel Bishop, the lipstick maker, became a TV advertiser, its business income rose from $50,000 to $4.5 million in just two years.

With those types of results, advertising expenditures on television surged from $58 million in 1949 to $1.5 billion in 1959. More specifically, Procter & Gamble spent a mere 1.7 percent of its advertising budget on television in 1950, but 92.6 percent one decade later ($101.5 million). Broadcasters accepted the money gladly, cashing checks worth a total of $170 million in 1950, $1 billion in 1955, and over $2 billion in 1967.

Advertising depended heavily upon brand names, elite symbols of the communities of wealth. Advertisers loaded these special brand names with valuable associations—style, taste, quality, discernment. Owning a brand-name product, advertisements suggested, implied possession of those valued associations at the personal level. Particular names, whether in cars or soup, revealed a heightened level of insight which befitted a particular place within the communities of wealth. Social convention recognized the fact that the company president would, of course, drive a different brand of car than did middle managers, who in turn would have a different car than the line workers, and so on. The entire wealth-driven system encouraged employees to become consumers and consumers to purchase goods in ways that matched their roles in the hierarchical system.

During this period in American social and economic history, postwar institutions and the middle class blended their interests and needs. As a result, growth and an expanded standard of living became shared objectives. As part of this shared vision, institutions granted higher salaries, increased employee benefits and created financial security. In return, employees gave their loyalty, time and energy to those institutions—usually for life. The stability and predictability that this arrangement developed, and the ever-expanding economy that it supported, validated its reason for being.

A FINAL BURST

The social tensions that swept through society in the 1950s (civil rights) and 1960s (anti–Vietnam War) did not derail the communities of wealth. They advanced them. The early civil-rights movement sought to open middle-class life and opportunities to American blacks, and their efforts often brought results. In 1960, 13 percent of black workers were in middle-class jobs. By the end of the decade, that number had risen to 27 percent.

Meanwhile, the youth movement that sprang to life with rock and roll in the 1950s delivered a huge boost to the economy. The demographic bulge that came from postwar optimism eventually reached its teenage years, and, unlike prior generations, this cohort had money to spend. That meant new marketing opportunities, because, as one observer noted, "If you can buy as an adult, you are an adult." That observation gave expression to what was becoming more and more obvious: teenagers were a market. In 1959, teens were walking around with $9.5 billion in their jeans. They continued to spend their money right through the turbulent 1960s. Between 1963 and 1967, counterculture (alias youth culture) spending on clothing boosted sales of "duds" by 40 percent, totaling more sales in just four years than during any prior decade.

Despite social unrest, America's drive for greater wealth and a rising standard of living continued. Between 1960 and 1968, total personal income of Americans rose by more than 70 percent, and the gross national product nearly doubled. Even unemployment steadied itself, hovering around 4.8 percent.

In the early 1970s, America's long and successful drive to grow and expand ran into troubles that caused widespread concern. In 1971, the U.S. experienced a trade deficit for the first time since 1893. In the first five months of 1973, U.S. inflation rose at an annual rate of 9.2 percent, prompting President Richard M. Nixon to impose a 60-day freeze on prices. Despite this effort, annual inflation for that year hit 6.2 percent, with a 14.5 percent jump in food prices. The 1973 year-ending Arab oil boycott added to inflation pressures, prompting many Americans to wonder whether or not their leaders actually controlled the country's economy. Having witnessed the 1967 cost-of-living index peak at 100, Americans watched it rise to 133 just six years later. Meanwhile, the purchasing power of the dollar declined from 100 cents in 1967 to just 75 cents in 1973. Taxes started to rise, and inflation and unemployment edged upward, all of this creating a combination of rising unemployment and rising inflation, an unprecedented economic malaise that economists dubbed "stagflation." "You always used to think in this country that there would be bad times followed by good times," fretted a Chicago housewife. "Now, maybe it's bad times followed by hard times followed by harder times."

This economic unsteadiness ran headlong into political scandals which first forced Vice President Spiro T. Agnew and then-President Nixon to resign, both in disgrace. Soon thereafter, the clumsy and even embarrassing departure of U.S. troops from Saigon in 1975 captured a loser's image that Americans watched on their TVs over and over again. The popularity of the movies *Jaws,* which envisioned a subliminal threat deep within ourselves, and *The Exorcist,* which posited naively that somehow evil could be purged, revealed the worries growing in the American populace.

President Jimmy Carter sought to revive lagging American morale. In his 1977 inaugural address, he threw out the phrase "a new spirit" five times, and calmly stated, "I have no new dream to set forth today, but rather urge a fresh faith in the old dream." Events undid his efforts. The 1979 nuclear meltdown at Three Mile Island undermined many Americans' faith in government oversight and private industry. By the decade's end, American hostages were being held in Teheran, prompting *New West* magazine to rephrase Charles Dickens's famous first line from *A Tale of Two Cities.* The magazine sarcastically intoned: "It was the worst of times, it was the worst of times." Americans started wondering whether the steady rise in the standard of living, the thing that had held society together, was coming to an end.

In 1980, the Gallup organization revealed that 55 percent of the public believed that "Next year will be worse than this year," and that 72 percent agreed with the statement "We are fast coming to a turning point in our history. The land of plenty is becoming the land of want." American attitudes were changing as well. In the 1960s, nearly 60 percent believed that "Hard work always pays off," but as the 1970s ended, that number had dropped to 43 percent. "Increasing numbers of Americans," concluded pollster Daniel Yankelovich, "are questioning . . . the value of giving a particular kind of hard work in exchange for a particular set of economic benefits."

In a way, these were early warnings of the imminent decline of the communities of wealth, but the old institutions had enough life in them to create one last burst of growth. The 1980s were the baroque era of excess for the communities of wealth, a last hurrah for the aging institutions. What had been a miracle of growth became an obsession with getting ahead. Productivity reached new heights as manufacturers created more and more products; distributors imported more and more goods; marketers and advertisers turned to extremes; and efforts to expand corporate wealth became an obsession. Eventually the system that was so rationally put together nearly 50 years earlier became too slow and too antiquated to deal with such new realities as global competition, unanticipated currency fluctuations, consumer changes and new communications systems.

Many Americans hoped that Ronald W. Reagan's 1980 election would bring social stability and return the country's steady movement upward economically. "They say that the United States has had its day in the sun," President Reagan told the inaugural crowd. "I utterly reject that view." While he spoke, Iran released American hostages, and many Americans believed that the old postwar world of an ever-expanding economy would return. After a punishing 1981–1982 recession, inflation and unemployment started downward. Interest rates eventually declined, OPEC lowered oil prices, and the economy started a lengthy and steady recovery. The economic vitality that marked the last lurch of the communities of wealth made some sectors of the economy feel quite good. Overall, however, this economic boost was different.

Individuals focused on expanding personal power to leverage personal advancement. Gone was the team concept of the so-called organization man. In came the Yuppie (the "young urban professional") and the Buppie (the "black urban professional"), whose motivation in either case was clear: Get ahead, no matter how.

The push to succeed became strained as individuals sensed that the old "steadily rising career" approach was coming to an end. Many pushed for the big deal, the single "killing" that would take them out of the "rat race" forever. This push for immediate gratification involved a concentration on self-improvement. Self-improvement meant both enhancing the body's potential and expanding wealth acquisition as well. The roughness of competition found its training outlet in Outward Bound, a program that taught executives to survive in the woods and develop teams to overcome barriers. In 1986, Outward Bound trained 13,325 executives in how to get tough to get ahead.

Competition in business and careers turned metaphoric via the outstanding growth of road racing. Marathons, those long runs undertaken by solitary competitors (but not by the "team" of earlier business metaphors), became a stand-in for career, training, self-absorption, and self-motivation. By 1986, more marathons took place in the month of November alone than had taken place in all of 1976. The survivor, the winner, the celebrity—these images replaced the organization man as social model.

An Anheuser-Busch television commercial for Michelob Light asked, "Who said you can't have it all?" "You *can* have it all" became an all-encompassing phrase suggesting that the communities of wealth were bottomless in their resources, and that individuals could never fully tap those resources. Helen Gurley Brown, founder and editor of *Cosmopolitan* magazine, titled her autobiography *Having It All* (1982).

Having it all—the end product of years of growth and economic expansion—meant essentially buying it all, and the consuming passion for shopping that had given birth to the postwar economy now reached a fever pitch. "Shop till you drop" urged a certain sweatshirt, and just saying it often enough seemed to displace forever the more cautionary phrase from the seemingly remote past, "Save for a rainy day."

People now tended to believe that rainy days were simply not in the forecast. With the government deficit-spending to the tune of $300–$400 billion per year, a classic Keynesian economic boost coursed through America's economic veins. Consequently, the doubts of the 1970s about America's future and the ability of the country to right itself dissipated. Americans returned to their favorite method of pushing aside doubt: borrowing against the future. Between 1978 and 1986, consumer debt rose an average of 10 percent per year. When the decade started, 63 million Americans carried 120 million Visa, MasterCard and Discover credit cards. By 1988, 80 million Americans packed 224 million cards from those three companies. In the early 1980s, credit-card debt had hovered around $55 billion, but by the end of 1988, that figure had jumped to $175 billion. What had started as a long and steady effort to grow American institutions and expand the individual's standard of living was ending with massive consumer debt and with institutions encouraging even more such debt.

EXCESS SIGNALS THE END

Madonna, "The Material Girl" who wore lingerie onstage and flaunted conventions of public performance, bragged "I dress to excess." David Bowie, another performer who ignored celebrity conventions, stared heavy-lidded into the MTV (music television) camera and proclaimed "Too much is never enough."

These statements of excess nudged "having it all" to new extremes, hinted at the vulnerabilities of the communities of wealth, and hastened their demise. What at one time sought to expand everyone's standard of living was now celebrating a few people's extravagances, and what once sought to advance all of society's wealth now simply offered a stage for celebrity eccentricities. In essence, the pursuit of wealth had separated from the "community," creating greater disparity between the haves and the have-nots.

While movie stars and music celebrities pushed and shoved for air time before American consumers, business people also started to think of themselves as deserving "fame," a peculiarly 1980s pop-culture word that inspired a book, a film, and a television show. Lee Iacocca made his name familiar by appearing in Chrysler Corporation advertisements, assuming that a company's chairman would be more reliable than other celebrities, yet at the same time making himself a celebrity with the same questionable image. But it did bring him his moment of fame, and evidently made him the subject of some degree of envy.

"I envy Iacocca," confessed W. Jeremiah Sanders III, founder of Advanced Micro Devices. "If they asked me, I'd do a *Miami Vice* episode [on television]; I'd even do *Hill Street Blues*." Sanders was not alone in his desire for public adulation. In fact, public notoriety became a new currency, a different sign of wealth. "There is so much show biz in business today," intoned Felix Rohatyn, a financier of some fame himself, "that working with people who are not show biz is a real experience."

The power that drove this fame mania was the power to buy and sell; to centralize and decentralize companies; to move personnel around; and to create massive wealth and display that wealth through purchases and public displays. The leveraged-buyout craze added impetus to this obsession. Big money passed into the hands of those who could craft a change of control and facilitate the shifting of resources from one owner to another. The bigger the transfer, the bigger the compensation. A later study would reveal that 57 percent of the 300 biggest mergers completed between 1986 and 1996 created entities that lagged behind their competitors in terms of stockholder returns. But during the 1980s, media and corporate "players" characterized the merger and acquisition (M&A) craze as adding value to the companies involved.

Overall, only the people who created the M&A transactions thrived. Michael Milken made more than $600 million in one year (and similar amounts in other years) by bringing together buyers and sellers of companies and "crafting" the money deal to "make it happen." Stories appeared in the press about distraught investment bankers who made mere seven-digit bonuses, rather than the eight-figured numbers they felt they deserved.

These men were manipulators, not manufacturers; they were the white-collar worker in the extreme. They acted upon the assumption that a company was undervalued, and therefore could be rearranged inside and out to create greater value. These financial power brokers were the rising wealthy of the late and fading communities of wealth. Their actions supposedly would "save" these weakening institutions by shaving excesses and creating efficiency. In their own futile way, they were becoming extremely wealthy doing futile triage on aging institutions. But that reality did not deter the momentum of the practice.

The hefty rewards that the successful expression of power generated inspired the decade's fascination with power everywhere. "Power ties," bold statements worn to show how serious and aggressive the wearer was, and "power breakfasts"—business events crowded into the front end of what was assumed to be such a busy day—added ritual trappings and ceremonial processes to the atmosphere of getting ahead and crushing the competition as a way of life. Ted Turner, Victor Kiam II, Frank Borman, H. Ross Perot, et al., all used their business positions to spread their image across American media. Power images pushed power plays. For example, when several of Ross Perot's employees were kidnapped abroad, he mounted a private expedition to rescue them, despite U.S. State Department reservations. The mission's success led to an NBC miniseries. Too, J. W. Marriott, Jr. and Robert Jarvis, among others, squeezed their frames into Hathaway shirts to sell themselves. Also, Lester B. Korn, chairman of Korn/Ferry International, suggested a direction for this status-hungry era: "I expect to see the day when, just as most Americans can name 10 or 15 major entertainers and 10 or 15 major athletes, they [would be able to] name an equal number of corporate executives." For businessmen these were heady, even if decadent, times.

The 24-hour-a-day Cable News Network (CNN) kept Americans abreast of world events, while the full-time Financial News Network (FNN) narrowed that focus to events that would impact markets around the world. Likewise, night-and-day MTV kept American youth aware of which music products and clothing styles were hot at that moment. In a much more transparent way than that of the old *U. S. Steel Hour* or *Kraft Music Hall* of the 1950s, MTV brought advertisements and programming into one video moment onscreen. What the viewer watched was, in fact, what the viewer was expected to buy.

Indeed, MTV could well have been offering a service to teenagers, because keeping up with new products became increasingly harder. According to *New Product News* (*NPN*), a journal that kept tabs on "new releases" in all merchandise categories, 1984 broke all records for the number of new products introduced into the market. In the 21 years that the journal had watched the changing market, no single year had even come close to the 2,000-plus items released in 1984. If *NPN* had counted line extensions, then the number would have exceeded 7,000!

The onslaught continued. In May 1985, some 235 new products reached America's store shelves, the highest figure for any month on record. Grocery stores which had stocked 25,000 products needed to adjust to a list that grew to 40,000 by 1997. Department stores like Bloomingdale's in New York City rearranged their floor plans to put more items on display; and American car dealers who once could brag about stocking 50 models per year came to exhibit more than 300. In the years that followed, marketers annually broke all production records.

Like Madonna's excesses, which were part of her market appeal, other excesses in the marketplace screamed for attention. A willing customer could buy Yves Saint Laurent cigarettes, Adidas "computerized" running shoes, Ford Broncos with Eddie Bauer interiors, Saint Laurent gowns for Barbie Dolls, designer shower heads and can openers, 23 different kinds of Nine Lives cat food and well over 230 different products bearing the Pierre Cardin label. More than 200 companies, including American Express and Embassy Suites Hotels, paid licensing fees to use the Garfield cat figure in their advertising. Not surprisingly, advertising agencies enjoyed 12 percent annual growth in revenues throughout the 1980s.

Choice engulfed consumers, and so, stores hired what they termed personal shoppers to help customers make decisions. Image consultants helped consumers weave their way through the maze of products to locate the "ultimate" look for them, and personal trainers urged on many others toward reaching their personal-performance best, whether in the weight room or the board room. The baby-boom generation had taken affluence to new levels of both desire and abuse.

While many consumers had plenty of money, they had less and less time to spend it. Consequently, mail-order catalogs became a popular marketing tool to supplant in-store buying. In the early 1980s, more than 6 billion catalogs circulated through the U.S. mail. By decade's end, eager marketers dropped more than 12 billion catalogs into the nation's mailboxes, and the mailings found willing buyers. In the 1980s, Lands' End, one of the nation's hottest catalog retailers, saw its sales increase annually at a compounded rate of 49 percent.

If homeowners misplaced their catalogs but still longed to shop at home, they could tune their televisions to the Home Shopping Network. This was an extreme end to the process started back in the 1950s when *Kraft Music Hall* showed a recipe on the television screen and asked viewers to call for their free copy. The Home Shopping Network displayed and sold merchandise 24 hours per day. This kind of buying frenzy highlighted the message proclaimed from bumper stickers: "He who dies with the most toys wins."

Shopping *had* to become simpler because work was gobbling up time. Leisure hours shrank throughout the 1980s as work demands increased. In 1984, Americans managed only 18.1 hours of weekly leisure time, down from 24.3 hours in 1975. Meanwhile, the average work week edged upward from 40.6 hours in 1973 to 47.3 in 1984, the same number of hours spent at work during World War II when America had a shortage of workers and huge numbers of armed forces to supply. By 1995, work weeks had expanded to 50.6 hours, and leisure time hovered around 19 hours per week.

With the high-powered communities of wealth, individuals could have it all, as long as all they wanted was wealth. If they wanted more time, the communities of wealth were less accommodating. Even the ability of these institutions to deliver wealth had started to subside. From 1973 to 1990, American salaries remained essentially stagnant. In the late 1980s and early 1990s, home-ownership percentages actually declined for the first time since World War II, and by the mid-1990s personal bankruptcies started to edge back upward for the first time outside of a recession.

These types of weaknesses worried scores of workers, who began to rethink what they wanted from their business institutions. Certainly, American public and private institutions alike, in the decades since 1945, had created great wealth and increased many people's standard of living. Since the Great Depression and World War II, the communities of wealth had developed so substantially, and produced so many things, that consumers could argue with a straight face that they were entitled to "have it all." That was a sign of success for the communities of wealth, but it was also a signal of excess as well as one of imminent decline.

In the midst of these excesses, phrases like "enough is enough" and "get a life" started to surface, as people began questioning the viability and attractiveness of the quest for wealth. Rather than wanting more and more, some started to argue for less and less. Rather than accumulate greater wealth, individuals started to think about preserving time, even if that meant having less money to spend.

The long period of success for the communities of wealth was coming to an end, a terminus that would feel a lot like a collapse even before the dénouement. Nonetheless, many people in positions of responsibility, both commercial and political, refused to acknowledge even the decline. They should have recognized that *something* was very different when the recession of 1990 hit. For the first time ever, American political leaders, professional economists and business executives completely missed a recession. Since that had never happened before, right then leaders should have realized that the economy and consumers alike were changing significantly. However, still focused on the institutional model that had created so much success for so long, these very individuals completely missed this *new kind* of recession—the kind driven by changing consumer values and not by traditional economic indicators. *This* recession should have been a signal, but—unfortunately for those mesmerized by the communities of wealth—it was not. Still seeing only what they believed, they did not see the steadily increasing influence of secular forces in the economy.

CRITICAL INSIGHT:
Cyclical Versus Secular Change

In April 1991, after months of denial, the federal government announced that the U.S. economy was entering into its ninth postwar recession. Government officials used statistical evidence from the National Bureau of Economic Research, which had accurately forecast the country's previous eight postwar cyclical downturns. Twenty months later, in December 1992, government officials finally admitted that the ninth postwar recession had actually *ended* in the first quarter of 1991, even before their earlier announcement stating that it was just *starting*. In short, specialists charged with monitoring economic cycles had missed the entire economic recession. So befuddled over the reality that the economy had experienced a downturn when their historically accurate models suggested otherwise, one baffled economist, in exasperation, conjectured that the downturn was actually the result of "wild animal spirits."

Even when the economists acknowledged that their models had missed an entire recession, they used them again to forecast a recovery that they defined as "slow growth as far as the eye can see." But, in the months following that projection, the economy grew steadily and rapidly as the recovery proved to be much more robust and durable than the experts anticipated. Confused over yet another miscalculation, one economist looking at the healthy New York City area regional growth explained that "The recovery has become a puzzling economic phenomenon in its own right . . . [and] downright stranger than anything before it."

What the economists, political leaders and business executives all missed was that, for the first time since World War II, the American economy had confronted two different negative influences at the same time. Both *cyclical* and *secular* forces were changing. Consumer behavior had triggered an economic downturn that did not affect traditional economic indicators until it was too late. Conversely, when consumers reversed their behavior, they spent at a much more expansive pace than the old economic models had anticipated.

Historically accurate models were insufficient, the indicators monitored were inappropriate and the interpretations applied were inaccurate. Like many other professional fields in this period of massive social change, economics was caught with old models in a new environment. Characterizing the entire transitional era, Stephen Greenblatt, a professor of English at the University of California at Berkeley, concluded: "It's a moment of paradigms lost." The old models no longer worked, yet nothing had emerged to take their place.

The new economic reality was that two types of significant and far-reaching changes were taking place at the same time. Cyclical changes, which traditional economic models had reconciled, continued to move through their ups and downs. However, sweeping secular changes, working both with and against this cyclical pattern, moved the economy in ways that cyclical models had yet to measure accurately—with dreadful consequences for those who depended on these models.

Cyclical changes are periodic (and sometimes historically predictable) expansions and contractions in the fundamental operations of an economy. For those who study cyclical forces, the impact of cultural and social forces upon the economy is held constant—that is, they assume that nothing is changing in the noncyclical arena. They ignore these changes at their peril. Secular changes shift the cultural environment that envelops the economy. These long-term changes shift the "norm," which during regular cyclical movement is assumed to remain constant. In simple metaphoric terms, the cyclical change is an object moving over a surface; the secular change is the surface moving beneath the object. Since the late 1980s, both the surface and the object have moved *at the same time,* making the objects' movement appear unpredictable. Consequently, those focusing only on the moving object continue to make inaccurate assessments.

"In a time of drastic change," explained social commentator Eric Hoffer, "it is the learners who inherit the future. The learned find themselves equipped to live in a world that no longer exists." That reality has shaken the foundations of economic forecasting and has made decision-making difficult for business and political leaders who in the past have found these forecasts comforting and reliable. In the new environment, those models offer only a partial view of the economy. Moreover, the segment of information that is missing from the models has become more impactful in the economy.

The dual changes have created anomalies in typical economic performance, events which are counterintuitive or atypical of historical examples. These anomalies suggest that the economy is changing in *significant* ways. Consider just a few of these seeming contradictions from 1994, 1995 and 1996.

ANOMALY NUMBER ONE

In 1994, the fourth year of an economic recovery, corporations reported profit increases of 11 percent (after 13 percent in 1993). In the midst of this growth, they let go more than 516,000 workers, a figure that came very close to the numbers affected by the past recession.

INFERENCE

In an era of coincidental cyclical and secular change, unemployment is not a clear economic measure, and corporate profits are not a dependable signal of the economy's general health. A corollary to this inference is: The stock market no longer signals the economy's status, as either a leading or a lagging indicator.

ANOMALY NUMBER TWO

During the 18 months leading up to June 1995, interest rates rose seven times, but consumer confidence rose as well. In the first months of 1996, mortgage rates started to drop, but housing purchases declined with them.

INFERENCE

In an era of coincidental cyclical and secular change, traditional concepts concerning the impact of interest-rate changes no longer operate, and the presumed link between consumer borrowing and consumer spending becomes less secure.

ANOMALY NUMBER THREE

After four years of a recovery (1991–1995), salary increases for the first quarter of 1995 were 0.6, the lowest in 16 years. Despite this 16-year low, the Consumer Price Index rose by 4 percent in the first half of 1995, prompting the Federal Reserve to tighten interest rates.

INFERENCE

In an era of coincidental cyclical and secular change, traditionally accepted (and even assumed) connections between economic expansion and workers' salaries break down.

These few examples offer some critical insights into new economic realities, and also suggest an equally crucial need for new economic models—ones that take into account both cyclical *and* secular inputs in appropriate (variable over time) proportions.

Business executives, politicians and other decision-makers seeking to operate within these new economic realities will soon discover that the existing tools available to them are losing their effectiveness. Interest-rate movements may no longer have the effect upon consumer behavior that they once did. Consumer behavior has fragmented so much, and personal reassessment processes have changed behavior so extensively, that any effort to guide consumer behavior could have unpredictable and even undesirable results.

Recent confusion over the American economy diminishes considerably when using the cyclical–secular context. By keeping their eyes only on the object moving on the surface (as our earlier metaphor suggested), forecasters completely missed the massive shifts that took place beneath the moving object. In particular, what economists missed in the "animal spirits" recession was a "disposable income squeeze," a structurally forced consumer-spending cutback that resulted not from traditional economic categories like declining employment or higher borrowing costs, but rather from a range of consumer-expense items. Twenty- to 40-percent increases in car insurance, medical expenses, tuition costs, property taxes, and other nondiscretionary expenditures squeezed consumer budgets. That required an involuntary reapportioning of personal resources, and therefore discretionary budget items— those items which in part drove the "shop till you drop" mentality— were the first to go. Since the U.S. economy depends on consumers for 66 percent of its vibrancy, *any* substantial pullback in consumer spending can trigger a downturn. While historically accurate forecasting models showed continued strength in the manufacturing sector, in machine-tool orders, and in other traditional economic markers (i.e., the objects moving on the surface), they missed the surface movement beneath the objects (i.e., the disposable-income squeeze).

The problem for American business and political leaders is that *no* historical models exist to handle such a coincidental and contradictory mix of forces within the economy. A first step toward creating and adopting a working model involves accepting the fact that secular changes are not like cyclical changes: They will not reverse course any time soon, and return everything to the way it was: Secular change is *not* cyclical.

Looking back over the successes of American institutions since World War II, we can easily see why so many leaders in positions of influence have been unable to let go of the old communities of wealth and the postwar mentality. In fact, past institutional successes are blinding many leaders to the reality of these changes. Society's "learned," as Eric Hoffer explained, are actually at a disadvantage because they know too much about what once worked. However, even if American heads of public and private institutions misunderstood the meaning behind the missed recession, the urgent message should have become perfectly clear when American society went "out of control."

CHAPTER 3

A WORLD OUT OF CONTROL

W hen the *Challenger* shuttle lifted off the ground from Cape
Kennedy, nothing in the early moments of its 1985 flight suggested the disaster that awaited just moments later. The shuttle carried
six professional astronauts and a school teacher, Christa McAuliffe from
New Hampshire—someone, NASA public-relations experts hoped,
with whom Americans could really identify. The ensuing disaster did
indeed create an identification with that school teacher, and the resulting anguish gave way to an investigation that would cost NASA its public support. In the moments and hours immediately following the
disaster, Americans sat transfixed before the nation's television screens,
wondering what it all meant.

The explosion over the Atlantic Ocean created a twisted trail of
white smoke, a shape a visiting Soviet poet called "a white swan of
death." News of the explosion sent Americans racing to their TVs to
locate CNN, the 1980s creation that broadcast news 24 hours a day.
Once tuned in, they watched the tragedy over and over, wondering what
was happening to NASA and America alike. The poignancy of the tragedy and the depth of the emotional response would later inspire Americans to recall exactly what they were doing when they heard the news.
Such a connection between public event and personal history had not
happened since the political assassinations of the 1960s.

The NASA disaster heralded a series of other disasters, problems
and conflicts that led to an overwhelming feeling that the world which
Americans inhabited had simply gone "out of control," a phrase that
people repeatedly used in reference to society, work, personal lives and

politics alike. The troubles came in waves: the first destabilizing public and private institutions, the second undermining their viability, and the third severing individual loyalty to them. Once upon a time, before the world seemed to lose control, Americans had felt secure—but, after these experiences, they felt insecure. Once, the communities of wealth fostered a common focus on expanding everyone's standard of living. After the conflicts, Americans broke away from that single social focus and started to look elsewhere for security. Before the disasters, the communities of wealth and their leaders had kept society on track and had addressed and (for the most part) solved specific problems along the way. After the crises, those same institutions and their leaders seemed incapable of handling a significant number of the events surrounding them. Individuals came to feel so swamped by these events, and so alone in their battle against them, that they concluded, as did one victim of hurricane Hugo: "We're on our own."

In this world out of control, America's mental status passed through three different stages. First, Americans endured a "psychic shock," the result of their battle with the economic shocks that created a disposable-income squeeze. Next, they struggled through an "anxiety attack," realizing that their leaders were simply not capable of handling the problems before them. Third, they tried to deal with a feeling of "psychological unemployment," the uneasy realization that while they might be currently employed, nothing but another misguided business decision stood between them and the pink slip that could prove their ticket to financial disaster.

The world out of control undermined the relationships, beliefs and possibilities that had brought loyalty and commitment to the communities of wealth. The success they enjoyed, and the benefits they created, began to lose their appeal. As the institutions and their leaders proved incapable of solving so many crises, many concerned individuals pulled away, cutting the loyalty ties that had helped their institutions to cohere throughout the postwar period. Next, they started to piece together their own protective mechanisms, in order to address the problems created by their once orderly world's loss of control.

THE FIRST PHASE: SHOCK TO THE SYSTEM

While the *Challenger* disaster was still fresh in Americans' minds, the depth of the problems that lay ahead was not very obvious. Imbued with feelings of "a new morning in America," the slogan that President Reagan used in his successful reelection campaign of 1984, Americans were reluctant to accept the possibility that real troubles lay ahead. In the months that followed the shuttle explosion, however, signs of trouble did start to surface. Public testimony revealed that, months before the disaster, some NASA officials were aware of the craft's faulty O-rings (the ultimate cause of the explosion) and that memoranda had circulated exposing such a risk—and, further, that in-house suppression had kept the information from reaching the appropriate authorities. Viewed from a larger perspective, the institution itself was the problem; its very structure and its way of operating had proved ineffective.

Additional revelations soiled the pristine white labcoat image that the agency had so meticulously nurtured. The NASA crisis brought Americans back to the troubling times they thought they had left in the 1970s. This time, however, the troubles did not go away, and this time the institutions were incapable of getting society back on track for the old communities of wealth.

After the *Challenger* debacle, everything seemed to go wrong. Congressional revelations further discredited NASA's good name, and other troubles surfaced from the agency itself. In June 1987, as three NASA rockets sat on their pads at Wallops Island, Virginia, technicians huddled in their blockhouse to avoid contact with a passing storm. Suddenly, lightning launched the rockets. One flopped harmlessly into the sea, but the other two hurtled downrange, forcing startled officials to head for their tracking equipment. Embarrassed officials insisted that lightning could never—repeat, never—launch a rocket loaded with a nuclear warhead. Then, in 1990, the Hubble telescope space probe achieved orbit bearing a faulty $1.5 billion lens which, due to inadequate testing on the ground, produced fuzzy images. Even though subsequent contact with the probe corrected some of the error, the story of experts failing in their work remained. Meanwhile, in the public sphere, a study of air safety found that near-misses in the air had increased by 40 percent since 1981, and that accident warnings had doubled.

While the professional side of America's institutions lacked efficacy, Americans learned that their elected officials were not tending to their responsibilities, either. The Tower Commission reported, and the Iran–Contra congressional hearings confirmed, that President Reagan was not in control of diplomacy undertaken in his name. No sooner had that political crisis died down than citizens learned that members of Congress were operating a personal banking system that allowed them to "kite" checks (receive the cash before the money was actually in the account) with impunity—running, in essence, an interest-free loan system, a perquisite denied other Americans by law.

As the government went, so went religious institutions. The Reverend Jim Bakker, who had created, built, and expanded the largest televangelism empire, and whose Christian amusement park in North Carolina grew steadily for nearly a decade, was removed from the pulpit and eventually jailed, for mismanaging funds and gaining personally from his ministry. Bakker was just the most infamous of several religious leaders, including Jimmy Swaggart, Oral Roberts and several Catholic priests, who had sordid moral and financial revelations undermine their saintliness.

The "few good men"—as the U.S. Marines prefer to call themselves—charged with guarding the U.S. embassy in Moscow won financial and personal favors from Soviet citizens in exchange for access to off-limits sections of the embassy. Not only did their actions breech embassy security; they also damaged Marine Corps honor.

Meanwhile, from secret perches near and above Los Angeles freeways, people with guns started taking random shots at cars below, creating the "freeway shooting" craze that spread to the Midwest, and from there to the East. In time, that random violence moved into drive-by shootings, wherein gang members, as part of their initiation rites, would choose an innocent person standing on the street and simply drive by and kill him or her.

The health-care industry lost control as well. Tuberculosis, which health officials for 30 years thought had vanished, returned with a vengeance. The number of cases rose by 2.6 percent in 1986, and by another 12.3 percent in 1988, and headed up from there. Meanwhile, syphilis reached a 40-year high in 1988, topping 16.2 cases per 100,000 citizens. Without doubt, acquired immune deficiency syndrome (AIDS) became the era's most frightening medical disaster. The inability of medical science to cure or even control this new disease suggested that science was not up to the challenges of contemporary life. First discovered in 1981, the disease and its HIV precursor spread unabated throughout the decade, reaching epidemic proportions by 1987—when the medical community introduced AZT, a treatment that doctors thought would curtail the virus. Very soon, however, evidence revealed that science's AZT answer was not in fact an answer at all, and the terror of the unsolved epidemic (or "plague," as social critics claimed) returned. Meanwhile, a streptococcus mutation emerged as a "flesh-eating" disease that literally ate away at human skin. The press reported these medical events at home right next to international crises like the deadly Ebola virus rampant in Africa—further exposing the apparent impotence of medical scientists.

Nature itself seemed to go out of control. Sensational hurricanes brought unsurpassed damage to America's Gulf of Mexico coast, south Florida and the entire east coast. In the midwest, the Mississippi, Missouri, Illinois, and Kaw rivers rampaged over their banks more than once, devastating thousands of heartland farm acres and bringing yet another huge swath of the country into the "national disaster" category. Extraordinary mud slides in California merely anticipated the stunning Northridge earthquake that shocked the most stolid Californian into thinking "The Big One," the earthquake that would send much of the coastal territory of California into the Pacific Ocean, could be at hand.

Even pets followed Nature's call of the wild, turning on their owners and even innocent bystanders. The American Staffordshire terrier carried a bland enough name. However, the "pit bull" dogs, as they were more popularly known, went on a mad spree themselves, killing or maiming hundreds of humans in the late 1980s. "Pit bull! Pit bull!" exclaimed Warren Brodrich, executive director of the Santa Clara Humane Society. "The hysteria is just growing."

While biblical-scale disasters reappeared annually, human errors continued to surface as well. Investigators revealed that the savings-and-loan industry, the rock-solid financial system that stood for neighborhood banking and local Chamber of Commerce boosterism, was actually a snake pit of deceit, corruption, mismanagement and weak (and even complacent) public regulation. This institutional structure, a bulwark in the post–World War II drive toward greater personal wealth, had fallen victim to the excess mania of the 1980s. In the end, Americans would have to finance a $500 billion bailout of the "S&L" industry.

Other financial institutions furthered the feeling of imminent collapse. When the stock market took its October 1987 nosedive, many Americans wondered if the country was headed toward another Great Depression. The wild spending, the excessive leverage, the widespread corruption and the overall sense that the country's institutions were coming apart gave them good reason to think the worst.

Books like *Liar's Poker* and *Barbarians at the Gate* opened the doors to Wall Street's inner workings and provided Americans a peek into the huge megadollar dealmakers. It was not a pretty sight. Petty egos mixed with rampant greed had created a system that was riddled with corruption, insider dealing, special privileges, misogyny and raging illegality. When several S&L personalities and Wall Street financiers went to prison for their deeds, Americans sensed that they were watching a few take the blame for the many. They did not believe that either Wall Street or the judicial system had performed admirably, and they concluded that the "system" was rigged.

Even though the 1987 stock-market decline did not lead to a repeat of the 1929 crash, its resilience did not give Americans any additional confidence in other institutions. In the 1980s, the institutions that once promised a rising standard of living in return for loyalty and hard work had started to break their own promise. Between 1982 and 1987, real hourly wages had declined by 0.5 percent per year. Between 1980 and 1989, the real value of hourly fringe benefits had fallen by 13.8 percent, faster than the accumulated hourly wage drop of 9.3 percent. In the 10 years following 1980, families in the lowest tenth of after-tax income had lost 10.2 percent of their pay, and the poorest fifth had watched their taxes rise by 16 percent while their income had fallen by 3 percent.

For the first time since World War II, the percent of American home owners started to decline. Even though overall ownership numbers started downward after 1984, they were dropping rapidly in the 25 to 34 age groups, hinting at future problems for the economy. Salary stagnation stood behind home-ownership decline. According to a 1989 Lomas Mortgage USA (Dallas) report, the average U.S. household fell $4,300 short of the annual income needed ($49,900) to qualify for a loan to purchase that year's average-priced U.S. home ($142,400).

The first phase of the world out of control did two fundamental things to the American people. First, it brought back doubts that Americans had cast aside about the stability of American institutions and turned the country's historic optimism into endemic pessimism. People lost confidence in their leaders; they lost the sense that "We are all in this thing together"; and they lost the belief that the American Dream was reaching more and more people all the time. In its place, many Americans realized that they had to take care of themselves because the system no longer assured them security and stability. For some, this meant "make a killing and get out," and for others, it meant "pull back" (from dependence on these institutions).

The second thing that the initial phase of the world out of control did was to create new types of financial threats. Consumer budgets felt pressure, but not in ways that historical economists had measured. That is, the Consumer Price Index did not shoot up. But other nondiscretionary budget items like property taxes, tuition rates, and auto insurance costs, rose quite rapidly. This uneven but nonetheless real budget challenge created a "disposable-income squeeze," a noneconomic indicator that actually triggered the ninth postwar recession. The causes and consequences of this new consumer reality require closer scrutiny.

In many locales, property taxes rose fast enough to prompt community outrage. In Maine, discontent over climbing property taxes made tax reform the number one political issue of 1989, forcing the Maine legislature to program direct reimbursements to homeowners. Nationwide, rises of 20 percent per year were common, and increases of 40 percent to 50 percent were not unusual. Residents in some towns on Long Island, New York, actually experienced increases of 170 percent.

Soaring legal, medical and car-repair costs sent auto-insurance rates skyrocketing. Nationwide, auto-insurance premiums rose an average of 63 percent between 1982 and 1987, far outstripping inflation. Even though 26 states had instituted no-fault insurance programs, they were unable to slow the steady increases. Outraged voters in California passed Proposition 103, which rolled back auto-insurance rates to 20 percent above their 1987 levels. But insurance companies soon found a "fair and reasonable return" loophole and circumvented the most restrictive parts of the proposition.

Even though health-care costs started upward in the 1970s, individuals did not feel the pinch until the 1980s. Health-care cost increases of 20 percent to 40 percent simply made care too expensive for companies to pay for everything, and so they started to pass some of the expenses along to their employees. By decade's end, nearly half of all American companies in the manufacturing and retailing sectors required their employees to pay for some or all of their health-insurance costs. Many of the companies that did not require direct payment for premiums raised deductibles, forcing employees to pay more money out of their pockets to meet health-care needs.

Even adjustable-rate mortgages (ARMs) turned against their holders in the late 1980s. While mortgage lenders had "teased" potential clients into taking a loan with low initial interest rates, when interest rates started upward, the monthly mortgage bill rose with them. In 1988, for example, teaser rates were as low as 7 percent, but after six months, the rates reached market parity. By the end of 1989, interest rates hovered around 11 percent. Those with ARMs suffered a 43 percent increase in their monthly mortgage payments. At that time, ARMs accounted for roughly half of all new first-mortgage loans nationwide, which meant that the most financially vulnerable were also the most exposed to the rapidly rising rates.

These items forced Americans to reapportion involuntarily their personal budgets, and for the most part they took money from discretionary spending to cover rising nondiscretionary budget items. In terms of the economy, this meant that consumer spending declined, even though the same amount of money was moving through the economy. With

consumer spending accounting for roughly two-thirds of the U.S. economy, the disposable-income squeeze triggered a recession. However,
that squeeze was not just a single event that came and went. It continued. According to Labor Department figures, the typical U.S. household
in the middle quintile still spends over 46 percent of its income on housing, utilities and health care—up from 33.3 percent a generation ago.
Thus, when American corporations started recession-era tactics to reduce costs, Americans were already suffering from recession-era economics. And it was that combination which helped create a new type of
economy.

THE SECOND PHASE: GETTING AGGRESSIVE

After the disposable-income squeeze recession, the second phase of the
world out of control started. This time Americans found themselves
even more vulnerable to the disasters and setbacks. Security issues—
both fiscal and physical—became more prevalent, and tensions arose
between and among categories of people, creating a less civil and more
aggressive culture. As a result, Americans felt that things were getting
worse, with little hope of reversing course.

In 1991, personal bankruptcy filings reached 1 million for the first
time in U.S. history, suggesting that the budget squeezes were more
than many could stand. Three-quarters of the filings were Chapter 7,
which required a sell-off of property to pay for debts. In essence, filers
saw no hope of readjusting their finances, and decided instead to surrender what they had. The National Consumer Law Center discovered that
many more people could not even afford the filing fees, and therefore
let the creditors have their property. Stories surfaced that mortgage
debtors were simply mailing their house keys to the banks that held their
mortgages. In a related statistic, emergency food requests in the nation's
cities rose by 26 percent in 1990, and emergency shelter requests jumped
by 13 percent. Meanwhile, actual emergency food resources rose by just
4 percent, while available shelter beds increased by only 3 percent.

The personal budget squeeze quickly passed to public institutions
charged with supplying safety-net services. The monthly federal deficit

jumped by 62 percent between November 1989 and November 1990. State and local governments typically ran surpluses during the mid-1980s, but things quickly changed after the disposable-income squeeze recession. Typically, state and local governments' surpluses had reached $20 billion per year. However, in the third quarter of 1990, state and local governments ran deficits of $30.7 billion, and that figure moved higher thereafter.

With governments losing solvency and individuals facing daunting financial burdens, the economy headed downward. In the midst of this troubling economic news, Americans experienced still another round of social disorder. This time, no one anywhere was immune to this situation, creating *another* wave of the world out of control. When a tennis fanatic leaned over a viewing-stand barrier and stabbed tennis pro Monica Seles in the back, Americans drew a collective gasp. Even though the knifing took place outside the U.S., Americans still wondered whether personal safety was at last anachronistic. As one writer explained, the Monica Seles stabbing "stands as a symbol of what can go wrong." Wrong, indeed: If tennis pros, with all of their attendants close at hand, are not safe in public, then no one is safe.

Events continued to reveal just how dangerous the world had become. Florida tourist murders, shopping-mall carjackings, playground shootouts, workplace assaults and additional random gunfire on America's freeways, especially when extensively covered in the media, added to the fear that no one could hide from rising public risks.

The stories became heartrending as well as threatening. Fifteen hundred mourners appeared at the funeral of Polly Klaas, a 12-year-old girl kidnapped from her home in Petaluma, California, and murdered. Most of the crowd had never had contact with the young victim, yet they felt the vulnerability and sensed the danger. She had been stolen from the safety of her own bedroom, an event that heightened the feeling that no place was safe anymore.

Other formerly safe refuges were violated as well. A prominent computer-science professor opened an innocent-looking package in the usually protected confines of his Yale University office, and it exploded, critically injuring him. This happened just days after a professor at the

University of California at San Francisco opened another near-fatal package. FBI Director William S. Sessions warned all professors that the so-called Unabomber had targeted them and that they should be especially wary of unexpected larger mailings.

Not only were homes and educational institutions vulnerable: All workplaces were at risk. One day a gunman armed with automatic weapons and hundreds of rounds of ammunition walked into the law offices of Pettit & Martin on the 33rd floor of a San Francisco office tower and started shooting. He killed eight employees and wounded several others. When trapped in the ensuing chase, he committed suicide. Even postal workers learned how dangerous "the office" could be, and courtrooms turned violent in several instances. According to Southland Corporation, former parent of 7-Eleven stores, homicide became the number one cause of death among women on the job. The company warned its employees "not to assume that the workplace is any safer than the rest of the world."

The biggest scare, however, took place on February 26, 1993, when a 1,500-pound bomb hidden in a truck in the parking garage of the World Trade Center in New York City exploded, killing six workers and injuring more than 1,000 others. As one agent explained, it was "the biggest terrorist attack in U.S. history." Not only had so many American institutions gone out of control, but the chaos and incomprehensibility of international terrorism had come to America. When, two years later, an American, Timothy McVeigh, bombed a federal building in Oklahoma City, killing 168 people, shocked viewers of CNN's live coverage realized that their own countrymen had internalized the violence that had once marked fanatical, unbalanced societies elsewhere in the world.

Dean Kilpatrick, director of the Crime Victims Research and Treatment Center at the Medical University of South Carolina, summarized his discussions with the Center's patients this way: "There is a feeling that no place is safe. . . . You feel your home is not safe, your public facilities are not safe. You're not safe traveling. Where are you safe?"

The concern about safety, even at home, helped add a sales boost for home-security systems, and classes in Karate and other forms of physical self-defense. In 1992, home-security systems sales jumped by 35 percent, and in the same year, month-to-month increases in gun sales rose anywhere from 50 percent to 100 percent. Even the sale of whistles—to be used as private alerts—rose steadily. Parents created a boom in minivan sales as they refused to turn over their children to public-transportation systems and preferred to carpool to make sure that the children were under parental control at all times. Using the same reasoning, parents enrolled their children in ballet classes, soccer leagues, music lessons and a host of other supervised activities, all intended to keep the young ones safe as well as occupied. This focus on personal protection gave new life to the private-security industry. By the early 1990s, private-security companies employed nearly three times as many personnel as all the country's public law-enforcement agencies combined.

These realities created tensions that divided Americans, even as they found themselves facing the same crises and worrying about the same dangers. Racial incidents, attacks against women, public incivility and hate crimes surfaced in greater numbers. When the United Negro College Fund started its annual telethon in 1992, for the first hour operators in Jacksonville, Florida, had to endure racial-harassment callers who damned all "niggers" and praised David Duke, the highly divisive former Ku Klux Klan leader who had run for office in Louisiana. In the 12 prior years that the NAACP had held the telethon, nothing like that had ever happened.

In Dubuque, Iowa, the National Association for the Advancement of White People rose to fight the city's plan to encourage blacks to move into the predominantly white city. According to one representative of what members called "the new KKK": "It's us against the blacks" for the city's resources. In the past, Dubuque's NAACP chapter actually had a white majority membership.

The divisiveness spread to political constituencies as well. In California, state legislators undertook a project to divide the state in two, one northern and one southern. In southwestern Kansas and southeastern Colorado, citizens started movements to secede from their respective states and form a new state, because they were tired of "their" oil revenues leaving the area. A group in west Texas started a secession movement, filing legal suits throughout the region and thus forcing local officials to waste time attending court proceedings. The citizens of Staten Island, New York, launched a losing effort to withdraw their largely shorelined borough from the City of New York, to form an independent city. All of these efforts were part of a mood to restrict geographic boundaries in order to control the chaos.

Along a similar line, people started developing "gated communities," which they hoped would protect them from the unwanted social aberrations occurring so near. These private enclaves surrounded themselves with stone and brick fences, placed private security guards at the entrance gates, and hired on-street patrols to keep the outside world from coming in. One such community outside of Chicago enclosed its streets by using a high metal fence, even though the streets were public, and the guards posted at the entrance gate were actually public police officers. What had started as private-sector programs had become public-sector programs!

Where citizens could not either afford or build gated communities, neighborhoods banded together to keep out those who would bring disorder onto their streets. In Louisiana, neighbors in Jefferson Parish erected barricades to keep noncitizens of their territory from entering. While the Louisiana example had a tinge of racism, the citizens of Shaker Heights, just outside Cleveland, simply wanted to seal off their neighborhood when they, too, erected barriers that allowed them to control access to their streets.

On the more aggressive side, the National Survival Game became a highly popular way to spend weekends. Toting guns that would shoot paint balls at vulnerable opponents, thereby "killing" them and eliminating them from further action, players sought to take land and symbols from their opponents before their sides were depleted by the fatal paint blasts. The game became so popular in the late 1980s that Tippman Pneumatics, a former manufacturer of machine guns, introduced a splatter gun that could fire 600 paint balls per minute. Duquesne Systems, a software company in Pittsburgh, actually played the game at its national sales meeting, as a way to integrate new employees into its competitive culture.

With the growing interest in self-protection, hand-gun sales started to rise, and public support for gun control wavered. Cities like Miami and Jacksonville passed laws that allowed citizens to carry hand guns in public. And Kennesaw, Georgia, actually passed an ordinance requiring every resident to own a gun. In the second phase of a world out of control, growing numbers of individuals realized that the old systems of protection were weak and ineffective, and that they needed to take things into their own hands. Doing that brought, along with the positive feeling of physical security, nasty, uncivil conflicts. The people's central focus, however, remained on making their lives secure.

THE THIRD PHASE: ASSAYING THE DAMAGE

In the midst of so much insecurity and rising incivility, American corporations started shedding "unnecessary" workers. Using rationales like "global competitiveness" and "cost reductions," American business started doing in fact what Americans were already suspicious had been happening: ripping apart institutional cohesiveness to benefit fewer and fewer people. When AT&T announced over 70,000 layoffs (later reduced to over 40,000), newspaper articles quoted pink-slipped employees, who spoke angrily of selfish bosses who were profiting from others' suffering. Indeed, those same articles revealed how the personal stock portfolio of AT&T's CEO, Robert Allen, had jumped by $6 million because his announcement of staff reductions ignited a rally in AT&T stock.

The first layoffs came during the recession, a practice Americans understood. But when the economy regained an upward momentum (a time when, historically, companies had rehired workers), the shedding of workers continued. Unlike in past recessions, 56 percent of employee reductions made during this recession became permanent, and the ax continued to fall right through the recovery. In fact, American business let go nearly as many employees in 1995, the fourth year of the recovery, as it did in the heart of the recession. In 1994 alone, nine American corporations axed more than 10,000 employees each. Fully 19 million adults said that a lost job in the 1990s had precipitated a major crisis in their lives.

Unlike earlier recession-induced cutbacks, these staff reductions did not just affect blue-collar workers. By 1993, the U.S., for the first time in its history, had more white-collar unemployed than it did blue-collar unemployed; and, in fact, more workers with college educations lost jobs than did those with only high-school diplomas. Moreover, unlike with past recessions, those who returned to employment did not simply step into the same job at a similar salary. In fact, 52 percent of the job-searching white-collar workers accepted jobs for less pay than their prior position garnered, and overall only 35 percent of laid-off workers in the 1990s found jobs with equal or greater pay.

Something significant was happening to the U.S. economy. Taken in historical perspective, the U.S., in 1956, in the midst of its highly successful drive to put together the communities of wealth, created an economy that had more white-collar than blue-collar workers, signaling a shift from an industrial-based economy to a consumer-based economy. In 1993, given more unemployed white-collar than blue-collar workers, the U.S. economy had shifted again. This time, neither the employees nor the political and business leaders understood what that shift signaled.

RESPONDING TO THE WORLD
OUT OF CONTROL

Everything from super hurricanes to unbalanced economic realities signaled that something was wrong. Most Americans, however, felt ill-prepared to address these larger issues. In the 1980s, massive productivity created abundant choices that overwhelmed American shoppers, but in the 1990s, a wide array of seemingly never-ending disasters overwhelmed American abilities to respond effectively. Within a decade, Americans had fallen from abundance and excess to abandonment and distress.

As they struggled to understand what was happening, many citizens turned to alternative explanations. The inadequacy of so-called rational

explanations for why things were taking place, and the inability of rationally constructed institutions to address these problems, turned people
away. The National Opinion Research Council discovered, late in the
1980s, that those who believed they had contacted the dead had risen to
42 percent, up from 27 percent in 1973. At about the same time, a Gallup
Poll revealed that 57 percent of college-educated Americans believed in
extraterrestrials, up from a mid-40s percentage in 1978.

The level of confusion and disorientation that the world out of
control had produced found perhaps its best expression in a group of
businessmen in New Jersey. In Wildwood Crest, educated community
representatives became desperate when they heard reports that the
Atlantic Ocean had brought pollution to their city's beaches, an annual
source of tourist revenue. Lost over what to do, and convinced that public agencies charged with the responsibility could do nothing, they took
chlorine tablets to the water's edge and threw them into the ocean, under
the incredible belief that these little capsules could do away with the
ocean's pollution.

Otherwise educated community leaders tossing chlorine tabs into
the briny deep's tide to halt the inflow of pollution generated miles from
shore could serve as a metaphor for the hopelessness that Americans
were feeling about the chaos that enveloped them. What could they do
as individuals? Institutions were failing them, and the things that usually kept society working toward the same objectives were vanishing.
The immensity of problems forced individuals and families alike to
struggle just to retain what they had.

In this mood, the arts took a gloomy turn. "The young and wasted,"
one critic called a group of youthful writers who came to prominence at
this time. Jay McInerney, Tama Janowitz and Bret Easton Ellis captured
the decadence that the seeming social collapse nurtured and also revealed the extremely negative bent that Americans were taking. With
novels like *Bright Lights, Big City* (McInerney), *Slaves of New York*
(Janowitz) and *Less Than Zero* (Ellis), these writers chronicled failure,
self-ruin, out-of-control individuals and a society without accepted borders. The world described in these and other such novels, as one observer
noted, could be summarized rather simply: "Everything sucks."

Writers ground out nonfiction books with titles like *The End of History, The End of Nature, The End of Art* and *The End of Science.* Marietta, Georgia, a city next to the one that had mandated gun owner- ship, prosecuted a pickup-truck driver for displaying a "Shit Happens" bumper sticker. With society in such a confused state, elected officials there passed a pair of laws which implicitly told citizens "Speak cleanly and shoot to kill." T-shirts also added to the tough-edged "fight or die" mentality: "Life, Death, or Los Angeles," said one, with another brag- ging "New Jersey: Only the Strong Survive." And these were *positive* pub- lic relations!

"There is a sense at large in America today of dissipation," wrote one art critic, "of forfeiture—of something gone wrong without know- ing how to fix it. There is a sense that something precious has been and is being lost, and is not being replaced." Rap music became aggressive and overtly violent, while maudlin and even defeatist imagery popu- lated the albums of the Cowboy Junkies, Lou Reed and Don Henley. "American music is really tired," complained one record producer. "All American music is saying is: 'Let's do drugs'; 'Let's not do drugs'; 'Let's have sex'; 'Sex isn't safe anymore.' "

In the midst of this negativity crisis, the movie *Batman* captured both the feeling of lost possibilities and the exceedingly remote possi- bility that individuals could solve the problems. The movie's scenery of cracking buildings, dirty and dangerous streets and a horrifically blackened atmosphere visualized what Americans were thinking about society in general. The implied messages—that only future violence can overcome present violence, and that it takes someone with bigger weap- ons to halt those who have created the chaos with theirs—gave narrative form to the hopelessness that Americans were experiencing.

One cartoon showed a *Batman* marquee carrying the disclaimer, "Not as funny as it used to be." One reason why *Batman* was not so funny then was that the spoof and wink that was essential to all super- hero comics and television shows had disappeared, replaced by an aggressive violence that undermined typical writer–reader irony. That is, reality overtook fiction.

Coming out of World War II, when Americans set about creating and expanding their communities of wealth, movie heroes were either individuals who were thrown into extraordinary circumstances and rose to the occasion (the so-called democratic hero), or they were a group—once called the "foxhole heroes"—which included representatives from different walks of life joined in a common purpose. In the more modern movies, however, the heroes were extraordinarily talented and heavily armed professionals who took a sadistic pleasure in destroying the opposition. When Clint Eastwood, playing Dirty Harry, pointed a huge hand gun point-blank at a criminal's head and begged him to move (by saying "Go ahead—make my day."), so Harry could rationalize pulling the trigger, the new hero model was set. Soon muscle men and explosives experts like Rambo were the new heroes. No wonder *Batman* wasn't as funny as it used to be!

The art that best captured what was taking place in American society, however, was architecture. The 1950s skyscrapers were symbols of orderly, hierarchical organizations. Squared to the street, upright and huge, these monoliths encapsulated American corporate identity. Postmodern structures, however, added to the modernist skyscraper the idea that all of history could be mined for one or another glorious image. But deconstructionists changed everything. They designed buildings that had no right angles, straight lines, entranceways, or other details that architects once assumed a building must have. Every assumption of architecture was up for grabs, and, as a result, the art itself was up for redefinition. Anything was possible, but nothing fit together. Without historical assumptions, no basic structures could be carried forward without a complete rethinking.

What deconstructionist architects were doing for buildings, American political and business leaders were doing to American institutions. They were shredding them in ways that broke apart community, progressive movement forward, and any sense that the future would be better than the past. All of the rules from the past became inconvenient and counterproductive. While the communities of wealth required loyalty to grow so successfully, leaders focusing on the bottom line alone destroyed that fundamental value. The later-era leaders laid waste the communities in quest of the wealth.

AMERICA'S MENTAL STATE

The world out of control undermined confidence in the communities of wealth. Americans blamed institutions and their leaders for precipitating social conflicts and for being incapable of handling those conflicts which reached critical stages. The crazily gyrating world also put the country through stages of mental anxiety—social psychological states that members of communities shared. They first responded with shock at what they saw. Next, they grew anxious when they learned that their leaders could not handle the problems. Finally, they fretted over their own vulnerability when institutions started to come apart before their eyes. These psychological states offer insights into the era of transition between the old institutions and the new organization that would displace them—between the way things were once done and the way they would be done in the future.

In the 1980s, when society went "out of control," individuals sensed that they were vulnerable to dangers that they themselves had not created. Everywhere individuals looked, they saw institutions incapable of dealing with the problems that lay before them: executive-level corruption, uncontrollable killer diseases, skyrocketing nondiscretionary expenses, shocking crimes and crumbling institutions.

As a result, America went into "psychic shock," worried that events and institutions, having gone haywire, would only get worse. With each crisis story, its audience wondered what would hit next. The sensational stories turned individual against individual, as people looked for scapegoats. Americans felt vulnerable, yet political leaders told them that nothing was wrong, business leaders said the economy was strong, and news commentators wondered if something was wrong not with the economy, but with Americans.

This dissonance between what individuals experienced in their personal lives and what they heard from their leaders created an anxiety attack of sorts—a sinking feeling that their leaders did not "get it" and that they as individuals were essentially on their own. The institutions which theretofore had shielded them from disaster had become ineffective or indifferent. Like a horror movie in which a perceived ally becomes a monstrous adversary, those same institutions were even *causing* the troubles. This reality, and the anxiety attack it provoked, motivated individuals to reassess the fundamentals of everything they had once accepted as important, and further to revalue relationships, needs, habits and other behaviors in light of their experiences.

After the recession, still suffering through the psychic shock and numb from the anxiety attack, individuals as employees had to deal with massive corporate restructurings that led to pink slips—and the fear of future pink slips. The thought quickly spread to all levels of the economy that no matter where one dwelt on the economic scale or on the career ladder, he or she was just a telephone call away from financial disaster.

The fear of financial ruin created the next mental anxiety: "psychological unemployment." This feeling of financial vulnerability concentrated one's attention and resources on creating stability, security and balance. Federal Reserve Chairman Alan Greenspan told Congress in 1997 that "job insecurity" was responsible for the lack of economic vitality. In response to this new mental crisis, individuals started to rethink the viability of their financial future, making resource adjustments where necessary, and to reconstitute relationships and priorities, whether personal, professional, or commercial. That is, they started over.

At the end of this anguishing period of constant adjustment, Americans concluded: "This just isn't working for me." What had worked so well for so long no longer worked. Americans started drifting away from the communities of wealth and toward any organization or institution that could offer them a solution to the myriad of troubles they faced. The twisted plume of smoke that marked the *Challenger* explosion signaled the beginning of a world out of control which would deconstruct and vaporize the unifying theme of postwar America: growth and a rising standard of living. In the midst of this system-wide collapse, Americans watched in disbelief as their political leaders bickered endlessly about irrelevant minutiae, their corporate executives extracted exorbitant sums for salaries from company treasuries, and their grossly overpaid sports heroes went on strike for even more money.

The essential irony of this massive period of transition came from the fact that the leaders had become lagging indicators, and the followers were now the leaders. That is, while the followers were changing directions, the leaders were continuing down the same path. As a result, while society was moving into a period of massive social change, the followers were leading and the leaders were lagging behind.

These lagging indicators need to change their perspectives. They need to stop interpreting consumer, citizen and employee changes as temporary aberrations and to see these changes as the beginning of something new. They need a different way to acquire insights in order to develop a different and more fully realized context within which to act. They need, as we shall next see, a Magic Eye.

CRITICAL INSIGHT:
Muscle Memory Versus the Magic Eye

The post–World War II system of institutions has started to come apart, but many leaders continue to tinker with each problem as if it were the only thing wrong. In essence, leaders are looking at each specific problem but missing the systemic breakdown. The heads of major institutions learned what they know and rose to their positions of influence within the context of the old institutions. Consequently, they are having difficulty identifying, let alone adjusting to, a business environment without expanding markets, compliant and responsive consumers, loyal workers, effective marketing tactics and dependable economic models. They may see a world of confusion, conflict, chaos and possible collapse, but they still believe the only way to fight these perceived troubles is to do something that is consistent with what they have always done.

Most know that they must do something to deal with these new realities. Too many, however, have conscripted the latest management theory, trusting yet another consultant's answer, all in an effort to keep the old system going. They have reengineered their personnel, repriced their products, downsized and rightsized their few remaining followers and even made their normal quality-management effort into a Total Quality Management (TQM) program.

Most of these theories are merely more of the same thing, albeit loaded anew with special terminological flare. The comfort gained from reasserting managerial control, resetting productivity measurements or raising motivational goals reveals the power of organizational muscle memory.

In sports, muscle memory tends to override new learning; the mind has a new and better technique, but the body prefers to do what it has always done. An individual learns about a golf swing that is more appropriate to his or her body type, but the old techniques and habits actually block the changes that are necessary to improve the swing. Organizational muscle memory also seeks to override significant change and tends to reinforce old habits. After all, like the old golf swing that may have gotten the individual's score under 90, the old corporate methods did help the company grow through the era of expanding the standard of living. Moreover, using new efficiency-based tactics, such as TQM and reengineering, leaders can feel that they are addressing new realities with new techniques. They believe they are swinging the club differently.

As a result, when a new reality faces the company, executives redeploy old tactics, even when those tactics no longer address new conditions. In its hardest form, companies suffering from muscle memory believe that what used to be can be again, and that what has come apart can be rebuilt to look and operate even better than before. They are only kidding themselves.

Undoing organizational muscle memory involves first and foremost seeing that things have changed in a way that makes old techniques ineffective. Efficiency can go only so far in the new business environment. Sooner or later, effectiveness becomes the crucial competitive edge. Also, tactical restructurings as a way of becoming more efficient likewise run their course, necessarily giving way to strategic restructurings.

But how does one see new problems as being, in fact, new and *different*? One method lies in a series of books that surfaced in America just when the changing culture became the most confusing. *Magic Eye* (1993), the first in the series, sold over 2 million copies. *Magic Eye II* (1994) surpassed 2 million as well, and Volume III won even greater market approval, passing 1 million faster than either of the first two volumes. At one time, stocks of these books were consuming so much shelf space that booksellers started worrying about their success having a negative impact on regular book sales.

The challenge of trying to see below the surface of the page captured the reader's interest. Viewed with both eyes focused on the surface of the paper (normal viewing), images appear chaotic and unrecognizable. However, by letting go of the old focal point on the surface of the page and then allowing the eyes to look beyond the surface, the reader allows a three-dimensional image to arise from "beneath" the surface.

To experience the focal point shift, the viewer must let go of the busy image seen in the surface focus and relax the eyes to keep them from zeroing in on the surface chaos. In essence, the easily accessible surface chaos obscures the important image; changing the way of seeing corrects the erroneous perception. "They're almost meditative," explained one of the book's editors. "You have to concentrate and you have to relax."

As a social metaphor, Magic Eye offers a model for dealing with a world of information overload, a world wherein public information suggests an image of chaos, and where, in fact, those who present that information—many news providers—actually benefit from giving a sense that chaos is rampant. With so much information all telling of difficult times, with disconnected experiences jumbling the individual's mind and with unrelated data coming to our attention almost at random, the challenge has become to see "through" the information overload, eliminate the extraneous, and allow the significant to emerge. To have, so to speak, a generic "magic eye" to look past the surface and see what is essentially transpiring.

From yet another perspective, the wild success of the Magic Eye, coming as it did right in the middle of the most difficult times of the early 1990s, suggests that at some level of consciousness Americans concluded that they needed another way to deal with the chaos. A "see-through" skill, the book's buyers suggested, would enable them to operate more effectively in the real world. For many, "I see it" meant "I get it."

Even with a new and compelling way of looking at society's surface chaos, muscle memory can still overwhelm the viewer. Those who were unable to see the magic eye's deeper image were allowing muscle memory to control perception. In terms of information, those who were confused about the context simply omitted unappealing information. Many simply dammed the flow of information onto their desks and went back to doing what they had always done. Rather than address the new situation with a new perspective, many canceled subscriptions, stanched the inflow of information, narrowed the research, rallied to another one-answer theory, and acted from theory rather than observation.

Again, for the "magic eye" to work, the viewer must look at the entire image, but just look at it in a different way from the usual. To curtail "magic eye" information, the viewer could tear the image in half. That would certainly lessen the surface chaos and offer a more "controllable" level of input. However, while such an action might lessen the amount of information reaching the eye, it would also eliminate half of the submerged image.

Operating in an environment that requires a "magic eye" is difficult. The target moves constantly, the "noise" bombarding the eye clouds perception, and a guiding principle seems lacking. The old tried-and-true tools just seem to feel better, and trusting an entirely different way of looking can be scary.

Yet reality requires that leaders do see through the surface chaos. As the "magic eye" metaphor suggests, important patterns exist amidst many distracting details, yet many leaders depend upon those details to guide their decisions. Surveys come and go, and polls have their moment and fade. But polls, surveys and also studies do not accurately reveal the larger context. They are part of the surface confusion.

The important events are within the field of vision. Allowing them to take their own shape, to come forward and create their own patterns and to have their own impact, demands time, skill and above all, patience. The surface action is easier to use but in periods of significant change, like the present, the action has proven less and less effective.

The reason that the leader needs to release from muscle memory and let go of the surface chaos is simply that consumers, citizens and employees—all the same people in different social roles—have changed and are not going back to the way they were when all of those techniques worked and when leadership first developed muscle memory. Those old skills can lead to some undesirable results. Deploying tactical restructurings and cyclical techniques, examples of organizational muscle memory, reduces the business enterprise to a low-cost provider contest. That is a vicious cycle wherein dwindling revenues force additional rounds of cost-cutting, further reductions of prices, additional low-cost competitors and further margin squeezes.

Applying the "magic eye" to identify the extensive secular changes underway and to develop a plan for strategic restructuring leads to opportunities to expand margins and escape from the low-cost-provider cycle. It offers better connections to citizens and employees and the potential for regaining society-wide, shared objectives.

While the changes underway may seem like chaos, they are not. An observable pattern exists. While old tactics may bring comfort with their built-in muscle memory, they are no longer adequate. The reason is simple: Individual responses to the world out of control have resulted in a personal revolution. To confuse the personal revolution for surface chaos is to miss a tremendous opportunity to move ahead of the competition. Seeing through the apparent chaos means simply understanding what has taken place in the lives of most Americans. And that is what we turn to next.

PART II

The Pursuit
of Meaning

I ndividuals responded to the world out of control by starting a revolution—a personal revolution that would spread its impact across work forces, constituencies and markets. At first, they responded with anger against a system that was failing to deliver on its historical promises and against the leaders who proved inept at solving the problems that surfaced everywhere. Eventually, however, individuals realized that their entire relationship with existing institutions was simply not working and that something had to change.

They retreated from the world out of control and initiated a process of personal reassessment that rearranged priorities, recalibrated personal expectations and discovered new values, beliefs and interests. In essence, they became different people with a more workable balance between needs and wants. Throughout this period, women reached each stage of the reassessment process first, thereby becoming leading indicators of the widespread personal changes underway, signals, so to speak, of what was taking place.

This personal revolution negatively affected the old communities of wealth. As people reached the end phase of their personal reassessment process, the anger they felt toward ineffective institutions turned to ridicule, a final rejection of the source of so many problems. As they freed themselves from old loyalties, individuals started piecing together new organizations, groups and institutions that could effectively meet the needs they now found important. As people reached the final phases of the reassessment process, they altered how they defined "happiness"—an alteration that would have tremendous impact on business, elections and employment in the years ahead.

CHAPTER 4

A PERSONAL REVOLUTION

Two journalists for the Philadelphia *Inquirer,* Donald Barlett and James B. Steele, wondered why Americans were growing so openly hostile to, and frustrated with, public and private institutions. Why, they asked, were some people prospering while most were feeling like victims? With their curiosities piqued, they launched an investigation which led to a series of articles, which in turn provoked a surprisingly strong and favorable response from readers. In fact, the articles drew such a public response that the *Inquirer* filled 400,000 requests for reprints.

Reader demand prompted the Universal Press Syndicate Company to print the series as a book entitled *America: What Went Wrong?* (1992). The book's opening chapter cited quotes from America's political and economic leaders, all insisting that the economy was sound and that the country's future looked good. The authors then listed what most Americans were experiencing: downsizings, stagnating salaries, dislocations in economic rewards, and unequal changes in the tax structure. From this wild disparity in American experiences, the authors concluded that the middle class was vanishing. "You might think of what is happening in the economy—and thereby to you and your family—in terms of a professional hockey game, a sport renowned for its physical violence," the authors noted. "Imagine how the game would be played if the old rules were repealed, if the referees were removed. That, in essence, is what is happening to the American economy. Someone changed the rules. And there is no referee. Which means there is no one looking after the interests of the middle class. They are the forgotten Americans."

The reason why Barlett and Steele's work struck such a chord was simply that it gave a lengthy and detailed explanation for the dissonance between what people heard from their leaders and what they were experiencing in their daily lives. Throughout the book, the authors offered more and more statistics to outline the image that the middle class was sliding downward, the working class was losing ground, and only the very wealthy were experiencing an increase in their standards of living. Placed in the current context, the authors revealed that the old communities of wealth were failing in their historical mission, breaking the post–World War II deal of loyalty for rising standards of living. At about the same time, other sources were offering additional numerical pictures of changing American economic fortunes.

- From the late 1970s through the middle 1990s, the lowest-earning 10 percent of workers lost 10 percent of their earning power.
- For blue-collar males in general, hourly wages measured in constant dollars shrank 14.6 percent from 1978 to 1994.
- For the backbone of the blue-collar work force—men with a high-school diploma or less—wages fell at least 20 percent in real terms over the two decades ending in 1995.
- By 1996, the minimum wage had reached a 40-year low in real terms.
- More people than ever were working full-time and still living below the poverty line ($15,141 for a family of four). Indeed, nearly 20 percent of all American workers were taking home paychecks that left them below the poverty line.
- Census Bureau figures for 1993 revealed that earnings declined for 60 percent of U.S. households.
- The average hourly wage, adjusted for inflation, fell for the 20-year period from 1973 to 1993. In the 12-month period leading to March 1995, real wages plunged 2.3 percent, a figure that economic historian Bradford DeLong said was the largest yearly drop since the 1840s.
- Of the 120 million people who were working in mid-1995, 8 million held two jobs, a 38 percent increase in one decade.

- Of the 22 million part-time workers, 4.5 million wanted full-time work but could not find it. The number of temporary workers tripled in the same decade to 2.1 million.

  Behind these raw numbers were stories of people facing a world quite different from the one that post–World War II America created. People were suffering, even while their leaders kept saying that things were fine. As leaders looked at their cyclical economic figures and saw things moving steadily forward, individuals looked at their personal finances and saw serious problems. In 1994, for example, Terri Yates, a Kissimmee, Florida, cab driver, took home about $10,000 working full-time. But even with Terri working six-day weeks, and her husband Phil driving a cab all seven days, their personal cars were more than a decade old, and they were unable to scrape together the money needed for a down payment on a home. "I'm making less money than ever in my whole life and I'm working more," explained a frustrated Mrs. Yates. "I have no life. I feel lost. Now everything goes up but people's wages. Either you're rich or poor." Terri was one of the more than 10 million Americans that *Time* magazine described as hovering "one rung above welfare on the nation's 'ladder of opportunity' . . . people who tiptoe between paychecks and have no savings, who ride the bus to the discount stores, who sell their plasma until their veins scar, who don't bother to clip coupons for Cheerios because the generic version is still cheaper, and who can be wiped out by even a minor medical problem."

As workers at the low end of the pay spectrum struggled, the gap between them and the most affluent households grew steadily. In 1972, chief executives at America's largest companies made 40 times the pay of the average worker in their own company. By the mid-1990s, that ratio had risen to more than 140 to 1, and from there the number eventually grew to 240 times for some industries. During the 1980s, the total amount of corporate money spent on salaries over $1 million increased by 2,200 percent—50 times the increase for salaries between $20,000 and $50,000. Indeed, the richest 20 percent of American households owned more than 80 percent of the country's wealth, and the U.S.

became *the most economically stratified* nation in the industrial world. Moreover, studies of mobility across economic categories revealed that the U.S. had become *one of the least mobile* industrial societies, with only England below it. These were not the results most Americans sought when they willingly participated in the growth and expansion of the postwar economy.

Americans recognized this growing split between rich and poor, but their leaders either did not or chose to ignore it if they did. In the national election year 1996, under the auspices of a University of Texas professor, 476 Americans representing the entire population gathered in Austin to participate in a "process poll" (a study of how people over time respond to information presented in discussion groups), and also to see what Americans were actually thinking about the country's predicament. Unlike faster, less-definitive polls, the "process poll" encouraged participants to interact and learn. "We came as strangers," explained one participant, "and cried when we had to leave." The diversity of perspectives actually worked to the gathering's benefit, and its easygoing discussions stood in stark contrast to the rancor expressed over differing opinions in the nation's capital. Just two months before the Austin gathering, Washington politicians had shut down the government because they were unwilling to discuss and resolve important budgetary issues. At Austin, this wide range of individuals had a different experience. "I was amazed at how people from all walks of life could come together for a few days and have a dialogue on a variety of issues," offered one member. "I sat between somebody who couldn't read and a trucker from Pennsylvania, and yet we had a common ground."

That common ground led to some interesting discoveries about each other. Before arriving, 50 percent of the participants thought the average worker's salary was too low. After face-to-face discussions and hearing everybody's personal stories, 75 percent felt that way. Those who felt the government should get involved in this issue rose from 31 percent to 43 percent. While rancorous name-calling had become the news of the day in Washington, this representative sample of America held open, civil and successful discussions. While national political discussions routinely erupted into shouting matches about this character flaw or that ideological point, these Americans sat down and decided that the country's most important issue was the growing disparity between rich and poor, an issue that was not even on the national politicians' agendas. Not only was the disparity growing between rich and poor, but an equally large disparity was also growing between what leaders thought and discussed and what citizens thought and discussed.

The American middle class was living the dissonance. While salaries stagnated, newspapers reported huge bonuses being awarded to business leaders. While workers fretted over pink slips, news accounts published the huge profits that corporations were reporting to their stockholders. And while Americans cut back their lifestyles to adjust to economic realities, journalists noted that luxury items and top-level designer shops were doing quite well, thank you. These types of differences, cast aside in political and media discussions, amounted to an indifference toward what individuals were experiencing. Americans took note of that indifference and soon registered their displeasure.

THINGS MUST CHANGE— INDIVIDUALS RESPOND

"Rage," explained the lead rapper of the popular rap group NWA, "is a commodity." Indeed, rap music rose from the country's inner cities, giving a public voice to black teenage frustrations. The fact that this black rage reverberated so well among white suburban teenagers, and inspired one of the most popular forms of today's pop music, suggests that something else was spreading underneath society's calmer exterior.

For many Americans, talk radio became an instrument by which they might express their rage. Through this format, the public could complain to others about whatever frustrated, irritated or sarcastically amused them. Also through this format, Americans essentially took over the programming from local radio announcers. At one time, programmers chose the play lists of recordings, invited specific guests, or preselected which socioeconomic positions would get aired. In the talk formats, however, anyone who called dictated content. Announcers simply aided and abetted. Talk-show hosts, ranging in approach from Rush

Limbaugh to G. Gordon Liddy, the latter a convicted Watergate felon, encouraged callers to become strident, and they themselves talked "tough,"
some becoming radio's version of Sylvester Stallone armed with verbiage.
Between 1990 and 1993, stations switching to the news/talk format out-
paced all other formats, making it the hottest radio-program structure.
Overall, between 1990 and 1996 the format more than tripled its market
penetration, from under 400 stations to more than 1,200. The talk-radio
system gave rage an electronic presence and deepened the social fault
lines in society. What those who abetted these divisions did not fully
appreciate at the time was that people on both sides of the political arguments were actually expressing one common theme: *Things must change.*

The wide spectrum of American pop culture in the 1990s, did indeed
make rage a workable and market-ready phenomenon. Rage attracted
audiences on both talk radio and MTV. It drew crowds to outdoor political rallies and county tax-committee meetings. It undermined leaders
and changed public discourse. Those who had positions of responsibility with the weakening institutions faced growing anger from within.
The typical list of distrustable characters (e.g., used-car salesmen, politicians) now had some unusual additions (e.g., celebrities, athletes, business leaders, religious figures).

This attitude also reached the country's movie screens. In early
1991, *Terminator 2, Boyz N the Hood* and *Thelma and Louise* all depicted heroes and heroines responding violently to institutional hypocrisy,
ineffectiveness, indifference, and brutality. That summer, another trio of
extremely popular films, *Home Alone, Sleeping with the Enemy,* and
New Jack City, gave further expression to emerging public anger. In
these films, the lead characters were under attack and had to fight those
who were assaulting them. Not one of the six films that topped the box-
office charts in 1991 showed a functioning or effective system of public
or private institutions. Everything was corrupt, and survival depended
upon individuals handling their own problems. The lead characters
extracted gruesome revenge on those who threatened them, and the more
agonizing the punishment, the more vocal audiences became. Ticket
sales confirmed that Americans found such displays of violence to be
appropriate responses to failing institutions.

This anger continued through much of the decade. In 1994, white males in the working class vented their frustrations on Congress, rejecting incumbents and embracing anyone who challenged the status quo. Historically, white males split roughly 50/50 in the Democratic and Republican categories. But in 1994, white males voted for Republican candidates by a 2-to-1 majority, and the brunt of their ire were all incumbents, the majority of whom were Democrats. In essence, they rejected people they held responsible for the current situation. On a more extreme level, more than 10,000 white (and almost exclusively male) citizens joined ad hoc militias actually seeking to overthrow the government. Founded in 1992, the citizen militia system rose rapidly, opposing gun control, the North American Free Trade Agreement (NAFTA), affirmative action, abortion rights and all taxes. Explained one vocal member of the Michigan Militia: "There are three methods to effect change: the jury box, the ballot box and the cartridge box."

For most of society, anger fell short of militia activities, but nevertheless continued to grow. Militia anger resulted from the distrust of leaders who were, members thought, conspiring to rob individuals of their freedom. Middle-class anger resulted from a lack of faith in leaders who, suburban dwellers thought, were conspiring to rob individuals of their financial stability. *Both* thought that leaders wanted only more (power or money) for themselves. And events gave credence to the middle-class argument. For example, when Sears announced it was firing 50,000 workers, its stock rose by 4 percent, a statement of money against people. Similarly, when Xerox announced a 10,000-job reduction, stockholders boosted the stock value by 7 percent.

The most extraordinary series of events, however, happened in 1995. Mobil Corporation reported a profit of $636 million, a turnaround from its 1994 loss of $145 million. One week after reporting the profits, Mobil executives announced plans to reduce its work force by 9.3 percent. Later, Mobil posted soaring first-quarter earnings, and one week beyond that, executives announced plans to eliminate another 4,700 jobs. To confirm the perception that a few were benefiting at the cost of the many, when the executives announced the second round of cuts, Mobil's stock immediately rose to a 52-week high.

These events confirmed Barlett and Steele's description of "what went wrong" with America. To ever more Americans, institutions which once sought to help everyone grow wealthier appeared now to be skewed to favor a few at the expense of the many. Safeway executives told their northern California workers that competition from discount stores and superstores was forcing them to "redefine" health benefits, thereby shifting some of the financial burden to the employees. Shortly after making that announcement, Safeway released its first-quarter (1995) earnings—up 48 percent over the preceding year. Then, company executives announced plans to invest more than $400 million in store renovation and new construction. Safeway's stock, company spokesmen boasted, had soared 51 percent in 1994, and the company's CEO had taken home $1.26 million, not including his stock options and benefits.

The Safeway encounter resulted in a strike, but whatever public response resulted, clearly Americans were gaining the sense that institutions were turning against the majority and favoring the minority. Michael Mandel, in his book *The High Risk Society* (1996) explained that the anger cut across political lines because the new targets were from different sectors of society. The focus of the anger, he thought, was anyone seemingly immune from the economic risks. "The groups receiving most of the animosity—welfare recipients, government workers, the elderly, CEOs of large companies," he wrote, "are precisely those people who seem to be protected from the rise of uncertainty or seem to be escaping most of the effects of the high-risk economy." Leaders, celebrities and athletes all took their share of abuse during this era of anger, as evidence surfaced to reveal that many were abusive, indifferent, arrogant, greedy, and/or addicted. However, one specific fan reaction captured the frustration that people felt toward those benefiting from the system and those abusing it.

The baseball strike of 1994 left the dwindling number of loyal fans angry at the greed and indifference of the entire professional sports enterprise. On July 18, 1995, New York Yankee pitcher Jack McDowell, a multimillion dollar-per-year athlete, was leaving a game, having blown his start, when boos erupted from the crowd. Rather than concede that, given his salary versus his performance, perhaps the boos were understandable expressions of fan irritation, the defiant McDowell threw up his arm and gave "the finger" to ostensibly all of those in attendance. The boos escalated, and shocked parents withdrew in dismay. The ugly scene that McDowell created prompted editors at *USA Today* magazine to place "the finger" on the cover of their monthly issue and ask: "Is this the end of civilized society?"

LARGER CHANGES UNDER WAY

While the magazine's story suggested that the daring digit could well mark the end of civility, from a larger perspective the scene was actually a symptom of a society passing through massive individual change. Americans were pulling away from old institutions, and as of that moment nothing had surfaced to replace them. Talk radio, movies and music all struck a sensitive nerve because they exploited the distance that people detected between each other and from the old institutions. Their anger was not so much an expression of classic alienation (to use a hoary term), as it was an expression of disappointment, worry, insecurity, and isolation—that is, disillusion with the corrupted and skewed communities of wealth. Americans were realizing that unfortunately institutions *could no longer* solve the problems which they, the institutions, had created; individuals had to deal with those problems *alone,* consequently bearing the brunt of institutional ineffectiveness. Ultimately, they realized that they had to solve their own problems and reassert control because no institution or systematic response remained to help. For nearly five decades, public and private institutions had backstopped individuals against the vagaries of a changing and risky world. Now, those institutions had not only abandoned that relationship but were making things worse.

The police beating of Rodney G. King in Los Angeles tapped into several of the very themes that made particular movies popular and certain music successful. Viewers watched in horror as uniformed white officers (i.e., representatives of the old institutions) brutally beat an unarmed and seemingly passive black violator (i.e., victim of institutional corruption and abuse), while—unknown to the violent perpetrators—an amateur videographer (i.e., people taking back control) captured the entire scene for all the world to view. As a moment in television time when society shared personal involvement with an individual's plight, the Rodney King beating matched in its own poignant way the disparate *Challenger* disaster and sad Polly Klaas situation.

Individuals soon realized that the old institutional system was abandoning them, and that they needed to change their way of relating to those institutions. They required a new set of priorities to guide them through the troubling era. They needed to rethink issues and priorities they once took for granted. To do that, they passed through a personal reassessment process. Looking at example after example of these personal reassessment projects, we noticed a pattern. Individuals were moving steadily through a three-part process in an effort to recognize what was happening, organize themselves to address it, and set their own personal agenda for future behavior. The three stages involved: (1) "Turning points"—moments when individuals realize that the way things are organized does not work for them, and that something thereof must change. (2) "Grounding points"—a rethinking process where they first bring control back to their personal lives and then reassess the most fundamental aspects of their lives, such as what they believe, what they need, who they are, what they find important and how they want to live. (3) "Compass points"—guideposts established during their grounding-points phase that direct daily routines and energize personal behavior in the years ahead.

Each stage of the process inspired a popular phrase that caught the meaning behind each stage and that rose to common use precisely because they captured the essence of what was changing. Prior to the turning points in the era of the growing communities of wealth, people used the phrase "Get ahead," and most of their efforts were directed at moving up on the standard-of-living or wealth scale. After the turning points and in the midst of the world out of control, individuals sought to "Get a handle," a phrase that suggested efforts (grounding points) to bring the chaos under control. After control was reached, compass points sought to fulfill the last popular phrase, "Get a life." Here the "life" involves something more than jobs, wealth and success. Get ahead, Get a handle, Get a life: These are the phrases that gave expression to the major thrusts of the turning points–grounding points–compass points process.

At the end of this lengthy and involved reassessment process, individuals shifted priorities from what had been called "the good life," which communities of wealth supported quite successfully, to what could be called "a life that's good," which the old institutions were particularly inept at supporting. Throughout the unfolding of these personal changes, women have repeatedly reached each stage ahead of the rest of society. While they have not always been the nominal leaders in a particular effort, women expressed first the needs that led to personal changes. For that reason, their actions are leading indicators of society's process of change.

MISSING THE PERSONAL REVOLUTION

In "Planning for Uncertainty," an op-ed piece in the *Wall Street Journal,* Peter Drucker drew the distinction between types of social changes by using the metaphors of climate and weather. Weather changes are constant, sudden and within an identifiable period. Climatic changes, however, are gradual, overriding changes which actually direct the weather. The turning points–grounding points–compass points process represented an economic, social, political and institutional climatic change in American society.

For several reasons, business and political leaders have had trouble recognizing the changes under way. The lengthy success of the old communities of wealth blinded them to the depth and significance of the unfolding events. Those charged with providing direction for the country's institutions insisted that the personal changes were temporary, or cyclical, or needed only a tactical marketing or human resource adjustment to correct. Over time, however, they had to face the consequences of these missed perceptions. In addition, what many leaders missed about this widespread process of change as it spread through society was that individuals reached each stage at very different times, thereby creating clashing perspectives and overlapping interests. This was not a mass movement with leaders and an agenda. Rather, individuals came to their own turning points at different times, depending on their own experiences. They moved through the grounding-points assessment at different paces as well.

New Consumer — Evolution

Lost Connection with System
Metaphor: Challenger Disaster

TURNING POINTS

S & L Crisis
Iran-Contra
Washington Grid-Lock
Pension Plans Underfunded
Layoffs at "Secure" Companies
Bankruptcies

Benefit Cutbacks
Lower/Stagnant Salaries
Jobs Not Where People Are
Health Care
Insurance & Tuition Costs
AIDS
Disposable Income Squeeze

Result: Alienation

GROUNDING POINTS

We're On Our Own
Metaphor: Hurricane Andrew

New Definition of Value
Reapportionment
Self-Security
　　　Home Security Systems-guns
　　　Neighborhood watches
　　　Self-managed pension funds
Stretch your budget

Result: Need to Know More

Reassessment
Metaphor: Coffee Houses

Cooking classes
Fly fishing
Family & Home
Lower work priorities
"I'm Outta Here"

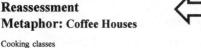

Get Smart
Metaphor: Murder Mystery Weekends

Book Sales
TV Magazine Shows
T. Rowe Price
"All Things Considered"
Lowered Expectations
Learning Vacations

Result: Personal Redirection

Result: Anger & Frustration

COMPASS POINTS

Looking for Solutions
Metaphor: Magic Eye

Context - Angels, Microsoft
Access - On-line, AOL, Internet
Resourcefulness - Books
Effectiveness - Debit Cards
Communities of Meaning

Misreading this evolving personal revolution, many marketers turned to tactics like "niche marketing" because they believed that society was simply splitting into smaller and smaller segments. They had missed the larger issue that change was sweeping unevenly through society. Despite the difficulties that leaders had in getting through the surface confusion and their inability to apply the Magic Eye's penetrating perception, Americans continued to progress through their personal reassessment process.

REACHING THE PERSONAL TURNING POINT

Turning-point changes first started to surface in the late 1980s and still continue to appear across all sectors of society. While some moments of insight were public and socially framed, others were personal and recognizable only because of the way in which individual behavior changed. Some responded so negatively to public events that this actually forced a personal turning point. Others may have become irritated over working harder and longer without tangible advances, creating a personal moment of reflection. Still others may have experienced a particularly nasty divorce that called for a personal change; and some, having found a pink slip in their mailbox, may have turned that crisis into a moment of self-examination. Whether driven by a social, economic, political or personal event, however, Americans reached their own turning points when it hit them: "This just isn't working for me, and something has to change."

Willow Shire reached her turning point in a most unusual way. When her essay "Managing in the Midst of Chaos" appeared in *Fortune* magazine, she appeared on the cover. The day after the magazine reached the newsstands, her marriage ended in a divorce, and six months later her CEO fired her just days before he himself was fired. She realized that managing in the midst of chaos was more personal than she had put in writing, and that her personal life needed to be both rethought and reworked. *She* had reached *her* turning point.

That same reality hit White House senior domestic policymaker William Galston, who suddenly resigned the post he had always aspired to have. What motivated his decision to leave was a handwritten note he received from his nine-year-old son outlining the fact that "baseball's not fun" for him because no one was ever there to watch.

"He let me know in various ways," Galston admitted, "that I was absent physically and emotionally from various important moments in life." Galston's lofty position was costing his son some important childhood experiences, and he took that to heart and quit. *He* had passed *his* turning point.

The "aha!" moments when individuals realize that things are just not working trigger the turning points, real moments in time when individuals acknowledge that continuing along the same path of behavior would only bring further disappointments and increased frustrations. As one psychologist commented, "More and more of my patients are coming in and saying, 'I have it all' or 'I'm getting it all'—and it's not making any difference." Claudia Shear, in her one-person Broadway play, *Blown Sideways Through Life* (1995), a look at work in America, explained the frustration and fatigue that work was bringing. After she went home from work, the day seemed wasted. "You're too fired up to go to sleep, so you sit at the kitchen table. It's late. It's quiet. You're tired. But you don't want to go to bed. Going to bed means this was the day. This February twelfth, this August third, this November second, is over. You made some money but nothing happened. Nothing. A whole day of your life is over, and all it means is that it's time to go to bed; a moment at four o'clock in the morning when you think that life is too hard, the tasks are impossible. There is no Grail. There is no treasure." With the institution-induced anxiety and its resulting financial insecurity, more Americans were experiencing what Shear expressed. And they wanted things to change.

From the changed point of view, old institutions become just another cause of the problems, and individuals slowly start pulling back emotionally and even physically from those institutions, whether they are employers, political parties or entertainment media.

At the turning point, attitudes about work start to change. In an earlier era, work and career defined a member of the communities of wealth. The simple question "What do you do for a living?" was an inquiry that initiated conversation at social events and also represented a way to understand a person better. What a person did for work somehow said something about who that individual was and what he or she stood for. After the turning point, work and career merely became a means to enable them to do the new kinds of things they now felt defined them.

Some individuals removed themselves physically by taking early buyouts from employers, retiring ahead of time, quitting and doing with less, finding acceptable work situations in small towns or changing to less-stressful jobs. Others, adopting "voluntary simplicity," simply lowered their emotional attachment to work by taking flex hours or switching to part-time in order to concentrate more on their personal lives. Even more remained at work and cashing their paychecks, but were in fact psychologically disconnected. All of these exit strategies were signs of the declining importance of careers in a post–turning-points mindset.

In *First We Quit Our Job* (1996), Marilyn Abraham and husband Sandy MacGregor discussed how his involuntary downsizing coincided with her voluntary exit from her job, and how these events led to a new and better life. "We were overworked, stressed-out, high-strung, short-tempered and had too many things to do and not enough time to do them," she explained. Then she added what amounted to their turning-point questions: "Why were we living this crazy life, anyhow?" Their answer sent them packing down the road in an RV, but for others the answer meant a different direction.

For many individuals, leaving a large institution in frustration did not mean leaving work altogether. Rather, it meant starting a business and working for themselves. Franchising became one area of opportunity. The Great Harvest Bakery Company, for example, is a chain of individually owned and operated bakers. The baking recipes come from the company's Montana headquarters, but each franchised bakery makes its product line fresh each day. The company hoped to expand their stores at a rate of 8 to 10 per year, and set the basic startup fee at $100,000. In the early 1990s, the company started receiving hundreds of inquiries per month and more than 300 completed applications each year from people interested in becoming bakers. In 1996 alone, the company received 5,200 inquiries and granted applications to just 14 applicants. By way of comparison, getting approved to open a Great

Harvest Bakery had become harder and more selective than being accepted at Harvard.

Downsizing at AT&T created a swirl of change that had, as of this book's creation, yet to stabilize. One employee who actually survived the cuts found himself with an offer to leave AT&T and take a spot on the ground floor of a new and growing software company. In the past, he would have routinely rejected the offer because he wanted to stay put for life. Lifelong employment had seemed inevitable at giants like AT&T. With all past relationships changing, though, he discovered his own growing tolerance for (indeed, even his pleasure from) radical change. "I found myself adapting to change so well that I started to say, 'How much change can I handle?'" He left the once-comfortable womb of AT&T and, with newfound confidence in his ability to deal with change, headed for the small-company experiment. "So here I am," he exclaimed. In essence, the traumatic events surrounding AT&T's downsizing had helped him realize that he could thrive amid major change and could easily survive without "Ma Bell."

While some found themselves in a swirl of activity that led to a new life, others worked slowly through that process. Joe Kita, a career-minded worker, decided to take time off, and wrote about his experience in *Men's Health*. He was changing jobs, and rather than switch immediately, he took 50 days off before starting back. He discovered that without the tiresome demands of a job he started to dream again; he lost track of time; his memory returned; he became more thoughtful about everything; he stopped yelling at his kids; he reconnected emotionally with his wife (heightening their sex life); he gained a new perspective on work, relationships and "life"; he felt less guilty; he looked forward to starting work again; and he realized that the "fun person" he once was continued to exist inside and was just waiting to find a way out.

Workers like Joe Kita, who remained with the same kind of work routines, sent indirect messages about the declining importance of work. Employee "dress-down days" became overt expressions of a changing work environment, all but eliminating the 1980s belief in a dress-for-success wardrobe. In 1995 IBM, "Big Blue" of the white-shirt-, dark-suit-mandatory school of doing business, changed dress codes to allow casual days—even at the corporate headquarters in Armonk, New York. In fact, the company told employees that if they did not meet, greet or come across customers, they would not have to wear the dark-suit costume again.

These sorts of corporate changes most assuredly had their impact. In 1989, men's suit manufacturers made 18.4 million units, while only one year later they made just 15.5 million outfits. In 1990, Hartmarx Corporation, makers of the Hickey-Freeman and Hart, Schaffner and Marx suit lines, lost $62 million and closed 65 stores. Similar changes occurred in women's clothing, and 1994 saw the sharpest decline in women's apparel prices ever. Meanwhile, Levi's new Dockers line of clothes (casual style, easy fit) found a new market and became one of the fastest-growing new casual lines in fashion-industry history.

Dress-down days signaled less than total commitment to work, but the simple switch in clothing hinted at wider personal changes. By the end of 1995, half of the respondents to a *U.S. News & World Report* survey said they had taken significant steps to simplify their lives. These steps included moving to a rural community that slowed their pace of life, reducing work hours to create more leisure time, lowering personal expectations, and rejecting job promotions. In the same survey, more than half responded that they would gladly take less money from work in exchange for more time to themselves, and the percentages rose as incomes increased. In another study, 67 percent said they would trade a day's salary for a day off. At their turning points, many individuals understood what Betsy Taylor, executive director of the Merck Family Fund, would later declare: "Increasingly, people realize they can't consume their way to contentment."

Individual interest in gaining more time, even at the cost of losing some salary, led to the creation of several organizations to help people live comfortably with less. Jim and Amy Dacyczyn and their four kids lived in rural Maine. Work routines and family tensions pushed Jim and Amy to their turning points. As a result, the Dacyczyns started a project to reduce expenditures in order to work less and have more time together. With wife and mother Amy leading the way, the family managed to reduce its yearly expenses to $17,580—less than half the $39,537 an average family of six spends. Reducing their need for money reduced their dependence on working for that money. In essence, cutting expenses bought free time. To help others shrink their expenses, Ms. Dacyczyn created a newsletter called the *Tightwad Gazette.* The best stories from the newsletter became part of a series of books with the same title. The newsletter became so successful, and created such a demand on Amy's time, that she eventually closed it down. The newsletter, which she created to help others discover the joys of a simpler life, had interrupted her own simpler life.

The whole idea of living simpler was not new in American history, but its appeal at this point in time and its spread into parts of society heretofore immune to its allure made this a different era. Books, professional advisers, and nonprofit organizations sought to lend support to individuals shifting from a life focused on wealth to one zeroed in on simplicity. Bob Lilienfeld founded Use Less Stuff to help people be more efficient with their purchases and waste. Janet Luhrs started a newsletter called *Simple Living* (also the title of her subsequent book), which focused its 2,500 subscribers on enjoying day-to-day living. "If you're continually consuming," Ms. Luhrs suggested, "you have to keep working; you can't get off the treadmill. It's the freedom thing, the way I see it." Too, Sarah Ban Breathnach's *Simple Abundance* rode the *Publishers Weekly* Best Sellers List for more than 90 weeks, went through over 20 printings, and sold well over 2 million copies; and her *Simple Abundance Journal of Gratitude,* which was ineligible for best-seller lists because of its journal format, still sold nearly 500,000 copies.

The Center for Plain Living, a nonprofit organization founded by Quakers, is a clearinghouse for criticism of technology-driven culture. It, too, hopes to redirect individuals away from the pursuit of wealth at the cost of precious time. Not only did the group's magazine, *Plain,* develop a national readership of several thousand, but the small southeastern Ohio city where it is published soon attracted hundreds of families who had left their homes and jobs to start a new and presumably simpler life.

At the same time, Vicki Robin and Joe Dominguez, in *Your Money or Your Life* outlined a step-by-step program to help people reach financial independence by getting by with less. Like the Dacyczyns, they argued that if people spent less money, they would need to make less money; if they needed less money, they could work less; and if they worked less, they could spend more time pursuing personally important, nonmaterial goals. Despite their suggestion that potential readers borrow but not buy the book, it sold over 600,000 copies. Meanwhile, the two authors, before Mr. Dominquez's death early in 1997, lived on $7,000 each per year by working, writing and teaching for free at their New Road Map Foundation, which was also dedicated to helping people enjoy lives with lowered and more personally balanced expectations.

Overall "voluntary simplicity" spread rapidly through society and became an attractive alternative to life on the other side of the turning points. Fran Rodgers, CEO of Work–Family Directions, a group that helps people balance work and family demands, summarized these movements: "There's an incredibly increased desire to have more control over one's life, to have more control over what is controllable, to spend more time with family."

Buying more time and simplifying routines often meant buying fewer expensive things. Second-hand stores and consignment shops rose to meet the demand of people seeking to cut back on clothing expenditures. Membership in the National Association of Resale and Thrift Shops grew at a 12 percent annual clip. One publicly traded company, Grow Biz International, Inc. of Minneapolis, actually watched its operation expand to 19 corporate stores and 1,000 franchises. By 1997, the company was adding 250 new franchises every year. While second-hand thrift shops have existed in lower-middle-class areas for years, the cutback mentality of the turning points reached much further (and farther) than that. For example, the Second Time Around stores, which sell used shoes, clothes and sports equipment, is situated along Boston's Newbury Street, right next to Brooks Brothers, Emporio Armani and Burberry's.

The relief and release that many people felt after reaching their turning points changed their lives. "I don't think we care about keeping up with the Joneses anymore," explained Carol Brooks—who (along with her husband, John) lost her job at IBM during a downsizing. "Going to

T.G.I. Friday's is just as good as going to a French restaurant. We don't miss it. In fact, I'm probably more peaceful now than I've been in memory." She went ahead to explain that they now have time to volunteer at church, to focus on weekly get-togethers with friends and to loosen their traditional work roles at home. "We talk more about cosmic realities, I guess," explained her husband, a former systems designer at IBM.

These realities, some forced upon individuals and some personally chosen, changed the way in which people viewed their lives. In a sure sign that more and more people were gaining control over their lives, Day Runner, one of the several successful schedule planners popular during the go-go days of career mania, reported sluggish sales at the end of 1996. Emotional upheavals helped individuals forge a new outlook on life; they were ready to move on.

MOVING STEADILY THROUGH THE GROUNDING POINTS

Communities of wealth had given individuals a sense of well-being, an identity and a sense of place. Now that the world out of control, plus ensuing institutional changes, had ended that comfortable relationship, individuals felt abandoned. Having reached their turning points, they knew that things needed to change, but not in what ways or how extensively. With these types of issues on their minds, individuals had to reassess what was personally important, what they truly needed and what they now felt like accepting. This process of personal reassessment led Americans to their grounding points—where they discovered the values, ideas, beliefs and behaviors that would become fundamental to their identity and essential to their sense of well-being.

During this period of reassessment, Americans, in almost naive amazement, rediscovered the centrality of family and home in their lives. In reaction to work excesses and as a sign of their separation from outside institutions, family activities—kids' soccer, gardening, redecorating, neighborhood parties, family dinners—rose in priority. Remodeling the home and creating a "more personal space" became important. The styles that gained favor spoke of historical identities—reflections of deeper needs that people wanted satisfied in their surroundings. Southwestern styles, native Indian patterns, and Ralph Lauren's worn look matched this turn inward to discover something fundamental to or essential in the environment. These types of interests created huge successes for the likes of Bed, Bath and Beyond, and Home Depot, and home-furnishings companies, sending those retail areas up by more than 14 percent between 1992 and 1994, even as the economy struggled to sustain a 2 percent annual growth. In 1995, consumer spending on home furnishings exceeded spending on apparel, for the first time in modern history. Not only did they decorate their interiors to suit their new needs; they also "did" the outside by personally planting and nurturing their gardens. By the end of 1995, approximately 78 million adult Americans said they gardened regularly—a 30 percent increase in three years. They created a $22 billion business, and made successes of magazines like *Country Living Gardener, Garden Design* and *Home Garden.*

Individuals in the grounding-points phase of their reassessment process lavished attention on their children, spending more time at their schools and at home helping with homework. They also spent freely on toys, pushing up sales at Toys "R" Us to record levels. As part of their developing interest in family time together, Americans looked more favorably upon holidays that brought family members together. Thanksgiving grew in popularity, as did Christmas. For Christmas 1992, the year after the grounding-points actions first started to surface, retailers enjoyed a 24 percent increase in sales, and holiday sales figures remained decent through the 1994 season.

The family and home were stabilizing discoveries for individuals in their grounding-points reassessment. But to regain control over the proliferating problems, they also had to "get smart," which is to say discover the sources of those problems in order to prepare to address them. In response, a revitalized interest in learning spread across a wide variety of areas. Book sales soared, increasing by double-digit percentages throughout the first half of the decade, making Barnes & Noble, Borders and other booksellers extremely profitable.

Oprah Winfrey had been the queen of television talk shows, but her ratings—like those of talk radio—started downward in 1995 after sufficient numbers of people had passed their turning points and started their personal reassessment. Venting anger over the airwaves, or watching others do the same, no longer held any attraction. What more individuals wanted was insight into events surrounding them. Attuned to audience shifts, "Oprah" (as she was most popularly called) changed formats and created "Oprah's Book Club"—and her ratings reversed and went straight up. The publishing industry soon discovered "the Oprah factor." When an author appeared on the daytime show, book sales rose immediately. Some of Oprah's programs even included lavish dinner sets, to encourage the feeling of table conversations revolving around books, and she also added parallel discussions via America Online (AOL). The surprising thing to publishers was that Oprah for the most part seemed to bring new book buyers into the market. In fact, Oprah Winfrey had simply linked into the rising interest in learning as a means of "getting smart" in order to get control over personal lives.

Book subjects soon included talk about this quest for learning. James Redfield's *The Celestine Prophecy* (1993) dealt with the discovery of an ancient tablet, the text of which actually revealed ten lessons that could make people happy. Each lesson revealed some new and wiser way to live within the world. In the book, church and state join forces to keep the document from reaching the public because its content would undermine the overseers' authority. Using this plot approach, Redfield not only tantalized the reader with a life-enhancing message many were pursuing in their personal lives (meaning in life, and the value of simplicity), but also exploited people's visceral distrust of huge institutions. The book quickly rose to the top-ten lists, coast-to-coast, and was still number one on the *Publishers Weekly* list 150 weeks after publication.

Interest in learning expanded into areas once considered esoteric and forbidding for the wider reader. Poetry-book sales at Barnes & Noble, for example, rose by 100 percent in 1995 and held steady after that. At the City Lights Bookstore in San Francisco, owners had once been ecstatic if poetry-book sales reached $9,000. With the new interest in poetry, sales figures surpassed $70,000 annually. College enrollment in poetry classes rose steadily. At Temple University, students filled and overenrolled every poetry class; at Earlham College, poetry enrollment doubled in five years; and at the University of Cincinnati, professors lifted course size limits because demand kept rising. And classes at the University of Pennsylvania overflowed into the hallways of Penniman Library. According to Robert Fagen, professor of literature at Claremont McKenna College in California, students turned to poetry because it was more spiritual, emotional and rebellious.

The surprise box-office hit of 1995–1996 was the Italian movie *The Postman*, which centers around a rural mailman who delivers letters to visiting Chilean poet Pablo Neruda. When Neruda helps the postman to discover poetry, the revelation changes the letter carrier's life. The movie's success not only spurred sales of the original novel, it also boosted sales of *Love: Ten Poems by Pablo Neruda*. The book sold out its first 25,000 printing and quickly moved on to a second printing— extremely unusual for the most esoteric poetry volumes.

The performance arts started attracting increasingly larger audiences. Storytelling and poetry readings, the latter at new clubs like New York City's Neuyorican Café and Cambridge's Cantab Lounge, attracted record attendance, and Broadway ticket sales started back up in 1995, reaching 9 million for the first time in 13 years. During the late 1970s, 60 opera companies performed nationwide—but by 1995, the number of companies had nearly doubled to 119. Also, attendance at those companies rose precipitously. For example, the Opera Company of Philadelphia had a 131 percent increase in ticket sales between 1990 and 1995. Between 1990 and 1995, the Sarasota Opera increased its audience numbers by 70 percent. For the same period, the Washington (D.C.) Opera saw its attendance grow by 50 percent, the same percentage enjoyed by the Los Angeles Opera. In yet another signal of how distant American leaders had become from most Americans, this surge in interest in the arts as part of the individual's get-smart quest came just as political leaders turned to discussing eliminating public funding for the arts.

Former U.S. Poet Laureate Rita Dove captured this change in needs: "In the '70s and '80s, we decided it was every man for himself, with a single-mindedness to get ahead. Then you get there and discover

'What's there?' What is there if you don't have a soul? The result of poetry is that it both speaks to your interior life and connects you with other interior lives."

The inner life and the soul became important topics in the grounding-points phase. In 1994, Thomas Moore's *Care of the Soul* started a 150-week run on the *New York Times* best-seller list. In the intervening months, publishers printed nearly 800 different books about the soul. A series of books called *Chicken Soup for the Soul* sold 24 million copies. When Martin Rutte released his *Chicken Soup for the Soul at Work* (1997), he volunteered, "I want to touch the heart and feed the soul of people in the workplace." To do that, he visited companies and read from his book. Another book, *Redefining Corporate Soul* (1996), discussed the institutional inner life. Robert Bly, M. Scott Peck, the Dalai Lama and even Aristotle (the last of whom wrote *De Anima, Treatise on the Soul*), all found a 1990s audience by discussing some aspect of the soul. Psychiatrist James Hillman's *The Soul's Code* (1996) suggested that the soul is in fact the individual's core identity—a thought that Ms. Dove had already suggested.

Bringing poetry and the inner self together, psychiatrists and other counselors found poetry to be a means by which to address deep personal problems. The National Association of Poetry Therapy saw its membership double between 1994 and 1997. At the same time, Ingram Book Company, one of the country's largest book distributors, revealed that demand for religious and spiritual titles had increased more than 300 percent from June 1993 to June 1995. Also, African–American nonfiction books returned to the best-seller lists because, as Avele Bennett, manager of Detroit's Shrine of the Black Madonna Bookstore, explained: "People are looking for answers. We're beginning to look inside ourselves. Not all the answers come from the outside. We have to begin with ourselves, to relate to that divinity within us."

The pursuit of learning and meaning changed consumer vacation patterns also. During the pre–turning-points era, when stress was a standard side-effect of getting ahead, individuals took vacations that involved plopping down somewhere and vegetating. Some stayed home, others drove to the beach and many tried to isolate themselves in fee-

simple vacations such as those offered by Club Med, which had advertised itself as an "antidote to civilization." Doing very little was the
attraction behind these vacations because doing very little was about all
that interested fatigued workers.

In the post–turning-points era, however, vacations became active
again. Americans with reassessed priorities traveled to anthropological
digs as volunteers, tagged birds in remote forests, counted bear "scat" in
the Maine woods, participated in field trips, drove across the entire
country with their children and enrolled in history and language classes.
This energized pursuit of learning experiences stood in opposition
to the energized work experiences that once motivated workers. In the
middle of this reassessment process, learning as an objective turned employees away from work and toward their newly discovered personal
interests.

Part of the grounding-points phase involved a rethinking of personal identity. The personal-identity quest made specific types of music
more appealing because they captured something essential about an
individual's identity, much as popular home-decorating styles had done
for domestic interiors. For one, country and western music gathered attention from a wider audience than at any time in history. To new fans,
country music expressed the essence of Anglo–American realities: hard
work and hard times, heartbreak and good times, disappointment and
simple pleasures. From 1989 to 1994, country-music sales rose by 400
percent, and album sales in 1994 and 1995 reached new twin peaks at
76 million albums each year. One country singer, Garth Brooks, broke
all records for album sales by a single artist in any field and any country.
During the first half of the 1990s, more American radio stations than
ever before used a country format. These successes in traditional music
happened when technology was assuming control over the office, and
individuals were getting comfortable with the Internet and on-line services. For many white Americans, this turn to country music was in part
a quick answer to the question "Who am I?" Meanwhile, Irish folk
music, Tijuana and other Latin music and international sounds from different parts of the globe all gave expression to the country's international citizenry.

While individuals in the grounding-points phase started getting smart about society and about themselves they also worked to regain control over their personal affairs. In this effort, they gave preference to products and services that were simple, accessible, functional and effective—all values that fit the grounding-points reassessment. Consumers made Intuit's Quicken software the third-fastest-selling piece of software in history because it helped the user to regain control over personal finances and fulfilled that role with the least amount of difficulty. They created market successes out of Charles Schwab & Co., a low-priced-stock broker; Morningstar Inc., a rating service for mutual funds; and CarMax, a used-car superstore—simply because they made things easy, accessible, less expensive and effective.

A key element in getting control revolved around a new sense of independence. As mentioned earlier, Americans spent over $126 billion in 1994 improving their homes, but the way they undertook those projects is also indicative of the grounding-points reassessment: Sixty percent of homeowners did the work themselves! "Working on a computer all day," explained one proud homeowner–repairman, "you don't really see your results. When you go and retile a bathroom or build a sun room, you see it, you feel it, you touch it. It's *there*. It's *real*. It's a real sense of accomplishment." Another observer added: "You get more choice, more control and more convenience by doing things yourself." The whole movement toward independence and control even caught the attention of Intuit's chairman, Scott Cook: "There's something big going on here, this move to self-reliance; something big and undocumented." The thing that apparently attracted and yet baffled Mr. Cook was a portion of the grounding-points phase having reached the marketplace.

READY TO EXPRESS THE COMPASS POINTS

After the turning points, individuals faced the personal crises of life without a clear sense of direction, and this prompted the reassessment of what was essential to them. They moved through their grounding points, motivated by a desire to get smart and get control, and to identify the bases for a new direction to their lives. Emerging from that period of reflection and uncertainty, those who moved ahead to their compass points and established new criteria for action started to work toward a new balance for their lives—not rejecting spending, but not indulging; not borrowing excessively, but not avoiding debt altogether; not following styles, but not passing up new things. From "Too much is never enough," Americans had moved through an era of restraint and "Enough is enough" and were now easing into an era of balance wherein they would seek to redefine "enough." As one employee at a kitchen equipment supplies store recounted: "I realized my life was imbalanced. I was so weighted toward work that it was getting in the way of work."

The search for balance led to some unusual life decisions. One lawyer who left his successful career at a major urban law firm moved to a small town to become a sole practitioner. "The setting and pace," he explained, "are conducive to practicing law and practicing life." A journalist who left a successful career at a major urban paper moved to a small town in North Carolina to teach at a small college. In an article entitled "Why I Left the Newspaper Business," he explained that it was not for the money, the nature of work, the work load, the lack of opportunity, a dislike of management or any other historically important ingredient in a career. Rather, he noted, "It was the quality of life." In his new capacity he was learning and helping others learn, and also was connected to a more gratifying way of living.

Many lawyers were often quick to move away from their disciplines and embrace the reassessment process. Thomas Dye, a civil-trial lawyer in Miami, who studied morality and ethics in his profession, learned that lawyers were leaving the practice of law in record numbers. Others were simply adjusting their life styles and schedules to downgrade the importance of law in their lives. Some students, having just completed law school, were not even practicing law. All of this befuddled many traditional lawyers. "This phenomenon you are observing," Dye told his colleagues, "is a lot of people trying to get balance back in their lives. Blind pursuit of economic wealth and neglect of a lot of other values are not bringing people happiness. People are looking toward a broader range of values to bring them balance. One of them is spiritual." In one

1997 study, a business consultant discovered that 120 of 150 people interviewed engaged in a spiritual or contemplative practice at work.

In a world where "practicing life" was becoming a top priority, education started shifting from a means to acquire wealth to a means to attain satisfaction. Just 3.3 percent of the 1996 freshman class wanted to be lawyers, down from 5.4 percent in 1989. Interest in business careers dropped from 24.6 percent in 1987 to 14 percent in the 1996 fall class. Meanwhile, interest in a teaching career rose to its highest level in 23 years. This new direction alerted educational administrators at Wharton School of Business, which actually added to its MBA curriculum a course called "Get a Life" on balancing personal and work lives.

Practicing life in a balanced way has given birth to several values that mark the compass-points stage of the personal-reassessment process. While it is still early for most people to have finished their grounding-points, a few interesting examples hint at what lies ahead. These and other values yet to surface will direct individual choices at work, in the marketplace, in the election booth and elsewhere in the years to come.

FAIRNESS

The 1996 national elections produced outcomes that kept journalists confused for months. They sought to explain citizen behavior through the fractionating prism of left–right party politics, and that led to the confusion. One of the tests that voters applied to contentious decisions was fairness and/or reasonableness, attitudes that transcended ideological categorization. Ideological purity (partisan politics) moved down the voters' priority lists. As a result, a referendum to end affirmative action passed in California, while another referendum to allow medical use of marijuana passed in the same state (and in Arizona as well). From the left–right perspectives, these were contrary positions, since conservatives supported rejecting affirmative action, and liberals backed the marijuana position. Yet the outcome proved that the same citizens voted for both seemingly contrary positions.

In these votes (which experts and leaders thought were contradictory), citizens decided that, from their way of looking at things, affirmative action was no longer fair and that withholding a scientifically validated medical treatment—marijuana—was neither fair nor reason able. Voters elsewhere carried the same message. In all eight states where voters had the opportunity, they passed state constitutional amendments extending rights to the victims of crime. Passing with an 85 percent majority in the eight states, victims'-rights legislation (or amendments) are now on the books in 30 states because they seem "fair."

In Florida, citizens rejected a "penny per pound" tax on sugar, to pay for Everglades pollution cleanup, but voted overwhelmingly to require all polluters to pay for the swamp's cleanup. They also voted to establish an environmental trust fund (for private, state and federal funds) to pro- tect and maintain the Everglades. The fairness issue involved whether or not to stick one category of participant (sugar growers) with the entire bill. The voters decided to accept some responsibility (and expense) themselves, while at the same time forcing all industries responsible for the pollution to pay for the bulk of the cleanup.

The reasonableness slant on public issues also affected voters in Maine, who rejected both extreme positions on logging, one an absolute end to clear cutting and the other an end to all controls on clear cutting. Turning away from both of those lines on the ballot, they chose instead to vote for a negotiated settlement between timber and environmental interests. Voters liked the fact that the compromise acknowledged the worthiness of both positions, while also recognizing that neither extreme was workable. Overall, a fairness and reasonableness filter affected decisions, no matter what the partisan bias suggested.

ACCEPTANCE AND INCLUSION

During the anxious years of the turning-point transition period, a "we/they" dichotomy developed, and that division broadened during the grounding-points period. As people focused on their own identities, they emphasized distinctions and uniqueness. Race, gender, ethnicity and other categorical differences created social tensions as people some- times held to their own identity by drawing lines between themselves and others.

Actions in the compass-points phase, however, suggest that line- drawing distinctions are losing their appeal, and thus losing ground, to a desire for acceptance and inclusion. For example, in 1996, Harvard University eliminated all student-choice housing for incoming freshmen. In the past, students could select roommates and buildings, leading to preferential segregation by ethnic, religious or cultural subgroups. Now, the university housing office will randomly place everyone, including athletes. The hostile arguments that ensued revealed that not everyone has finished the grounding-points to compass-points transition.

Late in the nineteenth century, the white residents of Joseph, Oregon, ran the Nez Perce Indians out of the territory, creating the last major Indian war in North America. Now, the residents of Joseph are hoping to woo the remaining 4,000 Nez Perce back to their valley, to establish a cultural center. While the community admits it hopes to create a tourist center to replace dwindling logging and ranching resources, they nonetheless hope that the formerly ostracized can come together with them to create a better place to live for both groups. "They're opening the door for the trail home," explained a direct descendant of the tribe's former leader, Chief Joseph. "I never thought I'd see the day."

Finally, congressional hearings on health care expanded their focus to include mental illness, and for the first time open discussions concluded that the illness is a disease, not a failure of character. Such public figures as Florida governor Lawton Chiles, actor Rod Steiger, TV news commentator Mike Wallace, media mogul Ted Turner, country singer Naomi Judd and Heisman Trophy winner Earl Campbell, publicly revealed their battles with mental illness. Stepping down from their celebrity pedestals, they described themselves as quite human. In essence, then: Mental illness started to gain mainstream acceptance as a "no-fault" disease. After the public discussions, Congress changed the law governing insurance coverage for mental illness.

OPENNESS TO ALTERNATIVES

When individuals lost their loyalty to old institutions, they simultaneously opened themselves to alternatives, and they gladly experimented with new ways to solve problems. In the process, they discovered holistic medicine, electronic bulletin boards, Internet news services, and activities that personally satisfied them more than work (e.g., gardening, quilting, cooking).

Health care was one area of institutional weakness. Consequently, alternative medicine grew from a mom-and-pop, word-of-mouth business into a $25 billion industry during this period of reassessment. One 1995 study revealed that 25 million individuals regularly consulted alternative-medicine practitioners, and a 1993 study showed that one in three Americans used some form of alternative medicine, most without telling their doctor. They sought advice on chiropractic therapy, megavitamin regimens, homeopathic and herbal remedies, biofeedback, healing touch, hypnosis, massage therapy, naturopathic systems, acupuncture and other treatments shunned by the mainstream medical community. However, with this tidal wave of interest arising from individuals who were open to new ways of doing things, doctors who once condemned the entire field as quackery soon had massage therapists, chiropractors and even homeopaths working in their offices.

In due time, mainstream institutions were struggling to keep up. Harvard University started raising money to create an alternative-medicine center, and in the interim decided to offer seminars and special clinics on various alternative practices. Dr. Mehmet Oz at the Columbia–Presbyterian Medical Center incorporated into his operating procedures what qi-gong practitioners call "energy medicine," which tries to focus positive energy on healing parts of the body. Also, pharmaceutical companies rushed to discover "the medicine" behind herbal remedies that Americans felt brought them health. Meanwhile, the U.S. government created the Office of Alternative Medicine and soon gave a $1.1 million grant to Dr. Ann Gill Taylor, a professor of nursing at the University of Virginia, to see if magnets can alleviate chronic pain. Other grants sought to learn about alternative therapies for cancer, AIDS, muscle and bone pain, asthma and neurological disorders. The Cleveland Clinic added acupuncturists to its staff, and the University of Maryland Medical School added acupuncture to its regular curriculum.

Oxford Health Plan, a health-maintenance organization (HMO) added coverage of yoga, massage, nutritional services, herbal remedies and other alternative approaches to its insurance program, primarily because "the customers wanted it." America West Life of California included several alternative practices under its wellness program. By 1997, 45 states required health insurers to cover chiropractic services, seven required acupuncture coverage, and another two mandated coverage of naturopaths.

America Online (AOL) added a bulletin board on "Alternatives: Health and Healing." In addition, Georgetown University's School of Medicine brought prayer and spirituality into the recovery room, and Seattle's city council voted to establish the country's first government-subsidized natural-medicine clinic. In Washington, the state legislature mandated that any insurance company operating in the state must cover visits to the Seattle clinic. These and other changes resulted from patients' openness to change, not the openness of existing medical institutions. The old system of medicine for the most part addresses people only when they are sick, but natural medicine tries to keep people well in order to make doctors' visits unnecessary. That shift in perspective matched the changing perspective of more and more Americans to get control and move ahead.

During most of the 1990s, while circulation of mainstream daily newspapers declined, alternative papers blossomed. (In 1994, 17 of the top 25 U.S. newspapers lost circulation.) Meanwhile, between 1990 and 1996, members of the Association of Alternative Newspapers managed to double their subscription base. Newspapers like *The Met* (Dallas), *FW Weekly* (Fort Worth), *San Francisco Bay Guardian, Chicago Reader, Phoenix New Times,* and *Boston Phoenix* command a loyal readership approaching 13 million, predominantly from the attractive 18-to-49-year-old demographic group with an average household income of more than $50,000. Many of these newspapers print schedules of events in the city, and offer criticism of pop-culture activity therein. They also take an outsider's view of mainstream political events and concentrate on neighborhood and community alliances. They rarely print international or even national news and specialize in unique perspectives on local issues.

Other local connections have attracted an increased following, too.

In the past decade, 20 cooperative organic farms have come into existence in northern California, and 57 others have appeared throughout the state. These subscription farms connect a group of consumers with a specific farm, which grows what that group wants in return for guaranteed purchases. Andrew Scott, farming director at Hidden Villa farms in Los Altos, California, noted that the concept is growing rapidly. "Right now," he explained, "there is more demand for subscription-farmed produce than what Bay Area growers can supply."

On a national scale, Community Supported Agriculture (CSA), which is not strictly organic farming like the California examples, has spread to 600 farms in North America, feeding more than 150,000 members. Meanwhile, in 1995, natural-food sales, the alternative to industrial food production, surpassed $9 billion, and organic foods managed $2.8 billion in sales. Annual growth of these alternative foods exceeds 20 percent.

The growth in this latter area has come despite the fact that most natural and organic foods cost between 15 percent and 35 percent more than standard products. Part of the reason for the willingness to pay is the distrust of mainstream food sources, and part is a desire to reassert control over what the individual consumes. People who buy so-called health foods speak knowledgeably of concerns about pesticides, genetically altered produce and chemical preservatives. Linking with a farmer ensures some control over the food supply's creation, and buying organic foods assures the shopper of products untouched by chemicals.

CIVILITY

At the conclusion of an extensive reassessment process and the beginning of a revitalized interest in social life, being civil also acquired new appeal. Part of that appeal resulted from the contrast that civility offered to the nastiness that marked the turning-points phase. It became something to save and savor.

While the overall audience for daytime talk shows declined, *The Rosie O'Donnell Show* steadily increased her audience share. She banned "trash" talk from her show, regularly complimented her guests, and maintained a friendly atmosphere. In short, she was nice. Her success followed the demise of the talk shows that dominated the airwaves through much of the early 1990s. Shows that focused on sensational stories that belittled individuals lost favor as audiences moved beyond the abusive anger that marked their turning-points phase. *Donahue* lost 12 percent of its audience during 1994, while *Geraldo* and *Maury Povich* lost as well. When programs like *The Jerry Springer Show* surfaced, viewers seem to treat them the way they did television wrestling: as staged entertainment, not as presentations of real life.

In Springdale, Utah, tensions had run particularly high over decisions about development, reaching a point where city council meetings involved yelling at each other and little else. A few citizens convinced Phillip Kent Bimstein to run for mayor. As a transplant from Chicago, he had won support because of his activities on the arts council. However, being mayor of the city was something else. But he yielded. Bimstein ran an unusual campaign: He called people on the telephone and asked them if he could come over and talk about what was on their minds. That shockingly new approach complemented his other campaign method: civility. He treated citizens and opponents politely and told his assistants to "treat each citizen equally." That astoundingly simple approach won him the election, and it also made him an especially effective and popular mayor. Listening to the citizens (not telling them what *he* thought) and treating everyone politely (not shouting them down) turned the town around.

This attitudinal shift made things easier for a community-based program that sought to instill in young people the values that would yield public civility. Started at a conference in Aspen, Colorado, in 1992, *Character Counts* quickly installed programs in more than 326 cities and counties, and 47 states. Local community groups like the Red Cross, the Rotary Club, and Little League Baseball sponsored programs in various communities. *Character Counts* seeks to enlighten its participants on a nonpartisan but socially agreeable set of character traits: trustworthiness, respect, responsibility, fairness, caring and citizenship.

In Albuquerque, New Mexico, students paint billboards, create videos and perform plays to show how these personal characteristics help everyone. After the students of Albuquerque's Bel Air Elementary School adopted *Character Counts,* discipline citations dropped from 60 per month to just 20 a month. "It has touched people's hearts in a way I would never have believed," explained Mary Jane Aguilar, director of the 116-school Albuquerque program. "We're just desperate to believe in ourselves, to believe we're decent people."

Smokers have borne the brunt of society's negativity, suffering through ever-increasing levels of social rejection (as well as toxic haze). Whether or not society's attitude about smoking per se has changed, its feelings about how to treat smokers has. The Westin Hotel in Cincinnati created a more hospitable smoking space for employees, as did State Farm Insurance. Procter & Gamble installed smoking booths; and Motorola, which had announced the harshest policy in the country (no smoking anywhere on the property, including parking lots and open fields), heard strong negative reaction from its employees (both smokers and nonsmokers) and was forced to return to its former, more tolerant policy toward smokers.

Companies such as PepsiCo, Kraft Foods, Kellogg's, NationsBank, Chase Manhattan, BankAmerica, DuPont, McDonald's, Chubb and W.R. Grace signed pacts agreeing to mediate almost all disputes with industry rivals. They seek to change their lawyers' mind-sets from litigation to dispute resolution. By 1997, participants agreed that between 85 and 90 percent of more than a hundred disputes had gone to mediation under the pacts.

William Galston, the man who quit his White House job because of his son's baseball poem, resurfaced in Washington as executive director of the National Commission on Civic Renewal. The commission, cochaired by former Senator Sam Nunn and former Secretary of Education William Bennett, seeks to revive civility as a public virtue. "Americans in general," Galston insisted, "have said 'enough is enough.' "

SOCIABILITY

"Be nice" civility extended into a renewed interest in social gatherings. The personal-reassessment process, while rewarding, did isolate most individuals (at home, in the neighborhood, among coteries of friends).

In the compass-points phase, individuals are rediscovering their need to be more social via interacting more frequently with others.

Schaumburg, Illinois, came into existence as a mall-oriented suburb outside Chicago. People hoping to escape the concentration of the city sought the isolation that a home in a distant suburb could offer. As Schaumburg's senior planner explained, "[The people who came to Schaumburg] wanted separation. They wanted privacy. And they got it." Now, they want something else: a town square where they can socialize. The city started constructing a true downtown with shops, restaurants, a library, ponds, parks and even waterfalls. According to another local planner, "People want a sense of place, a feeling that they are part of a bigger whole." The mayor adds: "It will give people a place to gather, give us a place to bump into each other, give us a place to share."

The Entros Restaurant in Seattle combines a dinner party, salon, art commune, and Kiwanis Club with sophisticated game theory to create a night out that brings people together without the deflating yet typically required opening line to conversation. The dinner tables have games that necessitate more than one player, and people find seats wherever available. In a short period of time, customers are interacting over a game and sharing dinner. While all ages find Entros appealing, the largest segment of its clientele comes from time-pressed adults.

SIMPLE PLEASURES

Consumers look for products that help them restrain their spending, bring them solutions to their desire for control and offer them an occasional small pleasure (fun and comfort). In this last category, espresso bars and poetry readings fit perfectly. As individuals move into their compass points, they are expressing a desire to retain this interest in small pleasures.

Cigars, cocktails and crooners have come together to gain top billing across the country. "Cigar bars" feature deep, soft chairs in which to enjoy a stogie, hard-liquor drinks at the bar and crooners on the juke box. Johnnie Walker Red Label advertisements capture the new mood of the compass points: "Men are from earth. Women are from earth.

End of story." The we/they confrontation of recent gender battles gives way to simple, sociable pleasures.

The period of personal reassessment involves a wide range of activities which, viewed without a magic-eye perspective, may seem confusing. But a pattern clearly emerges once all of those different events are understood as being part of a larger context and process. People are spread out across this process of change, and their different actions along the way can cause confusion for marketers. Some individuals, and especially leaders, have altered their behavior very little, while some have changed considerably. Others are in the process of rethinking past behavior, and that leads to bursts of changing behavior. For many businesses, the simplest answer to this confusion has been to speak of "market segmentation" and to spend money developing technology to develop "mass customization," a way to address these different types of actions as if they were permanent. However, a magic-eye view of the surface chaos yields a new context: the turning-point–grounding-points–compass-points reassessment process. To use an earlier metaphor, this is the surface (culture) moving and shifting beneath the rolling ball (the economy).

This surface turmoil at the personal level is playing havoc with politics, marketing and communications. With the consensus of rising standards of living coming apart and with no clear model replacing it, managers have struggled to discover an effective model for addressing the new consumer. For those hoping to gain a better perspective on the changes underway, they might consider looking at (and to) women.

CRITICAL INSIGHT:
Women as Society's Leading Indicator of Change

Starting in the early 1990s, as widespread changes were starting to move through society, women were noticeably leading most of them. Their thinking, actions and responses repeatedly anticipated the broader society's eventual direction. While women were not always "leading" specific efforts to realize personal change, their action gave early expression to values and attitudes that emerged over time. Because women were among the first to reach each stage of the individual process of change, we characterized women's forward-directed actions as society's "leading indicators."

Women reached their turning points in time to affect the 1992 elections. For many women, the Senate Judiciary Committee's treatment of Anita Hill during the 1991 public hearings to confirm Clarence Thomas to the Supreme Court was "a moment of truth." Women who watched the hearings on television felt that the row of white males sitting on the committee had intentionally humiliated Ms. Hill because she was a woman who disagreed with them. Women later described "a click" that went off in their heads as they watched. They hit a turning-point recognition that things were not working for women in Washington.

In the months after the hearings, the Equal Employment Opportunity Commission received 1,244 complaints of sexual harassment in the workplace, a 70 percent increase over the year earlier. The bipartisan Women's Campaign Fund doubled its donations following the Judiciary Committee's public haranguing of Ms. Hill. Emily's List, a Democratic fund-raising group founded to support women running for office, and WISH, the Republican counterpart, both enjoyed hefty increases in contributions. In the 1992 elections, 150 women ran for the House of Representatives, compared to just 70 in 1990; and 20 ran for the Senate, compared to just eight two years earlier. In 1988, only 25 women won seats in Congress, while in 1992, 52 did. In state legislatures, the number of women candidates rose from 1,853 in 1988 to 2,375 four years later. In 1992, 60.6 million women voted, up from just 54.5 million in 1988, the prior presidential election year. A Pro-Choice rally in Washington, D.C., attracted 500,000 people, the largest number ever assembled in the capital up to that time. President George W. Bush's surprisingly quick turnaround in political fortunes from a seemingly unbeatable incumbent to a defeated candidate matched the time frame of women reaching their turning points. Clearly, women had hit a turning point, and their actions in the 1992 election reflected that change. In just two years, as we have already mentioned, working-class white males would reach their turning point, and force changes in the 1994 Congress.

At their professional turning points, women discovered that fitting into the corporate structure had lost its appeal. Fewer of them applied to MBA programs and to law school. Rebecca Maddox explained that she left corporate America not because of a pink slip or any other disappointment. She left her job as Senior Vice President for Marketing at National Liberty to start her own company because "I wanted to make money, wanted to have fun and didn't want to work with any jerks." Kathy Dawson left corporate America to start her own business because she figured it was the only way to "still have a life." Patty Stonesifer, who was the highest-ranking female at Microsoft, and who admitted "I have the very best job in the industry," nonetheless quit because "it is all-absorbing here. I want to switch gears and put more into my personal life." These three women, and others with similar moments of recognition, created a wave of female entrepreneurs who are leading society toward a different way of relating work to personal life. At the end of 1992, the 3.2 million women-owned businesses—mostly small-but-growing entrepreneurial enterprises—employed more workers than all the Fortune 500 companies combined. Just three years later, women owned roughly 7.7 million U.S. companies, with 15.5 million employees and $1.4 trillion in revenues. By 1997, 8 million women owned their own businesses, a 78 percent increase from 1987, employing 35 percent more people than the total of the Fortune 500. While the communities of wealth were contracting, companies headed by society's leading indicator were growing.

Women expressed their discovered grounding points and created compass-point values by their actions, especially in the workplace. Leaders like Frances Hesselbein, the woman Peter Drucker thought should have replaced Roger Smith at General Motors, believes in "challenging the gospel" and "questioning everything." Her managerial model is "flat" (i.e., nonhierarchical), with staff and colleagues allowed to move ahead without her stamp of approval. When she headed the Girl Scouts of America, she practiced her leadership theory, "The more control you give away, the more you have." She does not recognize absolutes, deals comfortably with ambiguity and gladly takes new directions. Flexibility, dispersed authority, constant change and sensitivity are part of her leadership model.

In a 1996 study of 31 key management categories, completed for the nonprofit Foundation for Future Leadership, women outperformed men in 28. Even though researchers did not intend to examine gender performance differences, the strength of female groups forced the striking conclusion that women lagged behind men in only one category: self-promotion.

Sally Helgesen, in *The Female Advantage* (1990), examined the managing styles of prominent women. Basing her findings on diary-keeping, Helgesen discovered that women focused on developing relationships, avoiding top-down power arrangements, strengthening and expanding communication pathways and emphasizing accessibility, participation and equality throughout the organization. In her next book, *The Web of Inclusion* (1995), Helgesen expressed surprise at the range of positive responses she had gotten to the first book, which even received favorable comments from the U.S. military, the ultimate top-down organization. Her surprise, however, would have been lessened had she noticed that women's examples repeatedly lead society, and that eventually society follows those models. The widespread, positive response she received was society once again following the leading indicator.

Deborah Tannen, author of *You Just Don't Understand* (1990), suggests that the difference between male and female managers is not derived from gender but from socialization. Adults train young boys to see things in hierarchical terms, her studies showed, while those same adults train girls to see things cooperatively. Whether that explains the difference or not, grounding-point and compass-point values do favor the person who thinks inclusively and cooperatively. As more individuals reach their compass points, they are expressing a preference for the cooperative and participatory models of organization—perspectives that women have been expressing.

Judy Mann, adviser to the University of Southern California's Women, Men and Media Project analyzed newspaper writing and discovered that men favored a "hierarchical and . . . confrontational" language. "If you read the words," she explained, "it's the language of conflict and controversy. Women tend to feel uncomfortable with that approach. They are much less interested in a blow-by-blow account."

Women are uncomfortable with the confrontational model of reporting; they have a stronger need for context and meaning in the stories they write (and read). Tina Brown, editor of the *New Yorker,* said her own media studies revealed that women do not like the endless stream of "unconnected, unassimilated, static bits of information," which is to say that they do not like the normal run of front-page journalism. Instead, women prefer "constructive uses of information." A Knight-Ridder task force corroborated Brown's findings. Women want more stories on education, social welfare, safety, health, parenting and ethical issues. In essence, women prefer personal stories that revolve around the quality of life. Meanwhile, their interest in confrontations between powerful groups or individuals—the stuff of most front pages—remains extremely low. As was mentioned earlier, the decline in newspaper subscriptions resulted in part from changed attitudes. That is, people now prefer to get their own information because they distrust other sources and seek to use their own evaluating system. However, another reason exists: Women just do not like the way that newspapers report the news.

Women's Wire, an on-line chat group, moved from AOL to the World Wide Web in 1996 and started receiving 7.5 million "hits" (i.e., visitors) per month. The discussion room's success happened because of the founders' clear concept. "We wanted to build a collaborative community," explained a cofounder, Nancy Rhine, "[and] a central clearing-house for information related to women. Things like health and career and continuing education, and fun things like entertainment and parenting." Women were putting together communications connections that trafficked in compass-points values.

By 1996, women's leading role in society was becoming clearer, at least as far as popular culture was concerned. Two female singers—Alanis Morisette and Mariah Carey—each received six different Grammy nominations, the largest number of nominations for any one performer. Joan Osborne was right behind with five. Even Joni Mitchell, long ignored by the award committees, received a nomination for best album. What these women had to say and how they expressed it had created huge record sales because they gave voice to what people were thinking.

Evening television had become a series of women's stories. *Roseanne, Ellen, Cybill, Murphy Brown, Grace Under Fire, Caroline in the City, Sisters, Hope & Gloria, Suddenly Susan,* and *The Nanny* led the list of what one journalist called "the feminization of prime time." The 1996 Sundance Film Festival featured so many female stories with female creators that the festival's titular head, Robert Redford, when asked if any themes existed for the festival, answered simply: "Women." Women even brought a different style to male-dominated arenas. Just prior to the 1996 Centennial Olympic Games in Atlanta, Georgia, *Newsweek* put sprinter Gwen Torrence on the cover to accompany the feature article, entitled "Year of the Women." Indeed, by the time the Games ended, America's female teams had won more gold medals than at any prior Olympics.

The tragic death of England's Princess Diana revealed in great detail how women were leading indicators of social change. Women were at the forefront of an unplanned yet nearly pervasive response to the death of the royal family's apparent outsider. Thousands of people filled the streets of London, and innumerable Americans voiced public expressions of mourning. Flowers flooded the streets around the palace, and millions around the world watched the funeral on television. The immense public display of feelings caught the House of Windsor, the media and most men by surprise. The House of Windsor had won great public approval during World War II and thereafter by maintaining a "stiff upper lip," a phrase connoting resolve, endurance and strength in the face of adversity. Their expression of just that resolve in this situation at this point in history, however, triggered an extremely negative reaction against the royals. In the new social environment, people (especially women) demanded a more open, personal and emotional response for the loss of a royal family member who also seemed "like a friend" to people who had never met her.

In New York City, therapists reported that in the days and weeks following Diana's death, women patients brought the Diana issue into their sessions and expressed a sense of personal loss, while men rarely mentioned the topic at all. Many patients identified the royal family as exemplary of what they confronted in their personal lives from relatives, friends or colleagues who were "emotionally unavailable."

The "floral revolution," as one journalist called the amazing outpouring of emotion (and flowers) after Princess Di's death, highlighted the distinctions between a world that was fading and one that was rising. The same journalist, writing in *The European* newspaper, explained that the entire situation gave expression to "a struggle between the new culture of informality, the personal, the feminine, the present, the human, the admission of weakness and vulnerability, humor, merit and the casual; and the old culture of tradition, suits, deference, the old school tie, solemnity, the stiff upper lip, protocol and hypocrisy." The writer noted that the "new style of behavior [included] a new transparency, a new honesty, a new accountability, a new public life based on merit and worth. . . . This is a very feminine revolution. It marks a new hegemony of the feminine in public life."

Clearly, women were not just the leading indicator—they were becoming the leading models for society's advances. Women moved ahead in the turning-points–grounding-points–compass-points process, and the values they expressed helped give society a new direction. The chart that follows offers two lists of preferences. One column lists preferences from the Old Frame of Mind, which had its greatest support during the success of the communities of wealth, and the other column lists characteristics from the New Frame of Mind, which is starting to gain support. The list is not an either–or categorization. Instead, it merely marks preferences that gather greater favor and enjoy greater support.

The popular press prefers to cover women's "issues" as part of a larger gender battle. Such a strong line may be the result of the pre–turning-points preference for conflict. In fact, women's actions are not so much cause for conflict as they are indications of societal changes. The fact that the old institutions have primarily male leaders may explain why some resent women's actions and see them as a challenge to

Old Frame Of Mind	New Frame Of Mind
hierarchy	dispersed power
confrontation	cooperation
control	delegation
take power	give up power
command	participation
routine	innovation
impersonal ("professional")	personal
rigidity	sensitivity
absolutes	flexibility
authority	persuasion
victory in conflicts	conflict resolution
assign responsibility	assume responsibility
image	substance
data	context
specialization (narrow focus)	larger picture
analysis	intuition
efficiency	effectiveness
quantity of life	quality of life
contentedness	happiness
money as currency	time as currency
law	ethics
physics (study of forces)	biology (study of living things)
MBA	social work
exclusionary clubs	affinity groups
binary logic (computer precision)	fuzzy logic (software ambiguity)
power	impact
photography	expressionism
fitness	health

male authority. However, the real tension—the overriding tension—is not about gender. Rather, the conflicts are between loyalists to the communities of wealth, and the advocates of an institutional structure just emerging. Their conflicts have become typical for this period of transition from the communities of wealth to the emerging communities of meaning—the subject of the next chapter.

THE COMMUNITIES
OF MEANING

Historian Michael E. Goodich, in his book *Violence and Miracle in the Fourteenth Century* (1995), stated that miracles occurred and angels appeared, with greater frequency and with greater social importance than ever in the 1300s, during the "breakdown of the medieval consensus . . . and the decline of its characteristic institutions, such as the feudal system, the papal church, and the democratic commune." The disintegration of these unifying social institutions "enhanced reliance on the mystical, irrational, magical and miraculous." When America's world out of control reached its zenith, many individuals also took an interest in angels—variously defined as messengers, protectors, friends, allies and guides, but all somehow connected to a world beyond this one. The book *An Angel a Week* went through four printings between October 1992 and July 1993, inspiring its publisher, Ballantine Books, to sign contracts for 16 more books on angels. Other publishers joined the market. *A Book of Angels*, by Sophy Burnham, went through 25 printings in the first three years of the 1990s, leading the author to write *The President's Angel*. Also, *Angel Letters, Angel Answers; The Angels Within Us; Ask Your Angel; Where Angels Walk: True Stories of Heavenly Visitors; Do You Have a Guardian Angel?*, and many more of similar perspective hovered around the best-seller lists for years. Lois Mendenhall, of The Happy Bookseller in Columbia, South Carolina, explained: "If it's got an angel on it, it's working. Angel titles are selling across the board; there is no price resistance . . . [and] the angel trend crosses age and denominational lines." Joelle Delbourgo, editor-in-chief at Ballantine, added: "People are bringing angels into their daily lives." Interest in angels spread to other media as well. Two 1997 movies, *Michael* and *The Preacher's Wife,* introduced angels as principal characters, and *Touched by an Angel* stayed in the Top Ten of weekly TV shows during the same year.

Much as did the fourteenth century, the late twentieth century has experienced the disintegration of once-prominent institutions—and, like people living in that earlier period, Americans (like so many others) have taken to nonmaterial phenomena. Whereas the institutions that were coming apart in the fourteenth century were systems of religion and authority, those deteriorating in the late twentieth proved to be the communities of wealth—the very institutions that had delivered prosperity to postwar America. The old communities of wealth came apart both voluntarily and involuntarily. The voluntary disintegration resulted from a variety of management theories that taught leaders how to tear the old institutions apart in defense of some large, amorphous threat they called "globalization." The involuntary disintegration came from employees and consumers who, having finished their personal-reassessment phase, simply drifted away, either physically or psychologically, from the ineffective institutions.

As they drifted away from the old institutions, individuals started piecing together their own groups, organizations and institutions. Individual efforts to locate or create new groups that could embody the new values led to the creation of communities of meaning, places where grounding-point and compass-point values could most comfortably find expression. Whereas the communities of wealth espoused and bolstered the pursuit of wealth and, more specifically, the ability to expand everyone's standard of living, their replacement, the communities of meaning, had the pursuit of learning, growth and personal fulfillment as their most attractive features. Certainly the communities of wealth had these latter aims on their agenda *somewhere,* and just as certainly the communities of meaning seek to make a profit—but the difference rests in the emphasis as well as in the relationship that the individual had or has to the institution. In the communities of wealth, the individual fulfilled a role and received compensation that depended upon performance in that role. In the communities of meaning, the individual seeks involvement at *all* levels and wants ongoing growth, development and learning as part of the compensation.

Communities of meaning emerged from individual needs and developed to fulfill and possibly expand upon those needs. Having passed through their period of personal reassessment, individuals started creating groups, organizations and even institutions that offered fulfillment, satisfaction and growth. These new groups encourage participation, depend upon learning and grow by expanding the individual's personal satisfaction. Essentially, the old institutions had at one time been the best route to wealth, but that objective was losing its appeal and those institutions were losing their ability to deliver that wealth to most people. The new institutions allow for a search and a growing, for learning and fulfillment, *outside* the quest for wealth. They reinforce the individual's new interest in meaningful work, play and living. The more that old communities of wealth try to keep their old operating rules alive, the more individuals shift their loyalty to the new communities of meaning. Over time, the burden for the communities of wealth has become how they could possibly restructure themselves to meet the new criteria for both creating and sustaining loyalty.

COMMUNITIES OF WEALTH	COMMUNITIES OF MEANING
Career	Learning
Profit	Growth
Success	Inner Contentment
Loyalty to Employer	Loyalty to Self
Financial Rewards	Personal Rewards
Promotion	Development
Brand Names	Whatever Works
Standard of Living	Quality of Life

DISINTEGRATING COMMUNITIES

The communities of wealth started disintegrating both voluntarily (or intentionally) and involuntarily (or unintentionally). The voluntary shrinking of American corporations began in earnest with the recession that started the 1990s. Historically, recessions brought worker layoffs and other employment cutbacks, but usually the ensuing recovery returned most of those laid off back to company. Typically, blue-collar workers faced the greatest employment volatility. This recession, however was different, and even when the recovery started, laid-off workers did not find their old jobs waiting for them. In fact, 54 percent of the job cutbacks made during the recession became permanent. Overall, from 1989 through 1997, American companies cut 4 million jobs from the old communities of wealth. Half of those were white-collar job-holders, and 38 percent were managers.

Downsizing eventually affected operational effectiveness. When Chemical Bank reduced one department from 15 to just one, for days the lone remaining worker sat in her office and cried. Delta Airlines cut $2 billion and 15,000 jobs from its operations, reducing the per passenger cost per mile from 9.26 cents to 7.5 cents. However, the company also destroyed the company's "one family" ambience, enraged loyal customers and soon exceeded the industry average for customer complaints. Soon, CEO Ron Allen was gone, and the company started rehiring personnel. As one observer noted, "What this points out is that cost-cutting is not just a labor issue."

Another part of the voluntary shrinking of institutions involved offering workers the chance to retire early. These so-called early outs were less devastating news to those who had worked for years, and even decades, for the company—but nonetheless they were sent the message that their experience, expertise, and even presence were no longer worth the salary. But a reverse antagonism erupted as well. When the U.S. Postal Service offered workers a chance to leave, executives hoped 3,000 would exit. They received 15,000 acceptances. The early-retirement programs ran headlong into individuals with new priorities.

When Connecticut Mutual Life Insurance Company offered its 1,650 home-office employees early retirement, company managers hoped to shed 400 workers. Although that was a lot, the company needed to downsize to meet the contractual obligations of a forthcoming merger. However, 1,200 employees decided to leave. Embarrassed that they had completely lost contact with their own people, executives countered with big incentives to staunch the flow, but only 220 decided to stay, still leaving the company with an exodus of 980 people.

The Connecticut Mutual story had a history. Just two years earlier, the company's new CEO had insisted that everyone submit his or her resignation and reapply for a whole new set of jobs. The mood within the company in the months that followed was anything but collegial. "A lot of people are fed up with the way they have been treated," explained an administrative assistant who accepted the early-retirement offer and refused the second-effort incentives. "They have been screwing around with everybody's job for two years . . . and people can only take so much."

Those who were left behind had to work longer hours, assume more responsibility and still try to maintain control over even wider areas. After AT&T announced its employee reductions, those left behind felt abandoned and deceived. Turning on the phrase "one big family" that Chairman Robert Allen used frequently, one employee called it "a dysfunctional family. . . . If anyone tells you this whole thing is O.K., they're lying. Or afraid." Another employee extended the family metaphor and spoke of being like an "abused" spouse. Still another worker, undercutting the theme of institutional loyalty, added: "These days, if you work for a company for 10 years, they think they're doing you a favor." In a similar vein, General Electric by the mid-1990s was doing three times the business it did in 1980—with half the work-force. To get there, executive vice-president Frank Doyle admitted, "We did a lot of violence to the expectations of the American workforce."

That "violence" became more apparent over time. For the companies that used extensive downsizing between 1990 and 1995, the remaining workers suffered considerably, and those companies endured bigger increases in medical claims for psychiatry, substance abuse, high blood pressure and long-term disability than did companies not downsizing. The contradictory result of increasing health-care costs while trying to reduce overall costs revealed that executives did not have the overall situation under control.

Leaving the company behind physically was becoming harder and harder for many workers as well. Those not discarded in the massive corporate downsizings spoke angrily of doing their own job *and* that of *several* downsized workers, a condition that created longer work days. At the same time, technology created a world of constant contact between "the office" and the individual, resulting in the disappearance of the barrier between private and professional lives. During the 1990s, pager sales rose by more than 15 percent per year, while cellular-phone sales jumped by more than 10 percent per year. As one IBM consulting manager, who had two car phones and three cellular phones, explained: "There is no such thing as leaving [work]." Work continued to put more pressure on the individual, and many supervisors made things worse instead of better. One company programmed its computers to respond to *any* employee's shortcoming. When someone on a project team missed a deadline, Lotus Notes flashed a frowning face on the individual's screen.

While companies reduced head counts and added pressure to those remaining, they also reduced the returns that the remaining individuals received. The nearly 84 percent of companies that in 1982 offered their workers defined-benefit plans (that is, retirement plans that ensure fixed payments after retirement, until death) dropped to around 50 percent by 1995. At least 25 large corporations eliminated health benefits altogether for retired employees—another signal for those remaining that an end to the amicable corporate–individual relationship was inevitable. While paying management consultants in excess of $12 billion per year (in toto) to find cost reductions and other efficiencies, American companies were slashing salaries, benefits and job stability for long-standing employees.

Not only were employees working longer hours for stagnating salaries, but also, the feeling within the company was that no one really cared. In interviews with 300 executives from medium-sized to large companies, roughly three-fourths insisted that their employees were the company's most important investment. However, when human-resources department heads were asked how many actually had a say in the company's strategic-planning process, only one-fourth said they did. Despite what they said, corporate leaders' actions revealed that human-capital resources were low in priority. In counterbalance to their lowered status, employees made the corporation lower on *their* priority list. All this of course created growing attitudinal conflicts within most organizations, but then upper management—financially safe and secure—seemed not to care.

Throughout the historic rise of the communities of wealth, successful institutions created incentive programs that sustained loyalty and encouraged advancement. They raised salaries routinely enough that employees could assume increasing personal wealth in the future. Those same institutions added personal benefits like life and health insurance that kept employees feeling secure about being able to withstand unforeseen economic and personal disasters. Those companies typically promoted hard-working employees, giving them a sense through their lengthening career that they were accomplishing something. Even bonuses and stock options—extra statements of value—moved through many of the institutions. The whole system of employment and compensation was the glue that helped the institutions to cohere.

In the late stages of these institutions' lives, however, incentives reversed course and, rather than helping the organizations grow, they actually reinforced efforts to tear the institution apart. Early-out offerings actually *encouraged* people to leave. As we have seen, when companies like Connecticut Mutual and such institutions as the U.S. Postal Service offered their employees these opportunities to take the money and run, workers headed for the door in droves. And among them went the best and the brightest. Years of invaluable experience and learning walked out of the office. In essence, early-out packages paid the freight for shipping out the tradition, operations and skills essential to the successful management of the communities of wealth.

At another level, those same institutions added incentives for leaders to fire people. Robert Allen of AT&T saw his personal stock portfolio rise by $6 million on the day he fired 40,000 employees, simply because the stock market boosted AT&T's stock price on the news. In essence, the larger stock market rewarded most executive decisions to cut corporations into small pieces. Other leaders, who had substantial stock holdings in the companies they led, also experienced pleasant increases in their personal wealth when they dismantled their own institutions—and Wall Street rewarded their actions with a jump in company stock value. The most egregious example of all, however, was the bonus given "Chainsaw Al" Dunlap, who received a special payment of nearly $100 million for firing thousands of employees and "saving" Scott Paper Company.

Firing (among others) the best and brightest, then claiming to have saved the company, was typical of the late stages of the communities of wealth. Such ahistorical behavior was, to use a youth-culture phrase, "like having sex to save virginity." Companies were undercutting employee optimism, destroying personal security, and undermining customer loyalty. These were core parts of the social contract that helped the communities of wealth function effectively. The whole mission of the communities of wealth was vanishing at the leaders' and stock market's behest. Sadly, these actions validated what a former CEO of IBM told us. "Most corporate wounds are self-inflicted."

The late stages of these institutions of abundance gave credence to a corporate "essentialism" that separated something called the company from employees, customers and even products or services. In their place, a corporate essentialism necessarily narrowed the value of American corporations to their stock price and shareholders. All the other pieces of the communities of wealth—employees, customers, societal role—moved down or off the organization's priority list. Leaders were capable of envisioning a corporate entity separate from its market and its employees, an institution that could be downsized, reengineered and renovated without actually talking to the customers or the people doing the work. Somehow this entity could be whittled away to some essence that was the corporation, and be "saved." The "corpus" (from the Latin word for "body") was simply taken away from the "corporation," which was then left with some undefined core—and usually one on paper, or in "the numbers," at that.

These types of practices were undermining internal support for corporate life in general, and the resulting disconnect between employer and employee led to the organization's involuntary disintegration. Employees simply started leaving, either physically or psychologically. In 1995, an Opinion Research Corporation study revealed that of 1,000 adults interviewed, only 1 percent aspired to be corporate managers. In 1990, 25 percent of the MBA graduates from Columbia University joined large corporations (i.e., companies with more than 1,000 employees). In 1995, just 13 percent did so. Nearly 70 percent of Stanford University's 1989 business-school graduates joined large corporations, but just 50 percent did so in 1994. The student president of the Kellogg School of Management at Northwestern University summarized his fellow students' perspective: "I don't know anyone who wants to be like Jack Welch or Jack Smith." In 1996, executive-search companies reported surges in demand for their clients, the biggest jump being by 56 percent in the chief operations officer (COO) category. In 1990, some 20 percent of new CEOs at small companies came from large companies, but in 1996 that figure jumped to 40 percent. In short, while companies voluntarily unloaded "redundant" workers, other talented leaders were voluntarily heading for the door.

American corporations lost their appeal to more and more Americans because the rewards offered in relation to the demands made did not connect with those who had reset their priorities. When quality of life entered the equation, then long hours, excessive electronic connections, low pay, no security and all the rest did not fit. As one Emory University student commented: "When a big company says 'Nobody has employment security, we don't pay very well, and we stand for continuity, not innovation'—where's the payoff?" Another student was more succinct: "Why sign up for a beating?"

"I'M OUTTA HERE": EXIT STRATEGIES EMERGE EVERYWHERE

One of the ironies of the dissolving relationship between institutions and individuals during this late twentieth-century disintegration period concerned control. When companies reduced their costs and cut personnel, business leaders felt they were regaining control over their organizations. Even though that control proved illusory, their actions nevertheless resulted in a true loss of control for many workers—who then had to confront the economic world on their own. In reverse, individuals who subsequently passed through their personal-reassessment process discovered their own type of control, which allowed them to exist minus the communities of wealth. As more individuals exercised this personal control, more institutions lost control of their markets and human capital.

The old communities of wealth, however, continued to believe that monetary compensation alone was sufficient to keep employees. In 1995, more than half of the firms surveyed expressed confidence that increased compensation was sufficient to retain at least senior employees. Alfie Kohn, author of *Punished by Rewards* (a study of how workers seek compensation), explained that financial rewards to new employees looked like threats. " 'Do this and you'll get that,' " the author said "is not much different from 'do this or else.' " While corporations plowed ahead with their money-based incentives, individuals with reassessed personal values were looking around for compensation packages that included learning, growing, developing and greater personal control.

The involuntary reduction of the communities of wealth (that is, reductions the companies did not plan) involved individuals deciding that their current employer no longer met their needs, including the kinds of compensation that they now found appealing. Employees at all levels started devising their own "exit strategies"—personal projects designed to develop, fund and eventually implement their exits from corporate America. For some, that meant leaving work altogether and starting a new life. For others, it meant cutting back on work commitments (both time and energy), to allow time for other endeavors. For many still, it meant a psychological departure, because even though they continued to cash their pay checks, the emotional attachment was over.

Unlike the early outs that employees took in record numbers, the departure of the best and the brightest based on personal decisions was an involuntary loss of corporate talent. With the reassessment process reaching peak numbers of people, those deciding to "get off the tread-mill," "get out of the rat race" and "leave the asylum to the inmates" started to grow. Headhunters for executives reported an increased number of clients looking to slow down. "[Our new clients] get to a certain level," explained one executive recruiter, "and say 'Why am I doing this? Can I get more flexibility, more balance, more fun if I get to a smaller place?'" Likewise, search organizations for the advertising business noted that small agencies in places like Billings and Missoula, Montana, Boise, Idaho, and Spokane, Washington, were receiving hundreds of résumés from agency people in cities like Los Angeles, Boston, Atlanta and New York. Moreover, they were all willing to take substantial salary cuts to make the move.

Those heading for the doors came from all levels. U.S. Air Force "top gun" pilots, the best trained and most loyal fighter pilots, started leaving in droves. In 1994, the service managed to resign 81 percent of those pilots eligible to retire. In 1997, only 30 percent "reupped." They all agreed that it was not the money but rather the schedule that drove them to civilian life.

Stephen Friedman, chairman of Goldman & Sachs, abruptly re-signed from his post in 1994, citing time pressures and family demands. Rejecting a job that guaranteed immense wealth, he turned to a simpler life. Jeffrey Stiefler, president of American Express, who had accepted his elevation to president with great enthusiasm, one year later quit. An American Express official explained, "He realized he could just walk away. It makes a lot of sense—except that *no one* in that kind of position just walks away." Stiefler did because, as he summarized, "I needed to have a better balance between work and my family, and have some time left over for me." While that did not "make sense" to American Express senior executives, it made sense to Stiefler. And Anna Quindlen, the Pulitzer Prize–winning columnist for the *New York Times,* decided to call it quits, even though she stood a solid chance of becoming the managing editor. Even though her work schedule permitted time at home to tend to her children, the decision to quit journalism resulted from both her growing preference for writing fiction and a concern about her own well-being. "When you have a job that is very high-powered," she explained, "you can never really divest yourself of your preoccupation."

Sherry Stringfield also walked away from fame and fortune. She was a star of one of television's most successful weekly shows, *E.R.* But she discovered that what she really wanted was "to live a more normal life." At her turning point, she wasted little time leaving, although she did have trouble convincing people that she wanted to go. What motivated her was a director who said to her, at the end of a long day's shoot, "It's not a race"—a clear statement of the irrelevance of working hard as part of a good life. Even though she admitted that she liked to work, she yielded to the desire to "drive more slowly, stop and roll in the grass." For someone 28 years old and enjoying national celebrity status, that was an unexpected and significant change. The jilted studio felt so deprived that it made her sign a contract saying she would not reenter the television arena for two and a half years. She accepted because doing so would keep her from "losing my head and agreeing to take another part that would lead to 15-hour days and no life."

Understanding the immense work required to bring institutions in line with new market realities prompted some leaders to reject offers to assume top positions. Some were politicians who decided not to run for reelection. Others were police chiefs and school administrators who retired early. Many were business leaders who just wanted to say "Enough is enough." In one year, senators Nancy Kassenbaum, Bill Bradley, Sam Nunn, William Cohen and other senior and distinguished leaders left the U.S. Senate, and all agreed that mainly the antagonistic atmosphere and the quality of discussion there had led them to say goodbye. Their original reason for running for office—to participate in positive efforts to help the country—had fallen victim to the government's equivalent of the downsizing mania and to menial political nitpicking. Peter Schweitzer, groomed for two years to move from his position as supervisor of J. Walter Thompson's largest office (in Detroit) to become CEO of the entire company, balked at the last moment. The new position meant more power and more money, but more administrative work and more trouble. Also, he liked the circumstances of his job in Detroit. As he started recruiting for his replacement, he realized his mistake: "The more I tried to sell the job to others, I had to say 'Wait a minute—this is it, the ideal job.'" What awaited him as head of a huge company that needed restructuring in the midst of an industry with an identity crisis just did not appeal to his reordered personal priorities.

Like Schweitzer, the deans of America's business schools started recognizing the futility of their struggles. With faculty entrenched in past models, with real-life business demanding that the school update quickly, and with competition rising from everywhere, the job became less and less appealing. Even if a dean (or any other leader) were able to diagnose the institution's situation correctly, motivating an aggregate of people (many of whom had yet to pass through any reassessment process) to undertake massive change seemed daunting. "It's like moving a cemetery," intoned an exasperated former dean. "You have to realize," added another, "that the relation of the dean to the faculty is like the relationship of a fire hydrant to a pack of mad dogs." In 1994, the deans of (among others) MIT, the University of Virginia, Yale, Dartmouth, the University of Maryland and the University of Rochester all retired and went back to teaching.

BEMUSED BY THE COLLAPSE

During this era of contraction and disintegration, the comic strip "Dilbert" monitored the insanity that paraded as reasonable business practices. Created in 1989, the feature soon became one of the most popular in the country, syndicating in more than 400 newspapers. The lead character, Dilbert, is intelligent enough to see that his employers do not know the personal consequences of what they do, and in many instances do not understand at all what they do. Yet he does not have the strength to confront them over such arrogant actions as placing an employee-location device around his neck; restructuring the hierarchy and making him lower than the janitor; and awarding a promotion "with no extra pay but much more responsibility" because "It's how we recognize our best people."

Dilbert cartoonist Scott Adams learned firsthand about why his audience identified with his characters when he himself went on line in 1993. "I heard from all of these people who thought that they were the only ones [who saw the absurdity and felt the anxiety]. . . . Basically, there are 25 million people out there, living in cardboard boxes indoors, and there was no voice for them. So there was this pent-up demand [for my cartoon strip]."

Adams took the time to explain his philosophy and its development in a book titled *The Dilbert Principle,* which quickly rose to the Number One spot on several best-seller lists. Adams directed his satire at managers, who are characterized as incompetents promoted to the level at which they can do the least harm. (This idea, which is the essence of the Dilbert Principle, represents a revision of the Peter Principle from the late 1970s.) The book's success matched the comic strip's success because Adams depicted those in charge of American corporations as

FROM WEALTH TO MEANING: THE CHART

	1946 — 1986 Communities of Wealth	1986 — 1994 Transition	1994 — Communities of Meaning
Concepts	"Feel Good Era" "Too much is never enough" Standard of living	"Anxious Era" "Enough is enough" Get smart/Get control	"Sensible Era" Redefine "Enough" Meaning in life
Values	"Get ahead" "Unlimited opportunity" Affluence Success Future Power Credit Luxury (Big Rewards) Law & Order Consumer culture Career planning Security	"Get a handle" Limited expectations Control Restraint *Carpe Diem*/Nostalgia Anger Debt free/Worry free Comforts (Small Rewards) Violence/Vigilantes Survey & opinion poll culture Financial planning Insecurity	"Get a life" Adjusted expectations Fulfillment Satisfaction Continuity Growth Overall plan Needs (Functional) Pragmatism Beliefs culture Life planning Stability
		Turning Points **>> Grounding Points >>** *Compass Points*	
Products/ Services	French wine BMW Armani, Klein, Lauren Credit cards Employee benefits Brands "Professional" medicine "Professional" journalism "Professional" investor "Professional" programming Mass marketing/Advertising	Espresso Ford Explorer Dana Buchman, Dockers Debit cards 401(k), Co-payments Generics/Store brands Alternative medicine Personal journalism Morningstar & Quicken Talk Radio (& TV) Database /Niche/Multilevel mktg.	? ? ? ? ? Holistic medicine Public journalism Holistic investor Interactivity Resource/"Cool" marketing

both out of touch and out of control. The rational systems originally put in place to operate companies were now irrational and incompetent. *The Dilbert Principle* appealed to those who could detach themselves from the subject—the boss and the company. That detachment allowed the sarcasm to work most effectively. The process of saying farewell to the communities of wealth started with anger and frustration directed at leaders. With the arrival and success of *Dilbert,* the response had migrated to ridicule directed at managers who sought feebly and futilely to sustain ineffective institutions.

Meanwhile, most people had already started to piece together new organizations, groups and institutions that did what they wanted them to do. Leaders looking for direction in how to overhaul their communities of wealth should look closely at what individuals can and do create when *they* have control of the power.

NEW COMMUNITIES TAKING SHAPE

Women have been a leading force in the creation of these new institutions. Studio publicists expected the movie *Waiting to Exhale* to attract an audience of black women because the stars were black. However, the movie attracted a wide-ranging audience of women—who saw the story as a representation of something they thought was crucial: friends in groups. Getting together to discuss issues and share thoughts, the film's characters realized that together "We can take that good, deep breath and exhale."

Tamara Traeder, coauthor of the book *Girlfriends: Invisible Bonds, Enduring Ties,* suggested that such groups create continuity in a discontinuous world. With large corporations coming apart and with marriages now harder to sustain, "Women are finding [that] their friendships with women are their true long-term relationships," she observed. More than even long-term stability, these relationships also further the personal search for identity and meaning. In their book, Traeder and coauthor Carmen Renee Berry explained: "Our girlfriends say much about who we are—where we are in our lives, what aspects of ourselves we value or are trying to develop." Rather than the independence and self-interest that facilitated the latter phases of career mania, women's groups created a different kind of stability and identity—one that transcended and yet incorporated work and career.

These types of groups more and more came to be the ballast in a world out of control, stabilizing aspects that reminded individuals of both who they were and who (not "what") they wanted to be. Communities of meaning are integral to the thinking of reassessed individuals. Participation, growth, development, fulfillment, sociability and learning are key elements of the communities of meaning. Unlike the communities of wealth which wring productivity out of the individual in order to enhance the bottom line, communities of meaning reach successful outcomes because participants move in that direction out of a shared interest in developing. The loyalty that communities of wealth once enjoyed when participants held common objectives has moved to the communities of meaning because participants now share new common objectives.

Institutional observers watched as individuals within large companies have created what they call "communities of practice," which are self-directed, self-organizing groups. According to the Institute of Research on Learning's Etienne Wenger, communities of practice develop over time and are defined in terms of the learning they inculcate. Also, this type of community has a purpose—an enterprise—but no agenda, because members gather around a desire to add value to something they are doing. Also, these communities of practice involve constant learning as part of their basic function, which leads them to develop their own way of dealing with their projects. That is, they find their own role, develop their own way of fulfilling that role and decide when to disband. Thus they cannot be "managed," but only watched and supported.

Communities of meaning are communities of practice—plus. People are drawn to communities of meaning not because of the enterprise alone but because of the way that organization *pursues* the enterprise. The way in which work gets done (including sociability, learning, participation, responsibility and fairness) is as important as final results to people who join communities of meaning. In the end, what participants treasure is not simply the enterprise's success but also the personal growth, development, satisfaction and fulfillment they receive from being part of the process.

Looking at some of the early communities of meaning can help clarify this picture of interaction between objectives and participants. The self-named "Lake Ladies" and the "Chainsaw Kittens," some of whom are married and others divorced, but all of whom attended school together, live in different places—yet they gather annually to invigorate their friendships. For example, the Lake Ladies' annual meetings in Indiana became so important to them that they purchased an A-frame home on that state's Rocky Fork Lake. Each year, they assemble there to exchange personal stories about the prior 12 months. They do not get together just to solve personal problems. Rather, they also share experiences and enjoy each other's company. In the end, individuals discover support and solutions for their personal situations.

Another group, a dozen middle-aged women who had attended a Chicago high school together meet annually at one or another members home, whether it be in New Orleans, Charleston, Boston, New York, or the Florida Keys. They support each other during periods of trouble (e.g., breast cancer, divorce), and yet they manage to laugh a lot as well. Still another group has created a shared-retirement plan that will bring them together should they eventually find themselves alone. Sarah Pillsbury, who coproduced the movie *How to Make an American Quilt*, speaking of her need to participate in sharing groups, says that getting together offers an opportunity to "tell our stories," a way of connecting personal narratives with those of others who have had similar experiences. That personal link is crucial to the new organizations that people are forming.

Sociability, one of the core compass points, has moved individuals out of their homes, to which they had retreated in order to regain control. Sixteen women with an average age of just over 63 years started a group to study stock-investment strategies. While they certainly wanted to increase their wealth, members of the Beardstown, Illinois, Ladies' investment club admitted that learning and socializing were the main reasons they created the group. This unusual model of learning and socializing before investing worked. Their portfolio growth exceeded the Dow Jones Index, and the professional manager's average, as well. For 10 years running, the group claimed an annual rate of return of 23 percent. Eventually they wrote a book, *The Beardstown Ladies' Common-Sense Investment Guide* (1995)—which also turned a handsome profit, selling 100,000 copies in five months and eventually landing on the top-ten list. Professionals smirked when analysts revised the rate of return down to 9 percent. But they missed the point. The ladies first gathered to learn, and that they did abundantly. Hitting big numbers was not part of their agenda.

Women's groups cross all ages and all economic categories, and their success points society toward a new model of joining together to get something done. The Knitting Guild of America had 550 members in 1984, but by 1996 it had more than 10,000 knitters happily talking away while making one or another new object. At the annual convention, attendance has steadily increased by 15 percent every year, and most of the participants are in their twenties and thirties. Swarthmore College has a chapter which had a knit-a-thon to create clothes for a homeless shelter. In a completely different area, Jacquie Phelan, who mountain-biked in three national championships, said she got her greatest pleasure meeting with the WOMBATS (Women's Mountain Bike and Tea Society). The group of amateurs, as well as professionals, gathers and takes rides, which lead to rests and conversations over tea. "WOMBATS don't have meetings," Phelan suggested, "we just have rides that gradually decline into relaxation." The idea is spreading to other cities.

In Chicago, Sandy Thomas, who has an MBA from DePaul, put together the Chicago Social Club to bring men and women together via touch football and other sports. Every Saturday, roughly 4,800 people from 320 teams meet, play their games, and then slide into an extended social hour on the field. The huge response caught Ms. Thomas by surprise, and so she added another round of scheduled games on Sunday. Word of the organization's success spread, and soon clubs in 16 different cities, from Atlanta to Minneapolis and from Boston to Los Angeles, sprang to life.

Some groups meet and evolve into another type of organization, suggesting that individual needs, not a group's stated purpose, are the best guides. For example, Meg Ross and husband Peter Shinkle in Baton Rouge formed the Babysitting Group, which allowed members to call on other members for babysitting duty. However, the social side of this functional undertaking took over, and the Babysitting Group evolved. This group and others like it eventually became monthly book clubs and vegetarian cooking cooperatives. Others gravitated toward quilting clubs, walking clubs, music associations and community gardening clubs. In essence, the functional group worked—and that evolved into a social group that could address other needs and interests. The important ingredient in all of this, however, is people's shared experiences being at the core of many different groups.

Utne Reader, a publication that the *New York Times* called "the *Reader's Digest* of the alternative press," asked its subscribers if they wished to help develop a literary salon system, coast-to-coast. The purpose would be to bring people together to discuss individual books, as well as literature in general and important social issues. Of course, socializing would be an important part of *any* salon meeting. In short order, 500 *Utne* salons were meeting to discuss literary and social issues. About then, Elizabeth Long, a sociologist at Rice University, started to study women's groups in the Houston area and found less than half a dozen concentrating on books. However, within a few years she could point to more than 100.

Book-, bridge-, sewing-, gardening- and bicycling-clubs are not the only ones growing rapidly. *Walking* magazine has a data base of more than 1,000 walking clubs created at a meteoric pace from a base of essentially zero just five years after the striders organized. In 1987, just 5,100 investment clubs existed, coast-to-coast. Now roughly 36,000 clubs meet regularly, and their numbers are growing by about 500 each month. In 1996, nearly 45 percent of the clubs beat the market index average, compared to just 35 percent of equity mutual funds. Perhaps they are growing so rapidly because their sociable, interactive approach is also effective.

SEARCHING FOR A
MEANINGFUL COMMUNITY

The effectiveness of smaller groups approaching personal issues of importance has led some people to flee the cities, and even the suburbs, in order to dwell in smaller communities. Between 1990 and 1995, 1.6 million more people moved to rural areas from cities and suburbs than went the other way. During that same time period, rural employment grew faster than urban employment, and rural unemployment dropped more steeply than did the urban. Also, income rose faster for rural residents (5.1 percent) than for urban workers (4.8 percent). That reversed a 20-year trend.

One new resident of Washington, Iowa, explained why the small town seemed right: "Having a kid changes everything. It's safe here. It's pretty. And the people are there for you. What's important is different in this culture, and I like that." In other words, while the urban media portray the move to rural America as an escape, the people who are there describe a culture change, a new set of priorities and a community feeling as their reasons. The 1950s wave of suburbanization involved expressing the rising standard of living in terms of where and how one lived. This new migration has much to do with a shift in individual priorities and actually represents a cutting back in the standard of living. These new rural migrants are not escaping from something as much as they are heading toward something else.

Heading toward something else has created a huge "learning vacation" market for museums, colleges and other learning-centered institutions. More than 150 alumni organizations at U.S. colleges and universities offer hundreds of trips worldwide each year. Led by professors who include seminars and readings as part of the trip, these traveling communities of meaning effectively mix socializing with learning. Stanford University's "Suitcase Seminars" are two-week cram courses that may travel to China or New Zealand. The University of California at Berkeley's "Travel with Scholars" program takes adults to such interesting places overseas as Oxford, Paris, Venice and Turkey, and (in the U.S.) to the likes of New Orleans, to study local culture and history.

"It's more than just a trip," the school's advertisement invariably proclaims, "it's an educational adventure." Alumni Travel Holidays, a wholesaler that handles arrangements for alumni groups, started with 25 trips in 1994 and within two years was offering 80. At present, roughly a dozen different wholesalers ply the market.

In addition to traveling classrooms, many universities offer alumni colleges, which are one- or two-week stints on campus, with students attending lectures and seminars and generally utilizing the university facilities. At Emory University in Atlanta, for example, each day of the week-long alumni college starts with optional sunrise T'ai Chi classes, then flows into more classes in preselected subjects and eventually ends in the afternoon with lectures and discussions on contemporary issues. Cornell University's summer seminars for adults wins high marks from participants, almost all of whom insist that the most valuable "take away" from these classes is the rediscovery of the joys of learning.

This type of classroom-based adult education matches museum efforts to create special seminars in their buildings and to add foreign seminars where possible. In 1990 just 30 museums (mostly large urban institutions) offered special tours. Now 80 offer such trips, most of them adding a seminar or lecture component. The Textile Museum sponsors a trip to Morocco, the Museum of Comparative Zoology offers a trip to the "exotic isles of the Indian Ocean," the Smithsonian Museum sends tours to everywhere in the world, and the National Geographic Society takes participants to such locales as the Amazon rain forest, Greece, and Russia. A bimonthly newsletter, *Educated Traveler,* monitors this expanding array of choices for interested individual subscribers.

A rather more simple vacation awaits workers when they exit their offices to take a caffeine-and-chat break at their local coffee house. In 1989, just 200 specialty-coffee outlets existed in the entire country. However, that exploded during the following period of transition and change, leading to nearly 6,000 such outlets as of this book's writing. "It's kind of like an office away from home," suggested one patron. "I can sit there and collect my thoughts." Special coffees are expensive— but they definitely are a reward for surviving work. Moreover, coffee houses themselves are small, transient communities wherein individuals share the feeling that personal time is important. Many book lovers use the store as if it were a library reading room, and lots of others find it a handy place to meet people. Whatever their reasons, customers are attracted to these oases for reasons other than making money.

Electronic communications have of course advanced this shared interest in community and learning. Even though Internet chat-rooms and bulletin boards do not actually have a physical presence, they do offer many people the chance to share ideas, to learn and to socialize in a particularly "cool" way. Every kind of group has found its own place on the World Wide Web, that graphics-enhanced offspring of the Internet, and full-motion video and real-time sound inevitably will enhance all sorts of community efforts.

Arthur Armstrong and John Hagel III, writing in the *Harvard Business Review* in 1996, discussed four types of "on-line communities" that have arisen with the Internet: (1) communities of transaction facilitate buying (e.g., Virtual Vineyards); (2) communities of interest bring together similarly focused users (e.g., Motley Fool investors); (3) communities of fantasy create new environments, personalities, or stories (e.g., ESPNet); and (4) communities of relationship focus on specific life experiences that encourage deep personal connections (e.g., the Cancer Forum). The fact that the authors described this interlinking of individual users as a community reveals how widespread the need for community has become. Even Internet business writers conceive of their models as communities! However, this description of four types of communities also reveals that users are drawing ever closer to services that respond favorably as well as swiftly to their need for learning, sociability and control.

Electronic communities offer at least *some* parts of the communities of meaning. The Garden Web, for example, is an electronic community in which individuals during on-line forums exchange secrets, discoveries and experiences related to gardening. Visitors learn about new plants and planting techniques, request help for unusual planting needs and carry out transactions. Parents Place makes available information about raising children and answers parenting questions. It also has a shopping mall, on-line diaper ordering and other services related to child-rearing. These electronic communities attract people who have a related need, as well as an interest in some specific area. While much of the information could be located in readily available books, participants in the Garden Web and Parents Place enjoy the shared interests and experiences—the community.

These permanent and temporary groups alike are expressions of individual needs. To one extent or another, these ad hoc groupings solve problems, grant individuals control, create communities and encourage learning. They are small communities of *meaning*. The fact that individuals (when allowed to pursue their own preferences) gravitate to these organizations suggests strongly that they represent the future direction of successful American institutional structures. Already, even larger communities of meaning have surfaced.

SOLVING BIGGER PROBLEMS
IN BIGGER COMMUNITIES

During the first half of the 1990s, Americans were starting community or neighborhood associations at an annual rate of 10,000 per year. Part of the reason for this explosion was a widespread desire to respond to the world out of control. These local groups—40,000 in Florida alone—protected communities from regional encroachment. They argued the neighborhoods' cases on zoning, pollution, development and budgets. Over time, however, they also became community-based social clubs, official-type organizations providing what was needed in order for neighbors to congregate and socialize. Nearly 200,000 of these associations existed by late 1997.

Community participation took an extremely positive turn in Chattanooga, Tennessee. Big cities reported bad news throughout the 1970s and into the 1980s, and Chattanooga added its bad news as well—an empty downtown, rising crime, increasing unemployment, vacant buildings and homes and a dwindling tax base. Then, in 1984, a broad array of citizens from the city came together under the auspices of Chattanooga Venture, a local civic organization, to discuss the city's future. Through this vehicle, more than 1,700 people participated in group discussions that developed a list of 40 goals for the city, all to be reached by the year 2000.

The group's first accomplishment was to reinvigorate the city's populace. "People had been angry and cynical because they thought someone else was making all the decisions," explained one citizen-participant. "But when we all got in the same room, we realized that *no one* was making the decisions. No one was creating a vision for the city." When they concluded their meetings, they had set new goals: res-urrecting a positive self-image for the city, revitalizing the downtown, improving public transportation, developing new job resources, and focusing on the city as a regional tourist center. Overall, the citizens had addressed health care, crime, education, the environment, recreational facilities and historic preservation, but all in their own way and with their own voice.

The project so energized the citizens that they reached all of their goals for the year 2000 by 1993. The downtown buzzed with activity, the city's transportation moved easily and effectively, a new performance center named for native-born singer Bessie Smith brought entertain-ment to the city center, recreation facilities from bike trails to pedestrian pathways wound their way around the city, 1,300 new jobs brought a $739 million investment from private and public sources, and a new city aquarium brought visitors to the locale daily. In all, Chattanooga embarked on 223 projects, including day-care centers and family-violence clinics, to address urban troubles. Rather than rest on their accomplishments, the citizens then reconvened—and worked through 2,559 more community-improvement projects, setting another 27 goals to be completed by the year 2000.

Socializing, participating, developing, learning, and taking action are key elements of the effective communities of meaning. The Maine Council of Churches created 55 study circles of between seven and 15 people each whose mission was to discuss education reform. Citizens read information supplied through local newspapers and nonprofit groups in order to help energize them and develop solutions. Their dis-cussions yielded a program aimed at focusing on preparing students for employment, citizenship, lifelong learning, and traditional basic values.

The success of that project led to others, for which the *Maine Sunday Telegram* published supporting information related to each week's study-circle discussion.

Study circles have gained momentum. When the Minneapolis *Star Tribune* asked readers to join study circles on different topics related to the city, more than 4,000 responded. Typically, study circles meet for two hours each week, sticking to one overall topic for several weeks and discussing subtopics each week. According to the Study Circle Resources Center, the idea originated with the Chautauqua Circle in 1915, but its current evolution differs in that it remains local in focus and strives to activate citizens and solve specific problems. Sally Campbell, associate director of the Maine Council of Churches, suggested these differences when she said: "The minimum result of study circles should be a change of some kind, even if only a change in attitude." She added that study circles do not have an agenda per se—that is, they do not adhere to a rigid program that forces participants to march in step. Instead, they have objectives and get there in any way the group decides works best. People feel better about participating and also feel a sense of accomplishment for realizing their objectives in their own ways. She also noted another reason why people join at all: "It's a way for people to share perspectives, and [study circles should] make that preliminary to doing something."

Larger groups with larger purposes have come into existence as well, but they still center on what the participants consider important, and they all help and encourage participants to grow, learn and otherwise develop. In 1996, Promise Keepers, a Christian organization that seeks to help men recognize their responsibilities, held rallies in more than 22 cities and attracted more than 800,000 participants (as many as 80,000 attended a certain stadium gathering). In 1991, when it was founded by former University of Colorado football coach Bill McCartney, its rallies attracted a total of 4,200 men. Ellis Cose, a journalist who has looked closely at this movement, explained: "Many ordinary men are indeed feeling a need to ask: 'What does it mean today to be a man?' or at the least, to have their feelings and uncertainties confirmed through those of other men."

Different from the tribal "male bonding" groups advocated earlier by writers like Robert Bly, these gatherings are larger, religiously focused and directed at men seeking confirmation of both their worth and their needs. What participants at the rallies did was, as one Promise Keeper revealed, "pray, cry, sing, chant, hug, cheer and mentor other men." Afterward, they were to return home, hold smaller meetings and mentor even more men.

In 1995, roughly 850,000 black men went to Washington, D.C., to participate in the Million Man March. Political and journalistic arguments raged about everything surrounding the march, except its purpose: to encourage black men to take responsibility for themselves, their family and their community. Even many marchers disagreed with the values of the event's organizer, Louis Farrakhan, but they took part anyway because it offered a positive force for personal change. That is, individuals were looking for something they felt they would find, and the leader's role was in essence irrelevant to reaching that personal goal.

While these two groups differ considerably in composition and political outlook, the fact that they both arose at this point in time with such similar messages suggested that they were simply successful responses to changing individual needs. The idea of developing the self, helping others, and developing systems to help even more, caught people's attention. Their simple but powerful messages served as the basis for a functioning, even if ephemeral, community of meaning.

The 1997 Million Woman March in Philadelphia reveals how these communities of meaning are evolving. The number of black women who marched in the rain far exceeded the number of men who assembled in Washington for the Million Man March and the Promise Keepers March. What is most surprising about the record gathering, however, is that women created this success without celebrity speakers, nationally known organizers or high-profile leaders. By contrast, the Million Man March sprang fully formed from Louis Farrakhan and the Nation of Islam and got publicity from mayors of major cities and leaders like the Reverend Jesse Jackson. Similarly, the Promise Keepers depended upon its national network of connections and funding and exploited heavy national media coverage.

Without blaring media coverage or national representatives talking on weekly newscasts, the women held what seemed like a leaderless rally, having basically assembled themselves. Local organizers distributed mimeographed handbills on city streets everywhere, used only local black media for advertisement and depended upon neighborhood groups to enroll participants. With this approach, women rallied nearly 1.5 million women (police estimates) to come to Philadelphia. Local advertisements actually played down keynote speakers, insisting that the trip and the march were good for the participant. The group was so low-key that someone forgot to send an airline ticket to Winnie Mandela, one of the speakers.

These types of communities—whether the smaller, even transient, groups (like alumni colleges) or the larger, ephemeral outdoor gatherings that teach moral lessons—tell of the consequences of personal change. Individuals moving through their turning points, grounding points and compass points are changing priorities which are changing their interests. Club Med's past popularity is losing ground to Stanford University's Suitcase Campus—not because of poor marketing, but rather because the individuals who comprise the traveling market are changing, and their reassessed priorities are causing different products to succeed.

Communities of meaning are *not* about rejecting wealth. Rather, wealth is not one of the top reasons why people are drawn to them. The women who formed the Beardstown Ladies did so, as one member explained, primarily "to learn." They turned their backs on the traditional model for investing—find an expert, ask him or her what is best and then do it. Rather, they wanted to understand market forces, corporate reports, socioeconomic dynamics and the entire range of influences that affect the performance of individual stocks. From this platform of self-acquired knowledge, they invested. For more than a decade, they outperformed many experts (even with the revised numbers) and did indeed increase their wealth. But their reason for creating a joint effort was to learn and to socialize. The greater wealth was a positive side-effect of the original purpose. The way in which they operated was as important as the final goals they reached. Taking all of this (and more like it) from a larger point of view, *Americans* have changed their attitudes about what makes them happy.

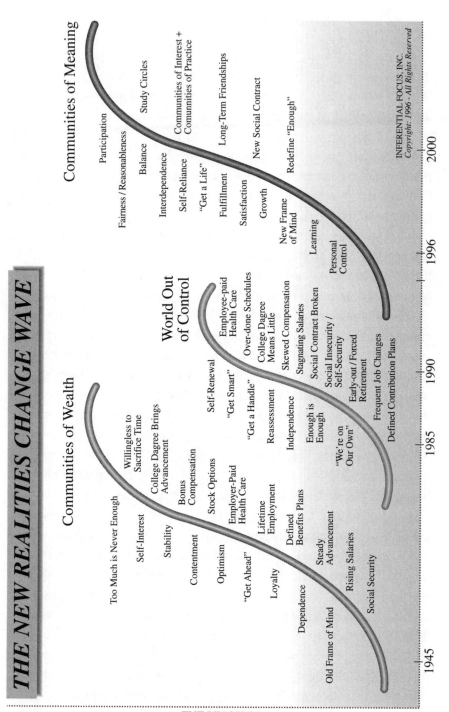

THE NEW REALITIES CHANGE WAVE

Communities of Wealth

World Out of Control

Communities of Meaning

MASS APPEAL

INFERENTIAL FOCUS, INC.
Copyright: 1996 - All Rights Reserved

1945   1985   1990   1996   2000

CRITICAL INSIGHT:
A Different "Pursuit of Happiness"

When Thomas Jefferson penned the Declaration of Independence, he originally ended the phrase "life, liberty and the pursuit of happiness" with "the pursuit of property." However, he marked through that first and more plebeian objective and added the more lofty but unexplained phrase involving happiness. Since that time, Americans, while rarely thinking about the Declaration of Independence, have taken that final pursuit to heart. In the twentieth century, seemingly every facet of American life (recreation and entertainment, advertising and literature, music and the arts, architecture and retailing) has focused on "lifestyles" that bring happiness—or, as in the instances of the blues, political protests and expressionist arts, on social ingredients that bring unhappiness.

Understanding what Jefferson really meant has been difficult enough for historians. Understanding what Americans, in general, at any given time in their history, have interpreted Jefferson's seemingly simple words to mean has often been confounding to everybody. The task of accurately assessing what contemporary Americans mean by that historical phrase has become even more complex because its meaning is still undergoing revision.

For most of the post–World War II era, American society openly accepted the idea that the pursuit of happiness fit quite comfortably with the economic drive for a higher standard of living. When institutions successfully generated greater affluence and managed to link that economic vitality to happiness, questioning what the pursuit of happiness actually meant seemed unnecessary. However, when the communities of wealth started losing their ability to deliver promised rewards and when an ever-expanding standard of living became more and more elusive, questions about happiness—or, at least, questions about society's objectives and whether or not they actually would lead to happiness—surfaced everywhere.

Those who have studied happiness have typically concentrated their efforts on the individual, not on society in general. Because of this narrow focus, the study of happiness has basically become the purview of clinical psychologists. These professional examiners of individual happiness have reached a near consensus on which personality traits are common to those who are happy. Understanding this profile and placing it in historical context offers a more grounded perspective on what lies ahead for individuals, markets and business.

Four traits appear again and again in happy people. First, those who believe they control the forces that govern their lives are among the happiest individuals. Second, individuals who socialize and regularly involve themselves in group interaction have a sunnier disposition, which gives them a feeling of well-being. Third, people who call themselves happy actually like the person they see in the mirror; they approve of the decisions they make, are self-aware and admit to a certain amount of self-approbation. Fourth, happy people feel good about the future and feel positive about life and what it offers. In short, the happy person has control, is sociable, has a positive self-image and is optimistic.

In the past, careers and the narrow pursuit of wealth lifted individuals toward these goals. The security and stability that institutions created offered participants a feeling of control over their lives. Office interaction and like-minded neighbors contributed to a satisfactory social life. Advances in position, compensation and economic standing gave those on the career ladder a positive feeling about themselves. Finally, all of these created a feeling that tomorrow would be better than today.

Recent events brutalized those same personal traits. The troubles that society's weakening institutions provoked actually attacked with vehemence the very happiness that Americans accepted as a reason to support those institutions. Individuals watched a society lose control—and, with that chaos, they struggled and suffered when their own lives went out of control. As schedules became stretched with more work and more chores, friends became less a part of each evening's activities. With personal lives out of control and with personal relations suffering, the individual's sense of self-worth took a beating. All of these together undermined what had traditionally been America's main strength: its optimism. Skepticism about America's future, about its public institutions and about its capacity to respond to the world's challenges became a common message in the media and in surveys.

Negativity became so overwhelming that when the Des Moines *Register* asked its readers what they most disliked about the news, they responded that it reinforced their skepticism to the point where they would choose to do nothing about society's problems because everything seemed too overwhelming. With this strong skepticism circulating through society, Americans turned against each other. The proportion of individuals who said most people could be trusted declined from 58 percent in 1960 to just 37 percent in 1993.

A DIFFERENT PURSUIT OF HAPPINESS

Americans who have passed through the three-part reassessment process (turning points, grounding points, compass points) are not returning to the old and narrow definition of the pursuit of happiness. They have started to shift toward a pursuit of happiness that includes something more meaningful and more personally rewarding, even though it remains less tangible than wealth. Learning, growing and developing are becoming part of the new pursuit of happiness. Personal fulfillment no longer depends primarily on financial compensation and the things it can buy. Rather discovery, responsibility, participation and interaction contribute positively to personal fulfillment, especially in the workplace.

The rise of a balanced consumer has brought about a different pursuit of happiness. Voluntary simplicity brings a feeling of control, while working especially long hours for no recognizable reason other than money makes one feel out of control. Being in control is better. The ongoing consumer reassessment has counseled restraint, and the satisfaction that personal control brings is part of the new pursuit of happiness. Individuals feel more secure when friends surround them, and their interest in socializing has expanded from workplace necessity to personal need. Like personal control that brings satisfaction, nurturing an expanding circle of personal relationships yields positive feelings as well. Developing those ties takes time, and finding that time will be part of the pursuit of happiness. Personal fulfillment is coming less from the answer to the "What do you do for a living?" question and more from questions like "What do you know about . . . ?" and "Have you read/ seen . . . ?" and "What do you think/feel about . . . ?" All of these things interact to create a feeling of growth, development and advancement—events that give individuals a positive feeling about who they are and what the future holds.

At one time, making money and developing careers created personal happiness. Now, individuals are finding other needs that must be met in order to create happiness. Personal loyalty is moving to the emerging communities of meaning—the places that contribute to the new pursuit of happiness. The difficulty that the communities of wealth and their leaders face is how to move from where they are to where their customers, citizens and employees are moving. Leaders and their institutions can make that move, but, at present, leaders are still holding on to what formerly worked. They should start by letting go and moving on toward more sustainable relationships.

PART III

Sustainable Relationships

Most American leaders have responded to the spreading personal revolution with indifference, even though this indifference could cost them a competitive edge when trying to attract and keep the best employees and also when trying to avoid customer turnover. Sustainable relationships with customers and employees will determine long-term competitiveness, and understanding the significance and durability of the personal revolution is a necessary first step to developing those relationships.

For the most part, American leaders are still "holding on" to the communities-of-wealth context and the managerial tactics that worked in that era. Some leaders, however, have indeed reached their own personal turning points and fortunately are "letting go" of past models and assumptions. After letting go, they can initiate their own strategic reassessment process for the organization before "moving on" into the new social/business context.

Developing sustainable relationships with employees requires a new social contract—one that reconnects individuals who have reassessed their values, needs and priorities with an institution that has also rethought its objectives, processes and relationships. In working toward these open-architecture relationships, institutional leaders will need to recognize an important metaphoric shift in the way they view their organizations. Specifically, the institution as lean machine is giving way to the institution as vital organism, a shift that favors systems dynamics over quantitative analysis.

Creating sustainable relationships with the new consumer will require a wide-open connection between company and customer. Leaders seeking to attract the new consumer must learn how to integrate that customer into the decision-making process and bring more company resources to bear on the customer relationship. The shift in emphasis away from "marketing to" and toward "interacting with" depends upon both making more knowledge available to the customer and creating new contextual connections between company and customer.

CHAPTER 6

HOLDING ON, LETTING GO, MOVING ON

James Redfield's *The Celestine Prophecy* tells the story of an ancient document and its impact on all those who read it. When the document is found, its wisdom threatens church and state alike, and they try to suppress the news about its discovery, and to punish those who own copies. In one scene the narrator, having just encountered the first pieces of the document, is racing through the mountains above a small Peruvian city, trying to escape sure death at the hands of the military. As danger subsides, he experiences a moment of transcendence during which he feels at one with the world, and all worries subside. His quest for a deeper meaning in life has for the moment gone well beyond the search for some hidden document changes. He actually experiences the oneness that the document talks about. The fleeting epiphany becomes his new focus as he seeks to gain enlightenment and learn how to recover that feeling through quiet contemplation. During these moments of meditation, he can let go of his transient goals and see the larger context emerge.

The desire to shed past assumptions, to see through momentary confusion and to embrace something new drives much of the personal reassessment process that individuals are experiencing. The examples we have seen of organizations that have successfully responded to this new individual suggest that American leaders need to have this same experience if they are to lead their institutions through a needed reassessment process.

The three phases of the personal-reassessment process parallel the three phases of institutional reassessment—or, more precisely, the strategic restructuring. Institutions and their leaders who have yet to reach their turning points are locked in an increasingly frustrating battle to hold on to what they had before. This institutional mind-set continues to believe that the old communities of wealth can remain viable in the years ahead; that they can, in essence, attract customers and retain employees. To sustain profitability in this pre–turning-point world, leaders have necessarily taken some short-term and potentially harmful actions, ranging from margin-pinching price cuts to huge, loyalty-busting staff cuts. Despite these extreme actions, however, more and more companies find themselves walking in ever-more-challenging terrain with dwindling margins, sliding customer loyalty and lagging staff resolve. At some point, managers start to recognize the diminishing possibilities resulting from trying to hold the old world together. That recognition is the institutional turning point.

When corporations and their executives reach the turning point and realize that the old practice of "more, better, faster" has crossed the point of diminishing returns, they let go of old practices and start their own quest for new fundamental strategies that can guide their institutions in the years ahead. By letting go of old-style accounting and marketing, they can switch their focus away from current, efficiency-driven practices, reassess their fundamental strengths and reconnect with what might be called their effective basic culture.

After they have "righted" themselves within the new cultural context, companies and their leaders are then in a position to move forward. They can address new consumers and new markets in the confidence that a connection has taken place, and they can feel confident that the company's internal vibrancy and loyalty have returned. With these new realities, companies can sustain relationships (with customers and with employees) which will carry the company forward. The positive results from this institutional reassessment process can also increase its stock value.

While the personal-reassessment revolution for most individuals has passed its midpoint, a few corporations have actually moved through a strategic restructuring process. Consequently, we can start comparing results. Looking at examples from companies along the three stages of the institutional restructuring evolution, we can better ascertain the liabilities of "holding on," the necessity of "letting go" and the competitive advantage of "moving on."

HOLDING ON

Retaining old institutional objectives and operations essentially involves employing the same market tactics—only faster, cheaper and, maybe, better. Unlike the formerly pervasive market environment that nurtured current institutional tactics, the new market environment subjects manufacturers, service providers and product developers to direct competition from a global marketplace where someone or other will *always* be able to provide the product or service faster, cheaper and, yes, do it better. In addition to these new competitive realities, American consumers, when judging product and service value, assume all market efficiencies (i.e., price, convenience) as a given, and they make spending decisions, where possible, on other product or service attributes. As a result, depending on price as a sustainable market advantage eventually loses effectiveness.

Reacting to these new competitive realities with tactical restructurings has resulted in customer indifference, employee disloyalty and managerial disarray. These consequences have in turn led to mad scrambles for mergers, takeovers and more products. During 1996, the sixth year of a steady economic recovery, American corporations cut more than 400,000 jobs, a 20 percent increase over 1995. So confused were the strategies behind these cuts that two-thirds of the companies letting people go were later hiring new employees, resulting in a net job increase for 27 percent of the job-cutting companies. Companies desperate for positive results after the downsizing wave ebbed turned to mergers and acquisitions to show growth. In 1995, corporate mergers reached $519 billion. The next year, an astounding 10,000 mergers took place, with roughly $660 billion changing hands. But in 1997, $1 trillion in mergers took place, 156 of them valued at more than $1 billion. In the three-year run, 27,600 companies merged. By way of comparison, 1991 and 1992 were in the low $100 billion range. *Fortune* magazine put the 1996 volume in perspective when it noted that merger handshakes took place at a rate of "more than one per hour, round the clock, all year long." Whether trying to attain growth through mergers or by cutting costs, American companies from 1994 to 1996 spent more than $30 billion on outside consultants to help them "reengineer," "reinvent," "total quality" manage and otherwise make their operations more efficient.

The more that corporations tried to hold on to the old world of win/loss, rising wealth and more–better–faster production models, the more they turned to accounting maneuvers or employee adjustments to raise bottom-line figures, and the riskier the situation became. In 1996, William Zuendt, the brazen president of Wells Fargo and architect of that bank's rapid acquisition program, pushed his company to take over First Interstate Bancorp, in a move that he thought would enhance his company's market share and create an internal organization that could be downsized to create the perception of growth. Immediately, he announced that Wells Fargo would fire a whopping 85 percent of First Interstate's employees. However, customers immediately started complaining about poor service and then started leaving Wells Fargo at the incredible rate of 1.5 percent per month. Wells Fargo's share of all deposits declined; its share of all loans declined; and its stock headed downward. These types of changes created unanticipated losses exceeding $220 million, which when added to the original cost of buying First Interstate made the purchase extremely unwise. In May 1997, Zuendt announced his retirement, leaving the mess to former chairman Paul Hazen to handle.

These buy-and-purge tactics, matched with a surprisingly higher value for bloated companies, yielded productivity numbers for the 1990s' economic expansion that were higher than those of the previous three recoveries (1970, 1975 and 1982). Specifically, nonfarm productivity for the 17 quarters after the recovery started rose by nearly 10 percent in the 1990s, whereas it had hovered around or just below 6 percent for the three prior expansions. Historically, American workers enjoyed rising salaries whenever productivity rose. Lawrence Katz, a former chief economist at the Labor Department, referred to this link between productivity and salary rises as "one of the strongest regularities of advanced economies." Yet the 1990s recovery did not bring salary increases. For example, for the first five years of the recovery, factory productivity rose by a stunning 5.4 percent, while factory wages rose by just 2.7 percent. For the 12-month period ending in March 1995, productivity rose by 2.1 percent, and salaries actually declined by 3.0 percent.

In essence, the huge corporate profits that annual reports proudly proclaimed came not from better products and service, but straight from the employees on whom every company ultimately depends for its connection to customers. During the wealth communities' greatest success, profits resulted from advancing consumer and employee standards of living, but in this late period, when institutional leaders decoupled the sense of community from the pursuit of wealth, greater profits actually resulted from lowering the employees' standard of living.

While merger and buyout tactics attracted many managers still holding on to the old model of business growth, others turned to cracking the whip on their remaining staff. Stories surfaced everywhere about managers working their remaining employees longer and harder, about companies firing tired and more expensive employees in order to hire fresher and cheaper ones, and about executives insisting that bigger and bigger numbers be met, or else. But more and more companies tried a softer approach in order to goad fatigued employees. For example, roughly 300 ministers and other religious advisers walk the shop floors and corridors of General Motors, Ford and Chrysler plants seeking to help individuals to cope with increased stress and personal problems. One company, Marketplace Ministries, now supplies clergy to 170 companies in 30 states—most of the growth coming since 1995.

Dr. Elizabeth Briody serves as General Motors' corporate anthropologist, studying corporate operations in order to locate solvable problems. Sue Squires performs the same tasks for Andersen Worldwide's Center for Professional Education. Tony Salvador works as Intel's first "engineering ethnographer," and Patricia Sachs uses her Ph.D. in economic anthropology to help NYNEX. Nearly 40 percent of U.S. employers offer one or another type of help for employees seeking to deal with workplace stress, a jump from 25 percent in 1985. All of these efforts seek to extract more productivity from the shop floor, while soothing over anxieties and problems that the same shop floor stress creates.

Another company tactic for growth without restructuring involved throwing more products at the customer, under the assumption that a bigger product line would control more of the market. In the first five months of 1995, for example, companies introduced 9,241 new products, a 20-percent increase over 1994, and more than four times the number of a decade earlier. Steinroe Mutual Funds of Chicago offered a particularly egregious example of a struggle to create new products: a mutual fund for kids, with the average age of the "investor" being nine.

The "more and more" mentality pushed the already overbuilt shopping-mall business to expand even further, despite vacant mall space and disinterested consumers. Each year, through the end of the nineties, 10 huge regional malls will open their doors, even though nearly 80 percent of the already existing malls do not make money, and even though the country already has more retail space per consumer than at any time in its history.

Not only have companies introduced more products and utilized more retail space, hoping to *force* growth—many have also launched those products with bigger and more expensive advertising campaigns. Increased "market noise," they have assumed, naturally leads to increased market growth. McDonald's, which was experiencing lagging same-store sales in 1994 and 1995, decided to spend $200 million to create the "biggest product launch in company history," hoping the new Arch Deluxe and the entire "Deluxe Line" of products would boost per-customer sales numbers. Having scraped the bottom of the price-war barrel, McDonald's decided to fight a volume (or market-share) battle. Despite the company's keeping actual sales figures to itself, the big-money effort did not change same-store sales figures, which in fact remained flat during the months after the launch. In September 1996, company executives insisted they would make the new product successful. Fallon McElligott, the advertising agency hired to sell the new product, soon resigned the account, saying only that the relationship was strained. In January 1998, McDonald's quietly dropped the Arch Deluxe from its menu.

McDonald's was not the only consumer-oriented giant that experienced troubled times with the new consumer. Going into 1996, Ford Motor Company declared that the completely redesigned Ford Taurus, which in its earlier design had been the country's number-one selling car in the three prior years, would have a higher price tag, and also that the company would not offer rebates or financing incentives to sell its hottest car. By the end of the first quarter, however, extremely weak sales forced embarrassed company officials to go back on their word and offer both $500 rebates and competitive financing incentives. Then, even before calendar year 1997 came around, Ford started offering $1,000 rebates on its new 1997 Taurus. Soon thereafter, when Taurus sales fell behind those of the Toyota Camry and Chevrolet Cavalier, Ford added below-market financing to help push Taurus sales.

Companies also turned more and more to gathering and sorting data to keep their marketing effort alive. Roughly 66 percent of manufacturers and retailers developed customer data bases, and nearly 85 percent believed they needed to create a data-base system to survive before the decade ends. With point-of-sale technology gobbling information as fast as new storage capacity can retain it, problems of digesting and analyzing the data became monumental. Fingerhut, for example, jumped its collected customer data from 600 billion characters to nearly 2 trillion. Meanwhile, Kraft General Foods amassed a list of more than 30 million users of its products and tried to exploit that group's buying habits when sending coupons. At the other end, American Express refined its data analysis through parallel processing machinery to such an extent that it started sending targeted promotions to customer groups as small as 20 people.

These types of actions become common when company executives refuse to acknowledge their own turning points. Of course, keeping the same old game going has drawn short-term bursts of applause from stock fans on Wall Street. But still, shop-floor ministers, hall-stalking anthropologists, margin-squeezing price cuts, expertise-draining mergers and the like send rather subtle (and presumably unintended) messages that the company's *employees* are the problem, that the company's services or products can only *lose* value, or that the company's leaders have run out of *ideas.*

Playing the short-term stock price game runs long-term risks. When *Forbes* magazine printed an article on Kellogg's, entitled "Denial in Battle Creek," the featured graphic was a rooster (Kellogg's corporate symbol) with its head stuck in a bowl of cereal. That could be a visual applied to many corporations refusing to reach their turning points. Kellogg's actually looks quite like the prototype of a corporation refusing to reach its turning point and clinging to its old corporate model. Historically, it has been immensely successful, what with quarterly earnings falling only once since 1945, with gross profits rising from 36 percent in 1980 to 55 percent 15 years later, and with the company in 1995 holding a 36 percent share of the U.S. cereal market and a 42 percent share of the world's portion of it.

Past success, however, has a way of blinding company managers to the need to rethink strategically their whole enterprise—that is, to get past their turning points. In 1988, Kellogg's held 41 percent of the U.S. market, but since then that figure has headed downward. During the summer of 1996, the company's market share had reached 33 percent. Operating margins had declined from 18 percent in 1988 to 10.2 percent in the second quarter of 1996.

Insisting that all of this troubling news was "just a blip," Kellogg's chairman, Arnold Langbo, dropped Kellogg's prices by 19 percent on two-thirds of the company's brands in response to price reductions by Post and General Mills. Given the cash-rich nature of the company, Langbo assumed that price wars would be a short-term phenomenon, and that with a little market jump-start the company would boost its market-share numbers upward. After all, this had worked in the past. Yet in July and August, the first two months after the price drops, shipments actually *declined,* and Kellogg's market share eroded still another 2.5 percent in volume. For the third quarter in 1996, in fact, Kellogg's revenues had fallen by 20 percent—which, according to sources at *Advertising Age,* was "one of the biggest declines [ever] for any of the food companies." By the end of 1996, Kellogg's sales had declined by 6.3 percent, and the company finally publicly admitted that it expected even worse news in the future.

Langbo, and the executives at Ford and McDonald's alike, perceived their market problems as simply temporary glitches. ("I don't think it's a secular change," Langbo intimated.) For them, holding on to what they had (e.g., traditional brand equity) and acquiring more (e.g., mergers), while waiting for the next big wave of consumer spending to hit, constituted their entire business strategy.

Holding on becomes less and less effective in today's new business environment. For example, a survey of more than 300 big mergers completed between 1987 and 1997 revealed that in the three years after the deals, 57 percent of the merged companies underperformed vis-à-vis their competitors, in terms of shareholder returns. An aggregate of other studies from different sources created the following total picture of recent business tactics:

1. Just 30 percent of the companies downsizing between 1990 and 1996 actually experienced an increase in worker productivity in the ensuing year.
2. Only 40 percent ever showed such an increase in subsequent years.
3. Downsized public companies outperformed the stock market for the first six months following their staff cuts, but lagged behind after three years.
4. The compound annual growth rate of market capitalization for companies that exploited downsizing amounted to just 11 percent from 1988 to 1994, while the same annual growth rate for companies that concentrated on revenue growth was 15 percent.

This devastating round of results on downsizing had parallel results for other single-answer management approaches. For example, roughly 80 percent of British firms using Total Quality Management (the previously mentioned widely embraced tactic of the early 1990s) showed no gain, and fully two-thirds of American executives who undertook TQM gained no competitive edge from their expenditures. Business author and professor Peter Drucker was particularly blunt in his criticism of this specific management theory. While acknowledging its utility for straightforward manufacturing procedures, Drucker noted that TQM was of little use now. "The great part about TQM," Drucker concluded, "is that it is for morons."

At the same time that TQM was losing its appeal, Tom Peters admitted that his book *In Search of Excellence* (1997), which sold more than 5 million copies, was only "right for the time." Given that two-thirds of the companies he touted eventually lost their competitive "excellence," he could only point to his latest books as better guides for the present. Michael Hammer, who along with James Champy wrote *Reengineering the Corporation: A Manifesto for Business Revolution* (1994), admitted that the entire reengineering enterprise was misguided—this after selling more than 2 million books and adding sequels like *Reengineering Management* (Champy) (1994) and *The Reengineering Revolution* (Hammer) (1995). "I was reflecting my engineering background," he told the *Wall Street Journal,* "and was insufficiently appreciative of the human dimension. I've learned that's critical."

Indeed, the employee as "critical" was becoming clearer. A *California Management Review* study showed that downsizing adversely affected employees' ability to innovate and change, thereby crippling the company's competitiveness. As a result of these pressures, employees were finding it less attractive to stay with unstable companies that condoned hostile working environments. In fact, nearly a third of new hires were leaving their jobs within a year; two-thirds of fourth-year employees were not "highly committed" to their employers; and more than half of all managers were similarly not "highly committed" to their companies.

Even while executives were slowly discovering that their hugely expensive factual restructuring concepts were a bust, the personal revolution was taking its toll on the market. In the midst of all these enervating efforts to create more efficient companies within, the world outside continued to reject price increases and force price decreases. And the latter were everywhere. Post Raisin Bran, Cheer, Era, Gain, Tide, Bounty, Sprint, Burger King, Compaq, Kleenex, Trix, Charmin, Toyota and other major brand names all had to lower prices in 1996. One observer exclaimed: "Every product. Every brand. Every price is under review." Indeed, the cost of holding on to past practices was rising steadily.

Rather than see all of these troubles as signals of massive change, many companies held tightly to old practices—and executives. Gillette offered additional incentives to keep its chairman and CEO, Alfred M. Zelem, from retiring in 1998; and Ford did much the same for its top executive, Alexander Trottman, who also had announced his 1998 retirement. Some companies, however, started to reach their turning points— those places where they could see that current personal and cultural changes are *not* temporary and that they, too, must change in order to stay connected to their customers and employees.

LETTING GO

When companies move past their turning points, leaders let go of tactics that have proved so successful in the past. Because many executives rose to the top by manipulating these same tactics, and because they may not have learned any other tactics, letting go is the hardest part of moving a company forward.

The agonizing reappraisal that precedes letting go reached the Army Corps of Engineers in 1996 and 1997. Massive floods throughout the Midwest during 1996 challenged the fundamentals of flood control that the Corps had developed over the decades. They believed that controlling the flow of a river was entirely in their power: Create a dam upstream, divert the river's flow downstream, build controlling levees along the route. But the Mississippi, Missouri, Kaw and Illinois rivers showed these and other "proven" tactics were ineffective. In fact, Corps intervention in river flows actually made the floods of 1996 *worse.*

New Year's floods in California overwhelmed levees and covered more than 250 miles of ground, destroying or damaging 16,000 homes, killing eight people and causing nearly $2 billion in damage. Again, the Corps' entire process of manipulation and control had made things worse. This time, however, authorities finally started questioning the power of humans to create huge flood-control programs that could work. Many engineers within the Corps called for more dams—that is, they refused to let go of the "tried and true" approaches of the past. But Walter Yep, chief of planning for the Army Corps of Engineers in California, Nevada, Utah and Colorado, realized that the Corps needed to learn some new lessons: "The values of 50 years ago—when we built dams upstream and we straightened our rivers and put them in concrete channels—need to be reexamined." Dr. Jeffrey F. Mount, author of *The Conflict Between Fluvial Process and Land Use* (1995), observed that things were starting to change: "The Corps of Engineers and the Bureau of Reclamation are undergoing gut-wrenching philosophical changes. The old tradition of when in doubt, pour concrete, is simply not going to work any more, for financial and environmental reasons." The Corps is passing through the difficult process of starting to let go.

A few examples from the business field add impetus to the need to let go. In the mid-1990s, Marshalls, a discount retail chain, fell on hard times, and discounter TJX, a major competitor, decided to buy the troubled retailer. TJX, however, did not use traditional turnaround techniques to revive Marshalls sales and profits. It closed just 40 underperforming stores (out of nearly 500 outlets) while opening six more, and it laid off just 100 workers (out of 58,000). Instead of the old slice-and-dice tactics, TJX simply slashed Marshalls advertising budget by 50 percent. Wall Street laughed. But sales went up, and the stock price more than doubled. Because of the Marshalls turnaround, TJX watched its own income triple in the third quarter of 1996 alone, even as overall retail sales struggled to beat inflation rates. Wall Street stopped laughing.

Strategists at TJX realized that Marshalls had in effect lost contact with its oldest followers. The chain originally did well because it attracted regular customers who were searching for a bargain and wanted to "discover" the best deal. That deal, regular shoppers knew, was not advertised, was not on the table next to the door, and was not marked with huge "SALE" signs. Customers actually enjoyed the "treasure hunt" process of finding that special deal. With targeted advertisements promoting "Buy One, Get One Free" specials on selected merchandise, the original store appeal—the shopper's individual quest for a bottom-of-the-pile deal—disappeared.

Bargain hunters flooded the store, "cherry-picked" the advertised deals and then left. In essence the company, through its advertising, had conditioned its customers to wait for their special-price ads before visiting the stores and then visit only to snatch up sale items. When the store cut its advertising budgets in half and stopped promoting special deals, "Marshalls customers" reentered the store without a specific product in mind, and once again were on the personal treasure hunt. In one of the more curious twists of the new business environment, cutting advertising helped Marshalls to reconnect with its customer, which in turn drove up sales and profits.

For a retailer with weak sales actually to *slash* its advertising budget is counterintuitive to the old marketing mind-set. For sales to rise steadily (and the stock to double) with *smaller* advertising budgets just seems impossible, especially to those still lingering on the other side of the turning point.

Procter & Gamble offers another example of letting go. Like Marshalls, P&G cut its advertising budget for the first time in recent memory—but it also committed to a program to lower its overall marketing budget from 25 percent of sales to no more than 20 percent. The company's biggest surprise, however, came when it seemingly changed what had been its practice of exploiting brand names by adding new products and line extensions. To take just one example: The company cut its haircare product line in half, yet increased its market share from 31 percent to 36 percent. That is, the company changed the one thing that according to the old way of thinking would certainly reduce market share (i.e., lower the number of products marketed), and it produced exactly the opposite result. These results verified that contemporary markets are different from their predecessors. With that lesson learned, the company changed its in-store systems to allow *consumers* to determine what appears on store shelves, rather than try to force sales onto the market. Twenty-seven types of promotions went into the trash can, and field salespeople started handling entire lines instead of competing among themselves for shelf space. The other positive effect of reducing special deals was that P&G lowered the number of retail invoices with mistakes from 31 percent to 6 percent, thereby dramatically reducing its operating costs.

The company had shifted its focus from market power to consumer awareness, and it enjoyed a boost in sales as a result. "It's amazing," exclaimed Lawrence Milligan, senior vice president and the company's top sales executive, "how much you learn if you simply ask other people." P&G had passed its turning point and had let go.

Part of the individual's grounding-point search involved discovering the basic values, identity and beliefs that felt right—that is, connecting with the fundamentals of social living. After reaching their turning points, companies "let go" of past accepted wisdom, then reassess their own basic relationships with the market.

As Marshalls proved, connecting with the customer is crucial. As P&G showed, reassessment involves rethinking the old idea of growth, which historically meant simply "more, better and faster." Another piece of a strategic reassessment involves rethinking the company's product value to the customer. In 1995, Bayer changed its approach to marketing aspirin. In place of the analgesic image, the company positioned aspirin both as a preventive against heart disease and as a pain reliever specifically for arthritis. After years of 5-to-8-percent annual sales declines, Bayer's aspirin sales *rose* by 11.4 percent.

With its declining sales, Bayer aspirin had been losing the battle of the analgesics because new medications had displaced the traditional pain reliever. Before the turning point, the company simply lowered its price, tried to expand its shelf space and actually agreed with Roche to market a competitor, Aleve. After the turning point, however, the company looked at what customers wanted (health solutions and preventative care) and recognized that the analgesic battle wasted the product's biggest strength. Bayer shifted its customer approach from relieving pain to preventing troubles. In essence, the company looked at consumer behavior and reassessed its product's capabilities. As a result, it reconnected with the customer.

One final and crucial candidate for a corporate let-go involves the company's social contract with its employees. The personal reassessment that individuals have pursued has altered their personal priority lists, and career and compensation no longer hold the same value. As a result, managing employees under the erroneous assumption that money will sustain motivation can be costly. In fact, reversing course can be quite profitable. In 1993, First Tennessee National Bank started assimilating family issues into its corporate culture—that is, company leaders started looking at personal issues as strategic business issues. Executives let go of the need to control employee behavior. Schedules became flexible, individuals took back control over their work routines, and programs to address employee family concerns became standard parts of the work environment. Since then, the company has retained employees twice as long as the bank industry average, and as a result of a more stable and satisfied work force, the company kept 7 percent more retail customers. Higher retention rates went straight to the bottom line, and company executives say those changes accounted for First Tennessee's surprising 55 percent profit gain in the ensuing two years, and put an additional $110 million on its bottom line.

Aligning company needs with individual needs can have a quick and positive impact on company morale, and ultimately on company profits. Xerox Business Systems (XBS) has installed within the larger Xerox corporate culture a cohesive learning organization that has no big-budget activities and no specific performance goals. XBS has instilled in its 15,000 employees a playful, experimental and "organic" mind-set. In essence, XBS, which does such simple things as photocopying and paperwork for its clients, has created a workplace ambiance that not only produces business results (40 percent annual growth, surpassing $1 billion in 1996), but also supports personal growth. XBS has let go of the old profit-is-everything mentality and has energized its work force.

After the turning point, company leaders let go of past assumptions and accepted wisdom, and reassess everything from top to bottom. The starting points for reassessment are the customer and the employee— and not mere lip service to these two key assets, but a real fundamental reassessment. If this reassessment is done right, then profit to the stockholder will follow.

MOVING ON

After a company passes its turning point and lets go of past assumptions, it reassesses its relationships to markets, customers and employees, and then develops a strategy that fits the new realities. The reassessment process, like that for the individual, can benefit from outside assistance (learning, development), but ultimately the answer comes from the interactions between and among the segments involved: employees, customers and company leaders.

Companies that are ready to move on have completed their reassessments. They have reworked their relationships with customers and employees, and set a new course—compass points for their institutions. For example, SAS Institute, Inc., the innovative computer-software company, has employee turnover figures below 4 percent per year, compared to the typical 15 percent for U.S. software companies. It has a 95 percent annual lease-renewal rate among its customers, and outside estimates concluded that in 1996, it had $300 million in pretax earnings from $600 million in revenues. SAS, which started as a university professor's consulting service in the 1970s, remains privately held, but analysts say that, should the company go public, it would be conservatively valued at $3 billion.

SAS is strategically structured and ready to advance in the new business environment. It has reconciled its customer-service approach to meet the new rules of engagement, and it has a vibrant social contract with its employees. The leaders are enlightened, and the institution has embedded learning as essential to its survival. Now comes the surprising bit of information. By Silicon Valley standards, SAS pays its employees less than the accepted industry wage. They have no stock options, no phantom stock, and no huge bonuses.

The mystery of SAS is really no mystery at all. Everything it does fits the new business environment; it attracts those who have personally gone through their own turning points–grounding points–compass points reassessment, and it has created an institutional outlook in line with what we have called "the new frame of mind." The company's products give customers unlimited variety in exploiting data-base resources, offering 16,000 variables to scan market profiles. This flexibility suits the new market paradigm of breaking down categories and eliminating unnecessary redundancies in programming software.

Beyond a quality product, the company maintains close links with its customers' needs and perspectives. Employees must put down in writing every suggestion a customer makes. Once a year, employees sort through these suggestions, rank them, and place them on a ballot which is sent to every customer. Based on the customers' returned ballots, the company ranks the top responses and implements them. This process brings the customer directly into the company's decision-making process. Improvement is customer-driven, not profit-driven.

Happy employees respond to such a positive and vibrant environment, but they also have more direct company contributions to increase their satisfaction: SAS has a 200-acre corporate campus, landscaped to encourage walks and outdoor leisure (including the ever-present Frisbee game). The company has developed thousands of acres next to the company acreage and offers them at reduced prices to encourage employees to build near the campus. A private junior-and-senior high school opened on the campus, allowing parents to have lunch with their children each day. Also, a 7,500-square-foot medical center, with two doctors and 10 nurses, sits on-site, facilitating ease of access to health care.

These types of benefits, which are nontaxable, extend to all employees the special kinds of tax-avoidance tactics once available only to top executives. They also eliminate the need for cultural anthropologists or stress-reduction counselors. Rather than apply Band-Aids to a fading corporate system, SAS has created a new corporate system.

This spread-the-good-works attitude also extends to the way in which all employees are treated personally: like university faculty members. They enjoy their own personal lives (which the company helps to make easier), their own intellectual interests (which the company strives to nurture) and their own ability to plan and execute their work (which the company wants to encourage).

Everything at SAS, from customer connections to employee relations, has advanced to the compass-points level. Individual customers and employees who have started along their own personal process of reassessment need the systems that SAS has put in place. The connection is so strong that both customer and employee retention are no longer a financial and time-straining problem. The individual's compass points jibe with the company's compass points. SAS is a community of meaning—and it is moving on.

What business leaders need as they move through the reassessment process is a new way of thinking about their constituents—both employees and customers. The reassessment process is not about borrowing another theory of change and applying it across the system. Rather, the process involves first changing attitudes and values, and then using the new values to move through a series of questions about what the points of contact are (and should be) between leaders, customers and employees. As far as the new attitudes are concerned, we can describe them best through two metaphors for leadership: natural horsemanship and fly-fishing.

CRITICAL INSIGHT:
Natural Horsemanship and Fly-Fishing

The Horse Whisperer, the 1995 novel by Nicholas Evans, enjoyed a long run at the top of many best-seller lists, and attracted the attention of Robert Redford, who with Disney decided to make a movie of the book. The novel introduces Tom Booker, a horse-trainer who recognizes the animals as psychologically vibrant creatures. With his quiet and respectful approach, he follows each creature through its transition from wild to tame. He learns from them rather than forcing them to submit to him. He has the ability to connect with his horses not by intimidation, control or traditional methods of "bronco-busting" but by a patient, open-ended process of communication that results in trust and shared interests. In other words, he uses natural horsemanship. "A lot of these things you can't really teach," he tells a woman who has sought his help with her horse (and daughter). "All you can do is create a situation where if people want to learn, they can. The best teachers I ever met were the horses themselves. You find a lot of folk have opinions, but if it's facts you want, you're better off going to the horse."

Howell Raines, in his 1993 best-seller, *Flyfishing Through the Midlife Crisis,* distinguished between what he called the Redneck Way of fishing and the fly-fisher's way. The Redneck Way essentially kept score. It involved competition, dead-fish counts and other machinations and devices that could measure how well a participant was doing. Someone fishing the Redneck Way could tout his or her success by counting the number of fish in the hamper, by ascertaining the length or weight of the largest fish or by telling how rapidly all the caught fish had been brought in. The Redneck Way, the method that Raines learned while growing up in rural Alabama, insisted that "Fishing that failed to produce an abundance of corpses could no more be successful than a football season in which the University of Alabama failed to win a national championship."

Raines ultimately realized that Redneck fishing merely brought anxiety, forced behavioral changes in the process of fishing, and changed his hobby into work. Because it was a measurable phenomenon, he discovered that he worked more on forcing some result rather than moving easily through a process of connecting with the environment. At this moment of insight, Raines discovered fly-fishing, which was less efficient but in the final analysis more satisfying. "Fly-fishing is to fishing," he realized, "what ballet is to walking." It was a more human and complete solution to larger personal issues. At some point in time, Raines concluded, nearly every fly-fisher realized that there were "holes in their souls [and that] this disciplined, beautiful and unessential activity might close those holes."

These two practices—natural horsemanship and fly-fishing—serve as metaphors for the ways in which leaders now need to think about their employees and customers. Natural horsemanship offers some clues on how to address the new employee, and fly-fishing offers insights into ways in which companies must approach the new consumer. Both deserve a closer look.

Tim Flitner practices natural horsemanship in real life. When working to convert a young or wild horse into a riding horse, he wears no spurs on his boots, and he does not yell at the horse to frighten it into submission. Historically, cowboys forced themselves onto a horse's back and rode through the bucking stage until the animal submitted, ultimately out of fear, to repeated riding. Flitner, however, approaches the horse with an outstretched hand and gently strokes its neck and back. He waits and works patiently for the horse to rise toward the bit and "ask" to be ridden. "You need to go to where the horse is mentally," he explains. Another practitioner explained it this way: "You have to stop trying to make the horse do something, and instead cause it to do something."

Dennis Reis, an advocate of the gentle approach, admitted that his partners and friends thought he had "gone off the deep end. . . . They say, 'Dennis, you're a cowboy! What's with all this touchy-feely stuff?' And I know how they feel. I had to give myself a 'macho-ectomy.' But I tell them: 'It's a lot less work.' " Reis has been quite effective in working his horses slowly through the process. "Horses . . . are looking for a leader," he insists. "If you holler at the horse, or whip it, he'll think you're a bully. If you sneak around, he'll think you're a wimp. And he has no reason to follow or trust anybody like that." Based upon injury reports on bronco-busting, the advantage goes to natural horsemanship. According to Dr. Doris Bixby Hammet, the secretary of the American Medical Equestrian Association: "A 'real man' might not do it this way, but a smart one will."

Tom Dorrance, the former rancher who first conceived of natural horsemanship, said the approach is not really "a method, because it's adjusting to the horse or the whole surroundings. It's becoming aware of what's going on within the horse and the person you're working with. It isn't a 1–2–3 deal." His book *True Unity: Willing Communication Between Horse and Human* (1994) outlines the approach. Nicholas Evans (who as we have seen wrote *The Horse Whisperer*) studied with Dorrance to learn natural horsemanship. What Dorrance explained to students like Evans was that control has nothing to do with working a horse, and that the ideal approach is to allow the horse to make and correct its own errors, that is, let it have control, and not to treat the animal like a subservient creature. One student, Ray Hunt, explained, "You're not trying to make them learn. You fix it up so they can learn. You're working with the mind." Hunt adds that a connection between human and animal is natural because to them learning is essential to living well. "I think when a person quits learning," he added, "it's a sad day."

Applying the natural-horsemanship metaphor encourages an executive to let go of the old structure and its deadening constraints and move toward a structure and culture that reinforce learning, encourage personal growth and support personal fulfillment. The natural horseman goes "where the horse is," and for the executive, going where the *employee* is means understanding the personal reassessment process and its consequences, seeing the need to develop a community of meaning and then initiating the institution's own strategic reassessment process.

In the early 1990s, sales of fishing supplies and equipment were heading downward. Yet, in 1993, in the middle of this decline, sales of fly-fishing equipment at Orvis jumped more than 40 percent. In that same year, Sage Manufacturing, which makes fly-fishing equipment, went into around-the-clock production to meet increased demand, which estimates placed at 15 percent per year for the entire industry. Also, enrollment in L. L. Bean and Orvis fly-fishing classes reached all-time highs in the fall of 1993. People were turning to fly-fishing in greater numbers, not just as an escape but also as a positive part of their desire to learn. In fact, more than 5,000 books on fly-fishing exist in the English language, and the majority of them are in print today.

Fly-fishing is not just another hobby. Individuals have pursued hobbies for decades (and some records suggest that ancient Romans enjoyed fly-fishing), but only recently has fly-fishing gained such popularity. Something about the sport itself matches what people need right now. To become adept at fly-fishing involves extensive practice on such techniques as fly-casting and fly-tying. For many, honing these skills represents a challenge that brings personal satisfaction. However, becoming adept at fly-fishing also involves learning about the river, the life in the river, the climate, the seasons, the time-of-day routines, the hatch process in and around the river and the whole environment in which the fish live—that is, learning the entire ecology. Learning both increases the enjoyment of fly-fishing and enhances the possibility of success. Techniques and skills alone are insufficient. Understanding the natural environment is crucial. Said directly: Stream-level observations are key to fly-fishing.

As a metaphor, fly-fishing speaks to the new ways that companies must address the new consumer. Thinking within the metaphor, one can see that past business practices have involved standing on the banks of the river and commanding the fish to jump into an awaiting net. Surprisingly enough, in post–World War II America this tactic actually worked. When yelling from the banks faltered a bit, larger speakers with greater volume (plus a few coupons) reignited the interest. However, new market realities have made this approach ineffective. Going into the stream for direct observations and thus learning about what the trout need are now fundamental. Reading most of the field's 5,000 books could prepare the fly-fisher for what to expect, but only direct observation and personal experience grasp the needs of each unique ecological situation.

The Ford Motor Company learned the difference within its own operations. As mentioned earlier, the car manufacturer insisted that its redesigned Taurus would never need to be supported with rebates, but soon Ford was issuing some of the largest kickbacks ever in hopes of boosting weak Taurus sales. However, those "too little and too late" rebates had only minor impact. At the same time, Ford's newly redesigned F-150 truck was a huge success. Deep inside the company a lone designer, James C. Bulin, using direct observation, created a truck that responded to new consumer needs and changing consumer attitudes. He studied market preferences that baby boomers had expressed in noncar purchases, and he learned about their changing values. In short, he designed a car based not on his personal stylistic predilections or his competitors' products but on what sort of behavior and needs consumers had actually expressed.

In the instance of Ford's Taurus, the company was still on the banks of the river turning up the volume on their loudspeakers—but with the F-150, the company was lucky enough to have a designer who believed in stream-level observations. When Ford introduced the F-150 to the public, company executives were there and so were most of the truck's marketing and advertising team. When James Englehart, company vice-president for light-truck development, sought to introduce the young designer, he learned that no one had thought to invite him. And that says succinctly where Ford's overall priorities were. In the past, it had created new models by looking at the competition and then reverse-engineering those models in order to create its own design—a process that had failed for fashion designers but which continued to have life in Detroit. Bulin's success has resulted in Ford's rethinking of its entire relationship between company and customers—no word yet as to whether this managerial enlightenment will spread to employee relations as well.

Natural horsemanship and fly-fishing as metaphors suggest that no one can with certainty mandate a desired result any longer, and that likewise no one can force a connection by merely yelling louder and louder. A leader needs to go where the employee is in order to develop a dynamic and successful work force and likewise needs to work at stream level to secure stable and lasting relationships in the marketplace. Past incentives like salary increases and cross-country promotions, all of which worked so well when careers gave shape to a worker's life, are losing ground to new incentives like learning, control, stability and personal satisfaction—all of which attract rather than command interest. Such marketing tools as massive promotions and bigger advertisements do not work as well as bringing solutions to the customer.

Taken together, the two metaphors reveal a crucial reality: Americans have developed new rules of engagement. Breaking broncos and net-fishing do not work in this new environment. Workers and consumers once accepted whatever came their way (with some clear limits), as long as financial growth, security or status resulted. Now, they are developing different priorities, needs and values—and they are also developing different requirements for any relationship with an employer, retailer or service provider. For employees and consumers (the same individuals in different roles), the new rules of engagement are the new mandates of the individual–institutional relationship. For institutional leaders, these new realities present new opportunities to construct a new social contract and to develop new relationships with reassessed consumers.

CHAPTER 7

A NEW SOCIAL CONTRACT

In 1995, *Utne Reader* printed a story by someone who had worked as a telephone operator for a catalog-related ordering house. He stayed on the telephone all day, taking orders and responding to questions. Enduring the manager's harangues about more orders and surviving lengthening time on the phone without a break, he finally quit and wrote his story. His essay looked at the general malaise of workers he encountered. "There's a feeling [among fellow workers] that's hard to pin down," he wrote—"a detachment that comes out now and then as rage or despair. Many of the people I work with are bone-tired from just trying to make it, week by week."

"For years," the worker/writer continued, "the working poor in this country have felt they had a pact with the powerful. Work hard and you'll be OK. Do your job well and you'll have the basics and a chance to move up. The rich and powerful, because they run the system, have been stewards of that promise. It means when the chips are down, the preservation of opportunity is supposed to come before the cultivation of privilege. . . . The promise has been broken." The broken connection between company and employee led to a new way of thinking about work.

After personal reassessment, individuals drew clearer distinctions between life and work and started looking for ways to develop nonwork skills and enhance the quality of their private lives. Work remained important to individuals, but only as it fit comfortably into new routines that had become even more important to them. Corporate recruiters on college campuses reported that top job candidates were asking different questions than they had just a few years earlier. Instead of responding to

"How much will you pay me?" now they had to answer "What are you going to teach me?" To the recruiters' amazement, these questions were arising in first-round interviews. *The Wall Street Journal* sampled the questions that recruiters faced:

"Do people who work for you have a life off the job?"

"Do your employees get to see their families?"

"If my job requires too much travel, can I change without doing serious damage to my career?"

"What support can you offer my significant other?"

"Does the location you're hiring for offer . . . [fill in sport of choice]?"

In 1996, Intel reported that interviewees asked about life-balance issues nearly 50 percent of the time, up from 20 percent just three years earlier. "Work is important to me and I really want to do my best," explained one female student who accepted an offer from Saturn Corp. because of its "quality of work life" and flexibility. "But that's not what I'm working for. I'm working to be able to afford the other values in life."

When he was CEO and chairman of Corning, James R. Houghton wrote in a brief essay that both the work environment and the worker have changed. The new workers, especially those "conceptual workers" who formed the center of his company, "will not be attracted by hierarchy, but by horizontal structure. They will not be attracted by security, but by the opportunity for personal growth. They will not be attracted by homogeneity, but by cultural diversity. And they will not be attracted by work alone, but by a perceived balance between work and leisure." More specifically, he wrote, old measuring systems about sales figures and the number of people reporting to someone will not be attractive. Rather, "Measures might include words such as 'mutual understanding' or 'shared responsibility,'" the latter including entrusting "employees with strategic ownership of the business." As if to prove Houghton's point, Baxter International, a medical technology manufacturer, asked its 14,000 employees what they wanted. To the company's surprise, the employees' number one answer was: respect.

Houghton's thoughts notwithstanding, most companies have done little to alter the old social contract. Because so many executives have yet to reach their personal turning points, they have yet to acknowledge the fact that the new environment requires a new social contract. They continue to assume that as older workers lose interest, new recruits will arise to replace them. But with college students asking the same "life balance" questions as the older workers, managers need to rethink their fundamental assumptions about human capital.

FIRST STEPS

The extreme importance of an engaged and productive work force has been a common emphasis of American business leaders for years. Yet their actions have rarely been quite as positive as their rhetoric. With the personal revolution creating new individual values and priorities, institutional actions will need to fulfill the promises included in public rhetoric in order to retain the competitive edge that a positive work force offers. That is, what they need is a new and better balanced social contract.

Investment in employees almost inevitably leads to a final payoff to shareholders. After studying 100 German companies, three members of the Boston Consulting Group learned that corporations placing employees at the core of the business produced higher long-term returns to shareholders than did their industry peers. The researchers looked for "employee focus" within the company, identifying two of its essential components: traditional human-resources processes and "intrapreneurship" (i.e., special freedoms granted to employees so they can pursue projects they see as important). In all 10 industrial sectors studied, the results were strikingly similar. Those companies with the highest scores on the two components produced greater shareholder returns than did their competitors. Also, companies that maintained an employee focus ultimately created the most new jobs as a result of growth and expansion.

Companies that raised long-term training budgets after job reductions were 75 percent more likely than before to show earnings. According to an American Manufacturers Association study, companies that invested in long-term training were nearly twice as likely to raise worker productivity as those which failed to make the expenditure. Despite this discovery about the companies in the AMA study, only 23 percent of companies that reduced their work force increased human-capital investments. In fact, on average, a 10-percent increase in employee education level created an 8.6-percent rise in total factor productivity, while a similar 10-percent increase in the value of capital equipment boosted productivity by just 3.4 percent. These results from the National Center on Educational Quality of the Workforce suggested that employees, not machines, make a company productive.

Although these numbers add great incentive to making substantial adjustments to human-capital allocations, most companies have lumbered rather slowly toward positive actions. While acknowledging that downsizing and other recent "silver bullets" of management science have not yielded what they anticipated (in some cases even exacerbating work force problems), leaders are still reluctant to commit to substantial change. Yet, some companies *are* committing to some changes.

American businesses have programs meant to address worker stress, excessive managerial authority, job security, salary decisions, work dynamics and various aspects of personal lives. Looking through these programs makes it obvious that a process designed to realign work and life priorities alike has begun in earnest. Starting with a recognition of the problem, at which point employers allow moderate adjustments to employee work schedules, some companies move to substantial reworking of employer–employee relations. These companies are definitely moving toward their turning points. The farther along in the process they move, the closer they come to letting go of past certainties and moving on to addressing the larger strategic issues of human capital.

SINGLE-ISSUE CHANGES

Many employers recognized that stress among their employees was having a negative impact on the workplace environment. Anxiety among workers increased tensions within the office, causing intergroup battles that ultimately affected the ability of many to get work done as expected and needed. Moreover, some workers under stress took more sick days, devoted less energy to work and ultimately were less happy with the day-to-day routine of corporate employment.

Granting permission to dress casually on selected days was one of the first executive efforts to lessen office tension. By the end of 1996, roughly 75 percent of American businesses allowed some sort of looser attire at one time or another. Anxious executives, wondering what this unraveling of standards would do to the workplace, turned to Levi's for advice because they wanted to create a "dress code" for dress-down days. In the three years ending in 1996, Levi's had visited and advised more than 22,000 corporations on how to handle dress-down days. Also, Target stores issued a videotape to help companies deal with the phenomenon, and both Levi's and Eddie Bauer opened special stores just for this easier style of dress.

The NPD Group, a market-research firm, discovered that morale increased among 61 percent of workers who were allowed to step down sartorially. Levi Strauss reported that four of five white-collar workers interviewed said their morale improved during the more-casual days, and roughly half said that a day with eased dress codes actually resulted in increased productivity. One employee confided that the dress-down day allowed her to relax and focus only on work, rather than on the image she had to present, given each day's strict attire rules. "I wouldn't trade it for anything," she admitted. Another worker added: "Everyone appreciates the opportunity to have a little more autonomy."

Employers also granted greater autonomy to employees through flexible-hours plans, allowing workers to select their own duty hours, control time-off schedules, and work more when work was really needed. This type of human-resources approach responded specifically to low morale among workers remaining after extensive downsizing. Employers hoped that greater control over personal time would ease the anxiety of doing more work with fewer people. When Citibank introduced its "flex-time" program, for example, the company wanted to eliminate the 9–to–5 mentality that caused many workers such stress, but it also wanted to overcome devastatingly low morale. They discovered that the program created a more personal one-to-one relationship between employee and supervisor because the two had to negotiate schedules based upon mutual needs. They also found that the program blended part-time employees more effectively into the work force and made job-sharing (more than one person "sharing" one full-time position) an easier tactic to adopt.

Other companies introduced sabbaticals—extended leaves from work—to soothe anxious and overwrought employees. IBM, American Express, Xerox and Wells Fargo Bank, plus others, introduced these benefits into their normal employment package. Helen Axel, an author who has studied this subject, considers a sabbatical a paid leave that employees may take at regular (but not short) intervals, returning to the same job each time. The Frank Russell Company, a pension-consulting firm, added sabbaticals because it was in the firm's best interest to allow employees to recharge themselves. This move would, company officials insisted, ensure future productivity. Because of that reasoning, the company *mandated* sabbaticals, thereby eliminating a problem that various other companies experienced: the refusal of employees to take leaves because the employer might become too comfortable without them.

Some employers went even deeper into the post-downsizing malaise and focused on issues of spirituality. Conferences on spirituality in the workplace attracted many human-resources directors and gained the attention of therapists across the country, but getting that perspective into the company was much slower. When the World Bank instituted its Spiritual Unfoldment program, few workers took the time to attend seminars and classes—but soon the sessions were attracting standing-room-only crowds and included senior management as well as young assistants. The sessions addressed what many employees were asking as part of their personal reassessment and now found relevant at work after the brutal effects of reengineering: "What does this all mean?" and "Why do I feel so unfulfilled?"

The spirituality-in-the-workplace movement brings new meaning to the office, creating an environment wherein individuals feel better about connecting with work. This focus on meaning and enlightenment led companies like Honeywell, AT&T, and Eastman Kodak to hire the poet David Whyte. His book *The Heart Aroused: Poetry and the Preservation of the Soul in Corporate America* (1994) brings poetry and its spiritual dimension into the office. The joy and quality of such poetic communications offer a way to express sensitivity and to recognize others as something more than colleagues. Poetry is magnificent at facilitating relationships, Whyte insists, because it nurtures creativity and allows workers to look deeper into personal and professional situations.

A look at the people who do not like the spirituality-in-business concepts provides insight into its depth and value. Former management gurus Michael Hammer and Tom Peters both quickly thought the whole movement misguided. "The word 'spirituality,'" offered Peters, "says that you're screwing around with a part of me I don't want touched." Hammer noted that "On the one hand, many of these books seem to me to be just a lot of pompous clichés strung one after another," but he allowed that "On the other hand, they clearly speak to something that's bothering people." They viewed the movement as something implanted in the organization, rather than something that is bubbling up and taking over the organization.

The old-style boss–employee relationship represented another thing that was bothering workers. The old model of command and control called for forceful leadership that demanded and got attention and subordination. A smoothly run community-of-wealth model moved ideas and concepts up through the hierarchy until they reached a level of decision-making authority. That top-dwelling authority figure made the decision, and action from the "direct reports" led to action throughout the system. The whole community worked best when all agreed upon the ultimate objective: expanding wealth. However, that top-down, inside-out process started coming apart when individual employees looked beyond money for positive reinforcement, and when consumers changed the way they shopped.

Changed employee values and priorities required changed leaders. Command-and-control leaders need to let go of that style and gain some understanding of the sweeping changes taking place. The movie *The Doctor* (1991) offered a good example of a leader's awakening. It followed a highly successful surgeon as he became sick and entered into a "hospital hell" as a patient. Without control over procedures, and indeed without control over his own life, the doctor learned a horrifying lesson about what his patients went through under his own care. Dr. Jack Mac-Kee, the doctor whose real-life experiences formed the basis for the movie, returned to his duties after his hospitalization and immediately instituted a policy that required all interns to spend three nights in a hospital as a patient—*without* the staff's knowing of his professional identity. The humbling experience of not being in control, he reasoned, would offer doctors the chance to feel what patients feel.

Law students at many colleges must now confront the "authoritative," "insensitive," "arrogant," "know-it-all" and "intimidating" attitude of the professional lawyer, in order to learn how *not* to practice law. The College of William and Mary's law school has a two-year program on client–attorney relations. The University of California at Los Angeles has a first-year program on sensitivity to client needs, and the University of Pennsylvania uses videotaped client–lawyer sessions to encourage students to be more sensitive to client conditions. "Clients want to be a part of the decision-making process and decide what risks they want to take," explained the director of William and Mary's program. "Lawyers have their own agendas. They don't listen."

Leaders not listening and retaining their own agendas characterized the old top-down model of company decision making. Old-model business leaders desperately need to rethink how they deal with people around them. As we have seen, some enlightened top managers have effectively altered work schedules and encouraged extended leaves. However, others have gone further and have started to attend more directly to the individual needs of employees.

Kingston Technology Corp. offers a powerful example. Owners John Tu and David Sun *know* if anything of a problematical nature is troubling their individual employees. According to cofounder Tu, who was born in China, his mother offered him the best leadership advice: "Don't bring flowers to those who have plenty. Bring coal to people when they need heat in the winter." Before selling the company, he and his partner paid salaries that exceeded the industry average by 20 percent to 30 percent, they routinely sent workers on paid weekend retreats, and *every* day was casual-dress day. They matched all 401(k) contributions and added another $3,000 per employee at year's end. They compiled 5 percent in pretax profits to disperse as bonuses each quarter, and they publicly promised that, should the company for some reason go under, every employee would receive one year's salary. They added individual touches as well. When their Web-page manager attended a difficult and lengthy trade show in Germany, Sun and Tu sent him to Paris and London to recuperate. When a coworker casually mentioned a childhood dream of owning a Jaguar, Sun immediately gave her his own.

"They're compassionate, patient, honest, loyal and trustworthy," explained one enthusiastic employee. "It's a joy to come to work here." That "joy" has resulted in positive company growth as well. By 1995, Kingston was on *Forbes* magazine's list of the 500 largest private companies with sales pushing $2 billion. Employee turnover, however, was below 1 percent, and nobody watched the clock. The advice of Sun's mother drove the company: "Money isn't the only thing. Treat people right, then they will help you when you need it."

That type of linkage among employees has also affected Hal Rosenbluth, CEO of the Rosenbluth International travel agency. "We're a company built on friendship," he insists. "When I was in college, I was taught not to work with friends because you can't get productivity out of 'em, you can't make the tough decisions." He discovered just the opposite to be true. Coworkers who are friends never let each other down, and in moments of trial and stress, friends make the best decisions for each other and willingly join the fray. Rosenbluth insists that every company meeting be open to anyone interested in attending, and any employee can sign up to "shadow" an executive for a day. When one employee asked to so follow Hal Rosenbluth, she found herself in Mexico helping the company to acquire an international travel agency. According to company officials, this approach contributes a "psycho-benefit" that helps the company to attract and retain the best qualified people.

Focusing first on going "where the employee is" (to paraphrase the horse whisperer's code), the CEO of Illinois Trade Association, Jack Schacht, identified his employees' reassessed value system and tried to respond: "We believe our employees don't work just for economic benefits. If people feel they can express themselves, it gives them a sense of meaning." When employees expressed an interest in alternative medicine, Schacht changed the company's policy to pay for chiropractic care, herbal therapy and related forms of health maintenance. Also, each employee can get a free massage once a month.

Schacht's concerns resulted from a recognition that losing employees is an extremely expensive proposition: "It's very important that we keep turnover to a minimum, because we put so much into training our employees." Thinking along the same line, American Bankers Insurance Group sponsored public schools at their work sites, as do nearly 75 businesses across the U.S. American Bankers spent $2.4 million to build a facility to house the educational institution on Bankers' office campus. Keeping parents who are employees happy lowered absenteeism by 50 percent and reduced turnover rate by 9 percent. Moreover, the training-cost savings from that one area alone will permit Bankers to recoup its initial investment in just 10 years.

Employee-friendly programs retain workers, and that benefit reduces training costs. A variety of companies have started to act upon this discovery. For example, Motorola added a long-term care provision in its employee insurance policy so that employees did not have to worry about the care that aging parents might require. Eddie Bauer's headquarters café stays open late so that time-squeezed workers can order food to take home for a family dinner, and the company offers employees one Balance Day per year, a day for the individual to balance personal needs against workplace demands. Aetna Life & Casualty extended new mothers' unpaid leave to six months, which cut in half the resignations from that group. As a result, Aetna saved $1 million per year in retraining expenses.

Family-friendly programs, like time-assistance programs, retained frazzled employees by helping them to address personal needs. Other companies assisted money- and work-strained employees by changing attitudes about worker retention and salaries. The 1990s upsurge in company layoffs left remaining employees to deal with increased work loads and the psychological unemployment we discussed earlier. Also, tightening compensation forced many employees to face a continuing disposable-income squeeze, which we also discussed earlier. Alert executives, however, have moved to ease these pressures on their employees. Northern Telecom (Canada) recognized the anxiety that cost-cutting caused employees and took action to ease it. The company unveiled a college-level recruiting program that promised new hires a three-year employment guarantee. On a different level, Cummins Engine signed an 11-year contract with the Diesel Workers Union, and a significant part of that contract was the company's guarantee that its 3,000 workers had jobs until the year 2004.

Some leaders, however, tried even more extensive programs. Steve Wilson, the West Point graduate who runs Mid-States Technical Staffing Services, created a way to refocus his employees' thinking toward growth and effectiveness. He established a policy to pay his employees cash bonuses throughout the year, whenever the company recorded an additional $75,000 in net profits. In addition, he opened the company's books to his employees, conducted lunchtime training sessions to teach everyone to read financial statements, and began posting budgets and income statements on office walls. The employees quickly realized that they could not only watch, but also control, the numbers. Salespeople could make a more determined effort and thus help each other because the ultimate effect resounded throughout the company. Office employees could track expenses more carefully, and operations people could minimize project costs for a "higher" purpose. According to company officials, employees stopped acting like employees and started acting like owners. From the start of the program in 1994, earnings ran double the company projections.

All of these examples emerged from executives who recognized that the workers had changed. Many leaders address specific worker concerns like time- or budget-squeezes, while others seek to alleviate pressures created by either larger social issues or narrower, more personal problems. While these efforts recognize that both employees and the work environment have changed, they nonetheless seek to extend the life of the old communities of wealth structure and incentives. In essence, executives, while acknowledging that things are different, have yet to let go of past models. They have probably crossed the corporate turning point in realization, but they have yet to start letting go and initiating the corporate reassessment process.

LETTING GO OF CONTROL

At Pacific Data Images in California, *predictable* worker behavior has little appeal. Even though the company offers its clients cutting-edge technology, its employees enjoy boundaryless office antics. Pogo-stick races, marshmallow fights and radio-controlled car races have become typical office antics. The company encourages such behavior for very simple reasons: Frivolous antics unleash creativity, workplace tensions find release and fun begets innovation. Once, president Carl Rosendahl even stood on the company's rooftop and threw office furniture and watermelons into the parking lot below, while employees circled the site and applauded the spectacle. Berkeley Systems, another technology company, has a playground slide connecting the office's two floors, and officials at Emerge Consulting in Palo Alto swear by Silly Putty as a source of creative ideas during meetings. Childhood play as a way to subvert adult intellectualized processes (the core of a traditional MBA case-study approach) is a key to stimulating Silicon Valley's creative capabilities. However, it also means that some managers must surrender absolute control over office dynamics.

Executives at Pacific Data and Berkeley Systems have let go of old command-and-control models and have dispersed authority throughout the system. They focus attention on the employee, and they are releasing needed creativity. While pogo-stick races may not fit all office environments, letting go of central control *does,* in the new post–personal revolution era.

Self-managing teams have become a structural way for some managers to let go of some authority. These groups assume their own management responsibilities and call for necessary actions as they move through their work. For example, General Motors' Saturn Co. uses teams of as many as 15 people to make decisions about how to meet productivity goals. This process removes the manager's propensity to micromanage operations and structures workers into the management role. In another instance, Nucor revolutionized steel-making by vesting each minimill with the authority to set all goals and objectives. Teams of leaders then share the profits that their actions create. Similarly, self-managing teams within Marriott Corporation seek to create new businesses within the larger corporate business. "We do everything we can," explained Marriott CEO Bill Marriott, "to help people help themselves." Likewise, Hewlett-Packard advanced its market position when it restructured to grant near-total control to small business units within the corporation. In fact, the laser-jet line of printers, which spread rapidly through the market, arose from just this type of small-unit empowerment. Ralph Larsen, CEO of Johnson & Johnson, which also launched a similar self-managed team approach, has explained: "Employees come up with better solutions and set tougher standards than I would impose." None of this internal creativity comes to the surface, however, without leaders first letting go of control.

The charter-school movement has developed because to some extent educational leaders have let go of centralized curriculum planning and created a structure that allows groups of people to come together and open a school with the blessing of state school boards. By creating a curriculum and petitioning the state system, local leaders, teachers, parents, corporations or other entities can start their own charter school. Roughly 700 groups across the U.S. have done so. For example, teachers conceived and founded the Renaissance School, an experimental educational institution in Long Island City, New York. Teachers working there talk of a sense of liberation, strong personal satisfaction and the belief that work is acquiring real meaning. They no longer use ancient textbooks and do not complete lengthy lesson plans or make extensive daily reports. They create their own curriculum, set their own teaching pace, work with students in ways they decide are effective and integrate subject areas without regard to traditional curriculum categories. They remain with the same students for two to three years, and they use that more-intimate knowledge of the students to get them to perform better. The teachers are especially pleased: "I have to be honest," admitted one seventh-grade teacher, "in all my 23 years of teaching I have never seen kids as happy as the ones are here." Like First Tennessee Bank which had better customer retention when it had better worker retention, the Renaissance School has happier teachers who energize and inspire happier students.

Rockport executives let go of their traditional prerogative to control employee meetings and got much more back than they anticipated. The company's 350 employees gathered at an "off site" to discuss Rockport's mission. When they strolled into the room they saw no podium, table or stage—just a circle of chairs. When they sat down in this "tribal" arrangement, a facilitator told them that anyone with a passion for any issue should write it on a piece of paper and tack it to the bulletin board. Those interested in contributing to a discussion of that topic should sign their names on that paper.

These self-selected groups then went into action to solve the issues raised. The process worked better than anticipated, and by the end of the day, employees had raised, discussed and even resolved numerous issues. Volunteered Richard Roessler, the human-resources executive who structured the meeting: "We now have a book of ideas that vary from how to get suppliers to send shoelaces on time, to how to find out what our competitors are doing, to how to help Rockport's women succeed better."

Roessler had noticed that in past company meetings, coffee breaks often triggered the most active employee discussions, and he reasoned that this was so because employees could choose what they wanted to discuss. He created open-space, agendaless meetings to approximate the coffee-break atmosphere. This approach, Roessler thought, would support two strong points: The best people to discuss important topics are those who want to discuss those topics; and those people who have a chance to discuss things are the ones most likely to improve them. But, again, the important first step in the whole process involved *letting go of control.*

MOVING ON:
DESIGNING THE NEW SOCIAL CONTRACT

Corporate executives ease across their turning points. Once there, they start letting go of control. In this, their grounding-points phase, they rethink all operations, relationships and fundamentals. From this rethinking process comes the strategic restructuring which not only changes the way in which companies address their customers but also rewrites the social contract, that implicit covenant between employer and employee that guides all interaction, establishes all expectations and sets all goals. The new social contract blends the interests of the evolving corporation with the reassessed values and priorities of its employees. It recognizes the new needs that both sides have and seeks to reconnect the broken link between employer and employee. The new social contract confirms the creation of a community of meaning and seeks to reestablish the loyalty lost during the breakdown of the community-of-wealth model.

Companies that have undertaken strategic restructurings have discovered a process which, over time, has altered all relationships within the company, changed traditional concepts of management and ultimately created a community of meaning. Open-book management is one such process, and the most popular practitioner of this post–turning point, post–letting go management approach is Springfield Remanufacturing.

Under open-book management, every employee from janitor and receptionist to line worker and executive becomes involved in the intimate details of running the company, creating an annual business plan and tracking the numbers. In the 1980s, Jack Stack, chairman and CEO, took this radical concept and installed it in Springfield Re, a struggling division of International Harvester with $19 million in business and 170 employees. In short order, he had taken over a troubled company, reassessed its objectives and created an independent company attracting more than $100 million in business and employing 800 people.

Learning was the catalyst that made open-book management work at Springfield Re. "What we've got to do is teach people how they are evaluated," he suggested, "[and] the tea leaves of business are the financials." As a result, Stack launched a huge educational program within his company. When job candidates went through interviews, they were told first about their jobs, and then that they would spend just 60 percent of their time on that work—the rest would be spent learning about the company. "Understanding financial concepts is not an easy matter," confides Stack. "It's much more than just looking at a simple balance sheet." That difficulty means more learning programs inside the company. In fact, Springfield Re typically spends more money each year to educate existing employees about business in general, and the company in particular, than it spends on job-skills training.

Using the open-book model, Stack provides all employees with a copy of the company's financial balance sheet and expects everyone to work to improve on the numbers printed there. Each division meets weekly to compile its numbers and register its financial statistics. Every other week, representatives from the 22 divisions gather together to share the numbers and develop an overall picture of the company's health. Everyone knows how the company is doing, and they discuss and implement ways to make improvements. "I'm trying to get management out of the way," claims Stack. Quarterly bonuses and an employee stock-ownership plan help workers to benefit directly from their efforts .

SAP, a German software company, has another way to encourage worker efforts. It has installed "intrapreneurship" systems into its overall structure. These simply give employees the power to make all decisions relevant to their work, which in turn maximizes the individual's desire and ability to innovate and initiate. As SAP's human-resource director, Helmut Gilbert, has explained, "People need freedom to do their best." Individuals at SAP have total freedom over where they work and in what ambience. The company has "sitting halls," which are large rooms that facilitate multitasking and collegial interaction, rather than cubicle offices. Employees can take classes in any area of the company, and they can use the acquired expertise either in their own work or just to understand even better how the overall operation works. Outside of the eight board members, all 4,000 employees at the company headquarters are at the same level, and all have the authority to seek money to fund a business project they have developed. With this internally open and personnel-friendly environment, SAP moved from the fourth- to the second-largest software company in Germany, enjoyed a 20-percent-per-year sales growth and delivered 33-percent increases in shareholder value from 1988 to 1995—the largest in the industry.

While individual autonomy encourages creativity and innovation for the company as well as personal growth and satisfaction for the employee, the educational element to corporate change facilitates creating a community of meaning. People who are focused on learning about their company's well-being develop a confidence in the firm's situation and competence in running the overall operation. That reignites not only interest in work, but also the institution. Taco, Inc., a manufacturer of pumps and valves, created a Learning Center which includes a computer lab, a library and several classrooms. The Center teaches such work-related subjects as blue-print reading, auditing, statistics and customer service. But it also teaches conversational Spanish, Weight Watchers and other antiaddiction programs, arithmetic, algebra, art, gardening and a host of other subjects that enhance the employees' quality of life. In all, Taco's Learning Center offers six dozen courses. Situated at the company's headquarters in Rhode Island, the institution has had the governor come to speak, as well as the mayor of Providence and the chief justice of the state supreme court. (The latter has also taught a history course at the center.) Additionally, employees' children have gone on whale-watching trips with an oceanographer from the University of Rhode Island, have been taught by members of the Rhode Island Philharmonic to play musical instruments, and have participated in their own science fair.

Taco's owner, John Hazen White, spent more than a quarter of a million dollars on the Center and dispenses roughly $300,000 annually to keep it going—a sum which is just one-half of 1 percent of sales. In his way, White changed the management role as much as did Springfield Re's Jack Stack. White changed his role from a leader to something else. "I decided to be a teacher," he explained. The importance of the program does not lay in the numbers. "Does it come back to us?" asked the owner of the privately held company. "Of course it does. It comes back in the form of attitude. People feel they're playing in the game, not being kicked around in it." When the company hit hard times, the employees did stick with the company, and the Learning Center became central to the effort to restructure the company to be more efficient and more effective. With its focus on learning, the company has held its turnover rate steady at just 1 percent, and with prices scarcely moving, Taco enjoyed a compound annual rate of increased labor productivity of roughly 20 percent.

Another model of the strategically restructured company comes from Brazilian businessman Ricardo Semler. He coaxed suspicious managers, unions and executives to accept shop-floor democracy and participatory management. Managers worried that they would be surrendering too much power, unions fretted that the arrangement subverted their role in negotiations with management, and executives worried that the new operations threatened chaos. Subsequent events proved all of them wrong. When Semler inherited the bloated company in the early 1980s, he whittled the work force down from 800 to 200— but, rather than cut loose so much talent, he helped departing employees to establish private consultancies, which his company hired. He embedded his own open-book system that granted all employees access to company ledgers, involvement in setting production schedules and voting rights on the boss's performance reviews. Employees even set their own salaries—but, since all employees make decisions about the value of particular jobs, workers assigning themselves too high a salary risk losing their jobs when other employees learn that one's productivity does not match one's salary. In the midst of Brazil's struggling economy, Semler's innovative company prospered, quintupling its profits in the first three years of the 1990s.

Semler's story emphasizes the difference between efficiency, which power-based management can force, and effectiveness, which requires an involved work force. AES, a unique power-generating company in Connecticut, actually has employees setting budgetary categories. Workers on the line discuss what to do with the money created by their operations, even to the point of making outside investments with extra cash. "The more you increase individual responsibility," argues AES's founder and CEO, Dennis W. Bakke, "the better the chances for incremental improvements in operations." Indeed, one employee, given the responsibility for decisions about operations, realized that he could no longer pass along blame to others for any troubles. "I'd been blaming others for not getting the job done," he confessed. "I suddenly realized that there would be no one else to blame anymore."

Through this model of dispersed responsibility, Bakke's shared authority approach also "makes work a lot more fun." He hastens to add that "fun" does not mean Friday afternoons at the local beer hall, slapping backs and telling stories. "Fun is when you're intellectually excited and you are interacting with each other. . . . It's the struggle, and even the failures that go with it, that make work fun." By spreading responsibility, Bakke has embedded more firmly the stated "core values" that underlie overall operations: "integrity, fairness, social responsibility and fun."

Clearly, Bakke has crossed his turning point and has let go of past models. Beyond that, his focus on intellectually stimulating work across the entire operation serves as an aggregating force for a community of meaning. Bakke would also quickly add that more "fun" has meant more market success as well. AES's revenues rose 23 percent annually, on average, for the first half of the 1990s, reaching profits in excess of $100 million in 1994, a sixfold increase in just four years. Bakke acknowledged that the changed structure has in turn changed his employees even more. "They've learned so much about the total aspect of the business, they'll never be the same."

The examples in this section highlight the movement away from the operational principles and models that guided the communities of wealth and point toward what happens beyond the institution's turning point. The experience of experimenting in these areas is exhilarating, and (as the examples indicate) leads toward a new social contract which both embodies the growth motive and responds to the employees' reassessed values and priorities.

MOVING ON MAKES SENSE

The logic of strategic restructuring eventually leads toward an inversion of the way things were on the historical side of the turning point. The period of experimentation leads to a liberating impulse to let go of past authority and operational structures and imbue personnel with the power to make decisions and act upon them. One perhaps extreme example of granting individual autonomy may clarify the points here. Plainfield (New Jersey) High School took this action one step farther: Any student can join any club, any squad, any team—regardless of ability. The teachers and administrators realized that the dual purpose of the school was to educate and to encourage personal development, and qualifying restrictions for extracurricular activities ran counter to that objective. In the first year of the effort, the school had 72 cheerleaders, 234 choir members and 140 band musicians. Students, along with sponsors, then worked on making the larger membership a viable system. At the end of the year, fully half the student body was participating in extracurricular activities—a rate that more than doubled past levels.

These types of actions may sound extreme (and for public and private institutions charged with taking actions they may be), but they reveal the attitude surfacing throughout society in this post–turning-point era. Participation, involvement and responsibility are crucial to a successful institution, and shared rewards and losses facilitate that objective. The fully realized corporation in the new era has worked through these issues and is prepared to move forward. In the area of human capital, St. Luke's (advertising) agency in London is just such a company.

A placard on the wall at St. Luke's captures the attitude behind this enterprise's reason for being: "Profit Is Like Health: You Need It But It Is Not What You Live For"—a thought that only makes sense to someone who has passed through a personal reassessment process, and only works as an operational thought within an institution which has also passed through a strategic restructuring. Within the organization all financial decisions are vetted and voted publicly among all who have vested money in the company, and that means every person working at the agency. In legal terms, a trust owns the company and a five-member council runs the trust. The council consists of one outside lawyer, two representatives of senior managers and two representatives of other employees. All of these people are selected by election.

On the day this firm was founded, the owners distributed 25 percent of the trust's shares equally among the employees. Every year since, managers have had the company revalued, and have then issued new shares (equally to all employees) that match the new, higher value. When an employee leaves, he or she must sell those shares back to the trust for redistribution. Like other innovative companies, St. Luke's does not have desks, preferring instead "brand rooms," areas that contain and organize information on specific clients, where employees gather around a client's concerns rather than those dictated by the company's operating structure. Computers are everywhere and available to anyone.

St. Luke's came into existence as the London office of Chiat/Day, but when that company ran into difficulty and sought to merge into mega-agency Omnicom, Andy Law, St. Luke's chairman, decided to buy the London office, which he did for a seven-year payback based on company profits. Law immediately created a new agency environment by giving to St. Luke's employees the equity he had just purchased.

From that rebellious beginning, St. Luke's continued along an innovative track, focusing the company's dynamic energy on staff needs. "These people," Law says, "were adolescents when [Margaret] Thatcher came to power. These people were adolescents when AIDS reared its head. Their interests are self-motivation, personal growth and working for a company they're proud of." With the purchase and equity dispersal complete, the entire company went into retreat to create the company's identity and its future. Subsequently, Law institutionalized that retreat so that, each year, an off-site gathering recalibrates the company's objectives to suit the employees then working for St. Luke's. "What's relevant are the people in it today, their ambitions for it, and how they can make it work."

Employees speak of St. Luke's not in the abstract third person but as an embodiment of the personal values they have discovered there on their own. That is why candidates for jobs must interview not just in their area of expertise but with four people from other areas as well. According to Law, while that process can be time-consuming, when "giving away a piece of the company to somebody, you want to make sure you get the right person." Overall, the agency has moved to another level of purpose and endeavor. "We've created this company to live beyond us," Law proudly announced. "We're just renting resources. Remember that we're a collective here—everybody is equal. What's disappeared are ego and greed, the two major driving forces behind the advertising business."

St. Luke's and other companies that have passed their turning points and started their reassessment process are working their way toward a different social contract. Whenever the experimentation has landed on an organizational solution that feels right to those involved (as it has at St. Luke's), the company's level of performance rises, and its competitive edge becomes more obvious. In its first year of operation, St. Luke's became the fastest-growing agency in London, attracting more than $72 million in business, and meeting its 1996 revenue target in the first four months. That type of advantage awaits companies willing and able to undertake a strategic restructuring of human capital.

SOME COMMON FEATURES

Each company has a unique culture and unique employee skills, and consequently no single theory of needed changes exists. Individual observations on where employees are and what will work for that company—natural horsemanship—remain the most dynamic approach to strategic restructuring. Yet, in looking at the examples cited here, several characteristics of the successful experimentation process do appear repeatedly. For one, the most successful examples arose after the organization's leader reached a personal turning point. The person at the top *must* realize that things have changed so significantly that the old world is losing its effectiveness. The examples that simply tweaked the old system to keep the old operational model going a little longer result from leaders' having not reached their own turning points. To be successful in a strategic restructuring, the person at the top must start the letting-go process and allow that release to filter through the entire organization. Said another way: Personal transformation is the first step toward organizational transformation.

At that point, then, the transformation really begins. In every instance, observations of what really is in place become crucial to a successful reassessment process. Andy Law knew his employees—who they were, where they came from and what they wanted. From that perspective, he realized that distributed authority was not just practical but essential. Yet, even with such unique elements as these within each institutional culture, only a few types of actions have repeatedly worked, and the key word in every instance has been *open.*

Open-book management works throughout the system to invert old power bases, break down artificial barriers of expertise and eliminate petty competition within the organization.

Open-agenda meetings release the creative energy within the company and bring employees into the center of company decision making. As a result, they have "ownership" of the decisions being made, and that converts to responsibility for seeing them through to success.

Open schedules are simply releasing work time to individual employee discretion. They do the job; they know the time frame. With the constant interaction of open-book management, collegial pressure and the personal integrity of office friendships keep workers learning, growing and producing.

Open Access recognizes the reality of modern technology, which allows anyone to gain access to any information. As a result, withholding information—the ability to do so having once been a symbol of power—is no longer either reasonable or viable.

Open Office recognizes that walls get in the way when creative people decide to work together in a creative way. Unfortunately, breaking down walls and opening up office space has become a managerial technique to push productivity rather than to facilitate interaction among creative people. The walls of private offices cannot come down until *after* the entire strategic restructuring process has taken place and all other open processes are in place. Done anytime before that, it becomes another old managerial technique to "bronco-bust" employees into submission. Also, employees deep in their own grounding-points reassessment may value their own private space. Eventually, when they reengage with the work place, *then* interaction will become more important to them. In short, when the employees believe the walls are getting in the way, that is when the walls should come down.

This openness facilitates the creation of communities of meaning which will attract the best employees in the years ahead and yield the competitive edge that companies need. Learning and growing are inherent in open companies because the information flow is not dammed; and individuals need the resources and knowledge to understand what that information means. Learning and openness bring rising responsibility, which spreads self-motivation and self-monitoring throughout the organization. Overall, by letting go of the old organizational models and behaviors, the process of creating a new and more dynamic institution begins. One way to grasp the changes necessary is to envision the overall model for institutional organization as changing from the physical dynamic of force to the biological dynamic of organic growth—from "lean machine" to "vital organism."

CRITICAL INSIGHT:
From "Lean Machine" to "Vital Organism"

In 1982, the famed Italian film director Fedrico Fellini made a movie entitled *The Orchestra,* in which he vented his anxiety over the collapsing of Italian society. Using the orchestra as a metaphor for society, the film depicts an organization with great discipline and precision following its leader, adhering to every detail in the score and subsuming individual skills into the whole, as ordered by the conductor. Soon, however, things start coming apart. Musicians cease playing. Order disappears. Eventually a huge wrecking ball blasts through the wall, destroying the entire scene. While it was completely fictional, Fellini intended *The Orchestra* to be an accurate demonstration of what was taking place in Italy.

In 1997, Academy Award–winning filmmaker Allan Miller created the documentary *Orpheus in the Real World,* which explores the wondrous real-world accomplishments of a 26-piece orchestra named Orpheus. Either the orchestra has no "conductor" or it has 26 conductors, depending upon one's perspective. Every member has equal input into the group's interpretation and presentation of every piece, and each participant negotiates and persuades, in open discussions, trying to move the whole group toward better and better performances. Julian Fifer, the group's founder, explained: "The main principle of Orpheus is to provide a setting in which all the musicians feel that they can have a voice, and that their opinions are respected—and not only respected, but put into play." Each orchestra performance is a collaborative production which starts with the written composition, progresses without agenda toward a finished interpretation and evolves and shifts according to the input and participation of the entire group.

Fellini's collapsing orchestra serves as a good metaphor for the contemporary status of the communities of wealth, and the vibrant Orpheus group is, in fact, a community of meaning. However, the interpretations and comparisons go deeper. The difference between Fellini's version of an orchestra and that of Orpheus is the difference between eighteenth-century science (with its mechanized control, order, uniformity and constancy) and twentieth-century science (with its variability, fluidity, interactivity and openness). Fellini's orchestra requires a single leader with disciplined followers all around; Orpheus, on the other hand, is a self-organizing, self-regulating self-processing organization. The eighteenth-century version of an organization dominates the managerial practices of America's public and private institutions, while the twentieth-century version—even as we have come to the end of that century—is just now emerging as a model that better suits contemporary culture.

Institutions are mental constructs, and their organizational charts are also. Historically, those constructs have had models, and even metaphors, by which they could best be understood. For most of the twentieth century, American institutions have based their model upon Frederick Taylor's "scientific management." While certainly not "scientific" in any way, it was, nonetheless, a technological model that derived its cachet from its connection to analytical theory and a cause-and-effect model.

Likewise, Taylor's management theory, derived, as it was, from a mechanistic view of production, sought to extract maximum efficiency from an organizational process. He broke down every movement of every operation into its component parts—that is, he analyzed the over-all operation. Workers could execute these tiny modules of work repeatedly, then pass the object to the next person for the next component action, all faster than one person could perform all the actions alone. Accelerate movement at the front of the line, and workers must pick up the pace all along it. This operation as machine metaphor devolved in unscientific ways from Newton's laws of physics that likewise envisioned the universe as a big clock (or analogous machine) once set in motion by some force and then left to operate on its own.

Oddly enough, Taylor created scientific management just when Newton's eighteenth-century physics model was losing its hold on modern scientists because the old theories could not explain new observations. The work of such scientists as Albert Einstein and Max Planck better explained the latest phenomena. As physicists fought to make the new facts jibe with the old theories, their shortcomings soon showed them that the *basic* concepts were wrong, and thus that the standard way of viewing the world was inadequate to explain new subatomic discoveries. Even the very basis of what they were doing came into question. Albert Einstein explained the shock of realizing that what *had* worked as reasoning and proof no longer did: "It was as if the ground had been pulled out from under one, with no firm foundation to be seen anywhere, upon which one could have built." Out of his and Planck's quandary, quantum mechanics arose to explain the mysterious phenomena more fully.

Through most of this past century, management and economics remained tied to the "old-physics" view of reality. Using the analytical method, managers and economists reduced the whole into some constructed set of parts, then reduced *those* parts into increasingly *smaller* parts, all along creating enough cohesive theory to attach these parts to those parts—and so on. Because of this elaborate chart of managed interactions, managers could control one specific operation well enough to raise its productivity and/or increase its efficiency. Because of this analytical and mechanical model, business could write plans, create organizations, measure results and control outcomes—elements that tied together a business "strategy" and gave the illusion of making things happen: Add some managerial force at one point, provoke a desired reaction somewhere else in the "machine." Make great staff reductions here, enjoy higher profits there. Add a coupon or promotion now, take in more money later. Create lower interest rates and watch the economy pick up speed shortly thereafter.

The fact that this limited scope of thought might create consequences not anticipated in the models, or could actually be counterproductive in a way that the model could never understand, simply remained outside the purview of the "old-physics" way of thinking. Anomalies to the system—the scientific facts that caused twentieth-century physicists to rethink basic assumptions—created no stir among economists, management theorists and leaders. Economists and management theorists tried hard to make their social studies sound like hard science, seeking to apply the eighteenth-century model of force and counterforce into grandiose models of the overall economy. Like modern Wizards of Oz, each had a firm grip on the hidden controls, and nobody should pay attention to "that man behind the curtain." In the old frame of mind where everyone agreed on institutional objectives, the old machine metaphor seemed to work—at least enough to sustain its viability among the experts.

Like the early twentieth-century physicists caught with old concepts to explain new facts, contemporary institutional leaders must sometimes admit that *their* old concepts, borrowed as they are from outdated "laws of physics," do not fit contemporary realities. Margaret J. Wheatley, in *Leadership and the New Science* (1992), wrote: "The great shock of twentieth-century science has been that systems cannot be understood by analysis." As a result, the institution as "lean machine" is losing its usefulness (not to mention its accuracy) as a metaphor. The machine metaphor suggests rigidity, efficiency, cold technological indifference and forced command-and-control management action. It suggests everything that social institutions are not. It suggests interchangeable parts in situations where any person can simply step forward and replace any other person. Reality is pushing aside that whole metaphoric model. The new model is a vital organism—a model based upon biology, not on physics.

In *The Web of Life* (1996), theoretical physicist Fritjof Capra explained that the entire scientific enterprise was experiencing a paradigm shift from physics to ecology—from the force-and-counterforce way of explaining the world to the systems-within-integrated-systems way of viewing it. According to Capra, "The paradigm that is now receding . . . consists of a number of entrenched ideas and values, among them the view of the universe as a mechanical system composed of elementary building-blocks, the view of the human body as a machine, the view of life in society as a competitive struggle for existence, the belief in unlimited material progress to be achieved through economic and technological growth, and—last, but not least—the belief that a society in which the female is everywhere subsumed under the male is one that follows a basic law of nature." Because of this paradigmatic shift, "Physics has now lost its role as the science providing the most fundamental description of reality. . . . Today, the paradigm shift in science, at its deepest level, implies a shift from physics to the life sciences." In this light, the women as leading indicator becomes clearer. They have remained more in touch with natural processes than have men, who have pursued technological control of nature and people with greater focus.

Capra explains that the old physics was obsessed with quantification and measurement (like Howell Raines's Redneck Way of fishing), as if by giving something a number, the mind could control the subject. The more "precise" the number, the argument suggested, the more the control. The key to the new science is not quantitative exactitude but rather acceptable approximation, because organic systems change constantly and evolve steadily. Also, while the physics explanations encouraged hierarchical structures, the new science thinks in terms of nesting—systems within systems, interacting across all systems without regard to any artificial hierarchy. The "web of life" that Capra uses to title his book is made up of "living systems (networks) interacting in network fashion with other systems (networks)." Margaret Wheatley added to this thought: "Systems thinking is 'contextual,' which is the opposite of analytical thinking."

This type of systems thinking—a term Capra used interchangeably with *ecology*—has several key characteristics: Nothing can be isolated and controlled; systems nest within systems, creating interactive systems; systems thinking is contextual thinking. All of these ways of operating run counter to prevailing mechanical as well as managerial thinking: isolation of subject matter for the purpose of analysis and control; the part is merely a subset of the whole; and cause and effect dominate. This huge shift in scientific explanations, and the attendant shift in thought processes, signals a change as well in the way that institutions operate.

A single example highlights this shift. In 1995, the San Diego Zoo, the nation's preeminent animal-display park, started reworking its display system. Like most zoos, San Diego had organized its displays to match the scientific field of study, rather than the natural habitat from which the individual animals originally were taken. The taxonomic categories (e.g., reptiles, birds, mammals) served as the basis for deciding which creatures went where. That is to say, the zoo used the *analytical* side of science to decide how animals should be displayed to humans. The new system, however, turned away from that rational system and moved toward a *natural* system. Henceforth, animals would appear in their "bioclimatic zone," surrounded by an entire ecology (e.g., African rain forest, U.S. Southwestern desert). By switching to this system, humans observe animals in their context—not isolated and categorized as if the zoo were one giant physical experiment.

The San Diego Zoo has gone from the power of old science to control, to the purpose of new science to develop contexts. Forcing animals to live in isolation without their natural surroundings was the height of scientific arrogance. Creating their own natural ecology inside the zoo moved the display into the life-science metaphor.

American institutions must now make the same shift, from the scientific-management derivative that has dominated organizations for most of the postwar period to more vital, almost organic systems approach. They need to move the central operating metaphor away from "lean machine" and toward "vital organism." In doing so, they will effectively match employee with institution, creating a new relationship that can return loyalty to the employee–employer dynamic.

Once the strategic restructuring of an institution's internal operations has ended, it is at last ready to face the outside world—and also to deal with reassessed individuals in a different way—as reassessed consumers. That area of contact serves as our next topic.

CHAPTER 8

A NEW MARKET REALITY

art way through Steve Martin's play *Picasso at the Lapin Agile* (1996), Einstein is talking with a street-savvy woman who is working on the marketing of the scientist's revolutionary book on relativity. The book will start a process of change from the old Newtonian model of physics to the quantum-mechanics model that would disrupt yet advance modern thought, and the woman believes that everyone should read it.

> "In order for your book to have an impact," she insists, "you've got to have a lot of people read it; every man in the street has got to have one."
> "No," Einstein replies, "only one. Max."
> "Max?" the stunned woman replies.
> "Max Planck, a German physicist, very influential. If he reads it," Einstein concludes, "he makes my reputation."
> Reluctantly, the woman accedes, "Well, you're lucky. If your market is one person and you know his name, you can put a limit on what you're going to spend on advertising."

Here, some would argue, is the greatest physics "product" of the twentieth century, but it is aimed at only one reader, and needs no advertising. With the substance in his product, Einstein insists that just one central figure in his field will be enough to start the word-of-mouth that will guarantee the work's success. How different that simple understanding is from the way in which twentieth-century marketing developed! Spending money to create a noise to force sales is, in fact, a logical consequence of the Newtonian view of the world: Everything is cause-and-effect; force a cause and create the desired effect. Einstein's work led eventually to quantum mechanics and the systems approach to physics, something completely different from and much more dynamic than the force–response world of eighteenth-century physics. In the market realities of the 1990s, traditional marketing theory (especially advertising) gradually has lost its central influence on market development, just as Newtonian physics lost its central position in physics when Einstein published his theory of relativity. Eventually, like physicists with the advent of Einstein's theories, America's institutional leaders will *have to* accede to the new market realities.

In an article entitled "The Philosophy of Instability" (1989), research scientist Ilya Prigogine of the University of Brussels discussed how instability encourages adaptability and creativity, and how human discovery of larger contextual issues is changing human understanding of the natural systems' interrelationships. He states quite simply that the stability the old physics (and management) theory supports actually stifles adaptability and creativity, key elements to a living organism's survival. "Today, the world we see outside and the world we see within are converging," he concluded. "This convergence of two worlds is perhaps one of the important cultural events of our age."

Carrying Prigogine's thoughts forward, we can see that curious forces have entered the marketing field. For example, when First Tennessee Bank changed its social contract, thus creating a happier workforce, the company not only lowered its employee turnover rate, but it also lowered its customer turnover rate. This suggests that disconnecting employee relations from customer relations is counterproductive. The overall systems approach envisions the two as interrelated.

As this employee retention–customer retention dynamic suggests, relationships across traditional categories of management may, in fact, be essential to the health of any company as it moves from the "lean machine" metaphor of the old frame of mind to the "vital organism" metaphor of the new frame of mind. For example, when the founders of Urban Outfitters started to piece together a retail-store concept, they hired potential customers to run the shops. Outfitters' creators knew they wanted to sell apparel and other items to the under-30 generation, but understood very little about what that group liked or needed. Rather than hire an outside consultant to do a study, a survey, or a poll, or run a focus group on what this market segment wanted, the founders simply started hiring personnel from the group they hoped to attract. Next, they structured the company to give these consumer-employees the authority to order, decorate and operate the stores. Managerial walls between marketing and human resources became, as it were, transparent, creating a direct connection between consumers and employees.

Nurturing those connections and enhancing their flow could well be more important than further specialization, categorization and segmentation. Frederick F. Reichheld, in his book *The Loyalty Effect,* discovered (much to his surprise) "[that] business loyalty has three dimensions—customer loyalty, employee loyalty, and investor loyalty—and that they are far more powerful, far-reaching, and interdependent than we had anticipated or imagined." In essence, the new institutional dynamic involves adapting to reassessed individuals and bringing their values, beliefs and attitudes to bear in the workplace and the marketplace.

Individuals who have survived a world out of control and regained their own balance have changed the way that they respond to information beamed at them, whether that information be advertising, on-line data bases or speeches by political figures. At one time, the first response to any message involved asking: "What can I take away from the message?" But now the first reaction is: "Why should I believe any of this message?" and "What amount of time, if any, should be spent on it?" That screening skepticism eliminates most of what advertisers and politicians once thought had impact. To cite just one example, more than half of sampled television viewers in an early 1990s San Francisco study could not remember a single thing about the content of a special news bulletin inserted into the evening's programming. Of those who could remember something about it, the average score was one item recalled for every 19 broadcasts.

Selling has lost much of its impact because consumers greet advertisements, promotions and any new product with increased skepticism. In that type of milieu, creating a personal connection with the customer becomes more important than selling. One historically successful ex-

ample shows the way. Hoechst-Roussel Pharmaceuticals institutionalized the difference between selling (which it once did quite well) and
consulting (which it created to replace selling). In the early 1980s, the
company changed its emphasis from pushing products through the system to creating enduring customer relationships. One sales representative convinced an Alabama hospital that for reasons of service quality,
the institution was buying too many products from Hoechst-Roussel.
When the pharmaceutical company's sales orders from the hospital
plummeted from $17,000 to $3,000 per month, company leaders were
ecstatic. In the years that followed, Hoechst became the principal sup-
plier to a thankful hospital and watched its relationship there steadily
expand. In a similar vein, the pharmaceutical giant stopped calling
on 18 percent of its clients because their needs did not match the
company's strengths. Yet revenues increased by 20 percent from other
clients, because of the time available to consult with their buyers.
Encouraging customers to buy less, like our earlier example of Marshalls growing by reducing its advertising, is counterintuitive to the old
marketing model. Yet connecting with customers advances the bottom
line in the new business environment.

Letting go has in fact gained more believers than one might think
possible. Not only has Procter & Gamble greatly reduced its flow of
new products and other old marketing practices, as mentioned in an earlier chapter, but the idea has spread rather quickly elsewhere. In 1996,
according to *New Product News,* the number of new products reaching
the supermarket shelves dropped by 13 percent as compared with a year
earlier. That was the single largest year-to-year decline since the magazine started tracing this statistic in 1974. Specifically, in 1995, companies introduced 22,572 new products, but that number dropped to
19,572 in the next year. Along the same lines, company-issued coupons
declined by 8 percent from 1995 to 1996, and the number—a hefty
268.5 billion—was the lowest actual sum since 1989. Specifically, Procter & Gamble lowered its couponing expense by 50 percent.

Beyond letting go of new products and coupons, leading companies
have recognized that old sales strategies may be counterproductive in
the new business environment. Southwest Airlines, for example, started

doing away with airline tickets altogether and converted its advertising program into an information-delivery system. Rather than sell the company's image over and over again, the company started using advertisements to say when they were flying, where and at what prices. In essence, they went against all past marketing tactics—and in 1993 and 1994, when other airlines were reporting huge losses, Southwest was profitable. It continued to be so in the years that followed.

The disconnect between traditional marketing techniques and customers brings back the fly-fishing metaphor cited earlier. Standing on the bank of the river and blaring advertising messages to fish no longer gets them to jump into the net. In the era following widespread personal change, the response is different; the noise is now seen as toxic. Customers are moving away from the loudest and most prominent noise-makers, especially if they offer nothing for the consumer's new standard of value. In 1993, some 35 percent of polled consumers thought that star endorsers lacked credibility. Three years later, 53 percent thought those same media stars were no longer credible. Moreover, 63 percent thought the endorsers were just selling the product for a paycheck, and not because they actually thought the item or line had any merit. The consumer's new skeptical screen undermined the celebrity's credibility and made the product message into a purposeful lie.

These new market developments have been difficult to accept for those who enjoyed success using the old model, and that difficulty has prompted some testy statements of denial. In response to the celebrity endorser's lack of credibility in general, for example, one advertising agency representative insisted: "Consumers will say they're not affected by celebrity endorsers, but they are." Paraphrased, he was saying: "I know consumers better than they know themselves." Denial is not a new element in American business, but when combined with organizational muscle memory, it can throw the whole enterprise out of sync.

As with human capital, leaders have spread themselves along a line of responses to the new market realities. Those who have yet to reach their own personal turning points have likewise not recognized that consumers are changing. They continue to hold on to what worked in the past. Some, however, *have* reached their turning points, *have* let go of past models and certainties and *have* explored some ways to address the new consumer. A few leaders have moved past their turning points, through their grounding points, and into their compass points, having developed a full response to the new market realities. They are the only ones moving on.

The three phrases that captured the essence of the three phases of personal reassessment—"get ahead" (prior to turning points), "get a handle" (part of the grounding points) and "get a life" (compass points)—match as well the phases of a branded-products evolution. During the get-ahead period, brands worked most effectively when they could exploit the desire for achievement. Advertisers sought to connect personal achievement—whether it be as homemaker, career wizard or social butterfly—to their products. However, when the world went out of control, and individuals sought to take back control of their personal lives, the value of brands and what they represented changed. They became resources, ways in which people passing through their grounding points could regain some control, and even leverage, in the changing social and economic environment.

As that extensive process slowly gives way to the compass-points era, brands are moving into a period when they can no longer survive on image (achievement) or utilitarian answers (resource). They need to become part of a dynamic process, a collaboration between consumer and company to meet evolving and changing needs—that is, a dialogue. In the first phase, advertising sold the image; and in the second phase, it outlined the solution. In the third phase, advertising needs to initiate interaction—not merely broadcast an image of a product or service, but also create avenues for contact—and then let that interaction encourage the evolution of relationships. But, as we shall see, movement through the three phases is not easy.

CONSUMER DISCONNECT:
FORCING THE INSTITUTIONAL TURNING POINT

The great success of the communities of wealth continues to drive the marketing strategies of those who have most benefited from that success. Indeed, products and services successfully marketed *themselves* for most of the post–World War II era by deploying aspirational messages that harmonized with society's overall aspirational ideal. They created, expanded and exploited the link between brands and individual achievement. In this environment, companies grew by increasing manufacturing capacity—whether by lowering costs, raising quality, enhancing productivity or expanding production. Companies also grew by exploiting distribution skills, utilizing logistical maneuvers to place their services or products close to the consumer. They developed retail power, whether in winning "shelf space" battles or opening their own retail outlets. They added advertising to create an image that connected the brand to the consumer's sense of achievement in a society saturated with images of expanding wealth. All of these successful tactics—increased capacity, distribution power, retail access, advertising imagery—worked because consumers wanted what the brands offered and subscribed to the brand-aspirational model. In short, the concept of a brand as achievement fitted the shared values of the communities of wealth.

Brand names offered reassurance throughout a depression, a world war and a cold war. Brands were consistent, accessible and enduring, and consumers easily recognized their image. Moreover, that image revealed that the purchaser had realized these basic American values and had aspired to some level of affluence and control. These were positive values, and they attracted consumers. In a society that reinforced conformity in the effort to expand wealth, aspirational marketing of brands worked quite well.

Changing world conditions and changing American realities altered American values. Today, they are altering the ways in which individuals relate to institutions and their products and services. Reliability has displaced reassurance; quality has replaced constancy; effectiveness has become more important than image; readily available alternatives have counteracted distribution power; and massive manufacturing capability worldwide has lessened the leverage gained by volume production. This large shift in societal values has diluted the power of brand appeal and imagery. Old-line product names instilled confidence in the system by their mere presence. They had survived market-share battles and won

consumer loyalty. To a large extent, developing and expanding economies elsewhere in the world *still* respond to the brand-as-achievement
concept. Their level of development and their desire to elevate wealth
make the old model work. However, in the U.S., that era has ended.

With the shift in the consumer's desire for effectiveness, new products that do the job better automatically win market share. At one time
distribution power, manufacturing efficiency and image were sufficient
to win brand loyalty. Now, those links may be necessary, but they are no
longer sufficient to gain any kind of market penetration. To create a sustainable relationship, a new connection between company and consumer must take place, and it needs to take place even before those
once-sufficient marketing tools even come into play.

Because many leaders of America's largest corporations have yet to
reach their own turning points, they have yet to let go of past assumptions. Due to this reluctance to recognize real change and undertake the
arduous task of strategically rethinking their institutions' marketing
strategies, most leaders are holding on to the old model of brand as
achievement. If leaders hope to return higher margins to their brands,
they must let go of their old beliefs about the power of brands as symbols of achievement, and about the power of that symbolism to attract a
premium price.

The fashion industry held to the old model as long as it could
before realizing that something had changed. During the era of brand
as achievement, designers turned into fashion soothsayers who could
determine what consumers should wear. They became celebrities, with
magazine photographers following them to parties and there capturing
images of movie stars dressed in their uniquely designed clothes. This
concept became a mass-market reality as fashion names like Calvin
Klein, Donna Karan and Ralph Lauren joined such brand names as Izod
and Brooks Brothers as images that preceded, and even overwhelmed,
substance. That is, they became brands as *achievement.*

Two problems hit the fashion industry at once: competition and radically changed consumers. Competition came from companies exploiting the capabilities derived from the "new industrial revolution," the
manufacturing reality that said someone out there can always produce

anything faster, better and cheaper than the current market has. For example, during the fall 1993 Paris fashion shows, ABS USA executives watched designers send microkilts down the runways. The next day, they sent their staff through the thrift stores in Greenwich Village to locate old kilts, which they then used as design patterns. They stopped production on several other items, put their own microkilt styles into production, and then made them available to Bloomingdale's, Macy's and Saks Fifth Avenue before the fashion shows had even ended in Paris. What is the advantage of fashion design when manufacturing power short-circuits style leadership?

While manufacturing power took away design "originality," changed consumers altered markets in other ways. Essentially, consumers reassessed the role of clothes in their personal lives, and uniformly devalued them. As a result, they insisted on less-expensive items—a price to fit their new value. Used-clothing outlets, outlet malls, store brands and other acceptable alternatives stole business from upper-level designers who had moved down-market with second and third lines, and name-brand boutiques that had drawn customers into department stores. In fact, many reassessed individuals no longer even went to the huge shopping malls because navigating the expansive retail space consumed too much time. With time becoming more important on the individual's personal priority list, recognizing that shopping malls *wasted* time created a physical disconnect between the consumer and an entire distribution system for fashion-industry leaders. Clothes as an expression of stylistic achievement had lost the power to affect consumer markets.

The disconnect between consumers and those holding to the idea of brand as symbol of achievement has become clearer with time. Eighty-eight percent of the respondents to a survey of advertisers thought that consumer promotions could still build a brand's equity. Meanwhile, 65 percent of surveyed consumers said that store brands were just as good as the heavily advertised national brand names. This disparity between what marketers believe they "own" and what consumers think about that ownership reveals the schism between marketers still clinging to brand-image equity and consumers searching for products and services that suit their new standard of value. Meanwhile, 57 percent of large

branded companies have turned care of their brands over to top executives—not to brand managers. With so many issues related to a changing marketplace facing modern corporate executives, adding brand care
to the work load merely erects another barrier between them and their
turning points.

For marketers still clinging to the old image game, the only pathway
forward is dwindling margins. Cigarettes offer a simple example. In the
late 1980s consumers, pressured by their disposable-income squeeze,
looked to reduce their spending and take control of their personal
finances. One tactic they used was to cut back spending on higher-
margin items. As a result, between 1988 and 1993, the market share of
private-label cigarettes jumped from 5 percent of the category to 35 percent. This growth eventually started stealing market share from the category brand leader, Marlboro, which owned 22 percent of the market. In
what became known as "Marlboro Friday," Philip Morris announced on
May 2, 1993, that it was cutting the price of its premiere brand by 40
percent. By playing the low-cost game, the brand, over the next two
years, regained lost market share and even rose to hold 31 percent of the
market, an all-time high. But while this tactic regained market share for
Marlboro, the brand's contribution to corporate profit was $1.5 billion
less than in 1992 before the whole price race started.

Like cigarettes, automobiles have seen their brand-as-achievement
status reduced, principally because consumers have revalued their relationship to the automobile. As consumers looked across the wide array
of purchases they needed to make and the price tag they saw on those
items, they rethought the importance of image in the mix of reasons for
buying one car over another. The result of that consumer reassessment
was to reset the value of cars in the larger context of personal spending.
In general, the new value was lower. As a result, consumers turned to
leasing cars to lower monthly payments (and control budgets) and eventually focused on used cars as an appealing alternative. Like the fashion
industry, the automobile industry faced *both* changed consumers *and*
altered competition.

The principal market-control mechanism for the automobile manufacturers was the franchised distribution system. Franchised dealers

ordered cars, displayed them (keeping huge stocks on the lot), sold them and serviced them. With this organization, manufacturers limited market access to dealers beholden to them. In the 1990s, however, the system started to come apart. In 1950, roughly 50,000 dealers moved product in the country, but by 1997, just 22,750 dealers belonged to the National Automobile Dealers' Association, and 50 were failing every year. Chrysler announced a plan to reduce its dealerships even further, seeking to reduce the number from 4,612 to 4,000 by the turn of the century. The company also started a program to eliminate the 60-day supply of cars that most dealers carry, hoping to create a "custom-car" approach that would have customers order the specific items they wanted on a car and then have that car "made for them" and delivered within two weeks or less.

These actions, however, were simply responses to changes in the marketplace. Used-car superstores like Circuit City's CarMax and Wayne Huizenga's AutoNation were stripping dealerships of their lucrative used-car profits. These huge dealers had an extensive selection on the lot, offered financing right in the office and cut prices to the lowest possible margins.

Huizenga then moved into the new-car dealership business, buying franchises for Ford, Chevrolet, Dodge, Lincoln-Mercury, Saturn, Buick, Mazda, Isuzu, Oldsmobile and Hyundai. This new megadealership transcends manufacturer loyalty and makes the entire enterprise into a commodity-selling business. With their own financing systems, these emerging megadealers also take loan business away from General Motors and others. Moreover, with their size and volume, manufacturers face stiff bargaining for volume wholesale prices, which in turn further drive down the retail price, making matters worse for existing dealers. In essence, what Home Depot did to local hardware stores and "category killers" (huge price-busting retail outlets) did to retail merchandisers, the megadealer system is doing to automobile dealers.

Manufacturers can continue to hold on to the belief that they control their own domain, or they can let go of past models and past certainties and move toward a strategic reassessment of their way of thinking and operating. It appears from early industry reactions that automobile manufacturers have decided to take to the barricades and defend the old brand image.

In 1997, General Motors launched the most widespread marketing reorganization in the company's history, creating brand managers and line-vehicle managers for each of its 82 car models. These new, more powerful positions control everything from the design and manufacturing through the marketing and distribution for the specific model they control. In essence, General Motors, hoping to reverse their loss of market share, which in 1996 fell below 32 percent for the first time in recent history, adopted the same brand-management techniques that other marketers use to sell cereal and toothpaste. In making these changes, company executives revealed their loyalty to the old brand-as-achievement model, and their additional belief that cause-and-effect marketing can still force results in the marketplace.

The entire brand-management mentality is a game played against competitors, to force consumers to prefer a particular brand over another. What General Motors is ignoring, however, is the fact that new consumers no longer look at cars in the same old way. Consequently, the brand-as-achievement approach does not have the same impact on their decisions. In 1984, for example, consumers placed buying a new car third on their "wish list" of things they would like to do. In 1995, consumers placed new cars eleventh on the list. Consumers started buying used cars in record numbers, and keeping their own cars longer. In fact, automobiles on the road in 1995 were older than at any time since 1948. In July of 1995, *Automobile* magazine, which typically pictured the latest and hottest new cars, put used cars on its cover. Given that the average reader of the magazine had an income of over $72,000, the cover story about used cars suggested that the new cars' devaluation had spread across much of the American consumer market. How can a "brand manager," no matter what authority the company grants him or her, affect these consumer realities?

Many leaders may never reach their turning points—despite the widening disconnect between them and the consumer. They simply resurrect old explanations for market troubles, and redouble their efforts to keep the communities-of-wealth approach alive. Those who do reach that turning point, however, soon realize that the consumer actually does have different needs. Consumers moving through their grounding points are looking for answers, for solutions to the problems they face. They have stopped seeing the brand as a symbol of their rising standard of living and look to the brand as a resource, an effective solution to a specific problem.

A BRAND AS RESOURCE
FOR A WORLD OUT OF CONTROL

Consumers who have disconnected from older institutions have moved into a "get smart–get control" mode. They need solutions for the problems thrown at them by the world out of control, and they seek insights that can help them during their grounding-points reassessment. As part of this learning process, as we have seen, they have turned to books, learning organizations, information programming, on-line services, study circles, investment clubs, educational vacations, book clubs, and other resource-driven gatherings to expand their understanding of the changing world and to enrich their own personal-reassessment process. Overall, they have been sending a clear message that they are looking for solutions.

The consumer-solutions search resulted from a linking of learning and skepticism. The more individuals learned, the less they trusted "experts" and authority figures—be they doctors, teachers and lawyers, or traditional leaders like politicians, preachers and business executives. This change in perspective negatively affected what these traditional sources of information had to say. Tainted sources of learning (that is, those sources that have something to gain from providing a particular slant to released information) became suspect. The previously discussed skepticism that reached elections in 1992, 1994 and 1996 spread to consumer behavior. In the past, trust in brand value and convenience was sufficient for many customers, and as a result, consumers granted credibility to salespeople and listened to advertisements as input for decision-making. With skepticism undermining those resources, consumers started honing their own discovery skills to locate needed information and use it to make decisions on their own.

The combination of consumer skepticism and the solutions search created a huge opportunity for those offering access to information without the once unavoidable link to an ensuing purchase. Companies like Morningstar—which rated mutual funds according to their performance, thereby offering consumers an outside perspective on product value—exploited the growing disconnect between consumers and traditionally branded companies. Investors once asked their broker for advice on which funds or stocks or bonds to buy, and that broker, representing Merrill Lynch or Dean Witter or (more recently) a bank like Citibank, simply turned to the company's research and offered a recommendation, quite often connected to a product on which the company made a market or actually originated into a fund. But with the creation of Morningstar, consumers had an independent resource that rated *all* mutual funds and had *no* financial participation in which products were finally sold.

With this new solution available, consumers quickly decoupled their quest for information from their product selection, thus creating a huge opportunity for Charles Schwab and other companies that offered low-cost brokerage fees and little or no advice. Similarly, H&R Block lost its status as the lone tax source for the middle class to Intuit's TurboTax software package, which turned home computers into tax-form generators. Likewise, fee-only advisers—not associated with any insurance company—charge a flat fee to determine overall needs for their clients and then to recommend which type of insurance to buy. As a result, the new consumer reaches an insurance company already armed with the necessary information, bypassing the sales pitches of company-designated agents for a specific company's products. This consumer shift also created numerous opportunities for insurance companies without expensive field-sales representatives to grab business from branded insurance companies by selling directly to the informed customer.

The consumer who had disconnected from the old brand model and initiated a quest for solutions created a market opportunity for new products and services which essentially disintermediated the historically direct relationship between brands and consumers. Services, products and individuals successfully inserted themselves between the original brand producer (whether product or service) and the traditionally loyal customer, making it more difficult for the original brand provider to make direct contact with the consumer. Until recently, automobile manufacturers dealt directly with the customer through their franchised dealer systems. Today, a customer can go on-line and search for consumer-advocate reports on different automobiles, use a consumer representative to bargain for prices with wholesale outlets, and go back on-line to find the best rates on a car loan—all without making contact with the manufacturer or the manufacturer's representative (dealer). Should the consumer choose the AutoNation option, he or she will be making contact with a dealer who has no special loyalty to *any* specific manufacturer, and will even provide financing directly on-site. The brand-name leverage has vanished from the system.

Banks, credit-card companies, insurance companies, brokerage houses and many other consumer-finance companies face disintermediation as a market reality. Not only have consumers revalued products and services across the board, but also, new decision-support tools have arisen to make their choices easier and less expensive. In a survey of 2,000 Americans, 64 percent reported that reasonable price was the main consideration in their purchases, and less than half said that name brands had some degree of influence on their decisions. These brand entities once had direct contact with consumers, but more and more companies are disintermediating this relationship, turning huge branded companies into "waiting corporations." That is, without direct contact, they can only wait for consumers to learn about their product choices. Consumers read, download or otherwise acquire judgments about products. They seek independent advice and then make a purchase from a resource that has no loyalty to the producer. Meanwhile, the branded company waits for the consumer to decide.

Becoming a waiting corporation is the worst-case scenario in a disintermediated market and also the most likely scenario—given the reassessed values of a more skeptical and highly price-sensitive consumer. With new consumers and new market forces, the disconnect between brand name and consumer is complete. Waiting for customers to enter their stores became too costly for Boscov's, a Pennsylvania department-store chain. Shedding an outer image as a retailer, even in the case of its locally successful brand name, the store started a new approach. Rather than accepting Boscov's as a waiting company with inventory waiting for customers, executives wanted the store to be more actively involved in responding to its clientele's new values and priorities. Identifying with the consumers' quest for solutions, they started a "Campus of Courses" program. Consumers could look to Boscov's as a community of meaning that offered classes in Cooking for One, Spring Floral Design, Women's Financial Planning, Understanding Long-Term Care and "Honeybug—The Greatest Fishing Lure." Boscov's activity brought the consumer quest for solutions *into the store,* in this way creating a relationship based upon learning and assistance rather than on transactions.

In the waiting-game market (where branded companies hold on to the old market mentality), price often becomes the only competitive weapon. Whether they want to or not, companies disconnected from their customers drift into a market battle to become the low-cost provider. That reality is what drove many companies to overburden themselves with downsizing and reengineering projects in an attempt to rebuild margins and profits. Contrary to their original intentions, the projects in many cases resulted in dwindling margins and a less dynamic above-the-line. Cost-cutting lost much of its leverage because someone else always did the job cheaper, better and faster.

To get out of the margin-squeeze cycle, companies (as the fly-fishing metaphor suggests) must understand how the consumers now live in order to learn about their needs and to develop a way to reconnect with them. In a world out of control, helping hassled consumers get a handle on their daily routines has been a successful way to create a link. Recognizing that the individual in the midst of the grounding-points reassessment needs assistance to get smart and get control has opened the door for many new companies, which have managed to attract customers away from larger and rather staid businesses.

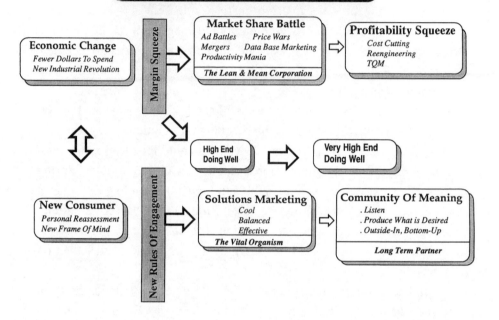

In 1989, grocery stores sold $8.2 million in prepared salads—in general, bags of cut lettuce. By 1996 that same product, having brought a solution to time-pressed homemakers, topped $1.1 billion in business. The price differential between a head of lettuce and these "prepared" salads is three and four to one. Clearly, consumers will pay for solutions.

At a Denver restaurant called A Piece of Quiet, parents "check" their kids at one door, and then go through another door to eat a quiet meal in the main dining room. In the children's section, new kids are met with some treats—healthy foods like apples and carrot sticks—but soon enjoy broader options, including pizza and hamburgers. This solution was so simple, and the ensuing demand so great, that the restaurant had to place a two-hour limit on the parents, who essentially did not want to leave.

For those who cannot even reach the grocery store in order to buy prepared salads, or load the kids to get them to a day-care-style restaurant, other options have arisen. Gourmet Taxi, Dinners to Go, Takeout

Taxi and other delivery services have created successful businesses delivering restaurant meals to homes. Customers who want ease and quality pay full restaurant prices, plus a delivery fee and tip. By the early 1990s, individual chains were reporting delivering up to 30,000 meals per week.

Consumer solutions in an out-of-control world have their moment, then eventually give way to other solutions that address more pressing problems. Still, their success reveals that consumers forget about the lowest price when a solution enters the equation. These companies benefit from consumers' thinking about saving time, for example, even before they think about specific ways to do so. As a result, when customers learn that restaurant food can be delivered to their homes, they take advantage of the offer and expect to pay more for the service.

Consumers in the discovery mode take nothing for granted, respond to different messages and think nearly everything through from their new point of view. Consequently, they now have *two* stages to their decision process: discovery (learning) and response (purchase). Companies wishing to reconnect with these new consumers must participate in the discovery-solutions process or risk losing the chance to participate in the response-purchase process. Without offering resources to assist the consumer in learning about a potential purchase, companies can find themselves relegated to the status of a waiting corporation—waiting for consumers to decide and then competing—mostly on price—against other waiting corporations. Meanwhile, those who facilitate the decision-making process have already established a link with the potential customer, thereby creating an edge going into the purchase process.

When leaders reach their personal turning point, they soon realize that the old mentality that guided the communities of wealth has become anachronistic and so has to change. They see that consumers have changed, and that the old ways of spending no longer work because today's consumers have different needs. Consumers in their grounding-points reassessment are rethinking their personal lives, and that offers an opportunity for companies that let go of past models and tactics to look afresh at what individuals are doing and how they are thinking.

Part of letting go of the old marketing model involves recognizing that the company no longer "owns" its brand, as it did when the brand-as-achievement model thrived. As part of the response to the world out of control, the brand became a facilitator or resource for consumers, and when it did, its "ownership" moved closer to the consumer. In the past, brands inspired people to act, but, more recently, consumers have been pushing back against direct selling, forcing brands to become facilitators in order to prosper. In this phase consumer needs, values and priorities establish successful brands. For a quick example of how this works, consider the difference between McDonald's, which in early 1997 lowered the price of some of its sandwiches to 55 cents, while Starbuck's charged nearly $3 for a cup of a certain type of coffee. One company was struggling to be the low-cost provider in the old marketing game, while the other was offering a reward, a moment of quiet, a solution in the context of a world out of control.

Moving beyond the world out of control and past the grounding points, consumers started looking to brands to be part of an ongoing dialogue between consumer and company. This dynamic interaction between consumer and company is becoming a central feature of successful marketing strategies. The new dynamic requires sharing information because companies can no longer "control" markets by retaining information. Like the opening-up processes that must take place within the company as part of the new social contract, an open-architecture relationship must also develop between company and customers. This open institution reinforces a consumer–company dialogue that can first create and then evolve successful brands in the communities-of-meaning era.

BRAND AS DIALOGUE:
RECONNECTING WITH THE NEW CONSUMER

Letting go of past practices and opening the organization to direct consumer input are key elements in any company's grounding-points reassessment. Companies that create open systems for employee relationships will find opening their organizations to consumer input equally necessary and effective. While many companies are spending sizable amounts of money on what they call "relationship marketing," they are still missing the larger issues. Relationship marketing seeks to deliver the feeling that a customer has a personal relationship with a company, usually through one employee. But what happens then? How does the company solicit consumer input and bring that input to bear on company operations and decisions? How much power to make real changes does the contact employee have?

The flow of information from outside the company is essential if a company wishes to be competitive in the years ahead. But that remains just one part of the necessary and sufficient restructuring that must be completed. The total renovation of internal relationships leads to the overall renovation of consumer relations—and relationship marketing, even if done with best intentions, is only a small piece of the overall renovation.

Having passed through their reassessment periods, companies, leaders, employees and customers alike are moving ahead to their compass-points/community-of-meaning structure. For brands, this means that having left behind the concept of brand as achievement associated with the communities of wealth and having developed a brand as a resource marketing approach to help consumers with their own reassessment, they now move toward a new concept: brand as dialogue. The open and interactive collaboration between customer and company—the dialogue—and the open social contract between company and employee help to convert a company from a community of wealth to a community of meaning. Thus, barriers between them come down, and interaction is constant. Profits then result from a different and better relationship.

Oddly enough, the best examples of this appear outside the business realm. Public journalism, community policing and primary nursing exemplify new strategies that allow citizens to set agendas and to drive the individual–institutional dialogue. For "professionals" in old-style journalism, criminology and medical care, this shift in focus has been at least difficult, and in many instances impossible. Top criminologists complain that community policing does not parade enough power in front of citizens. Influential newspapers like the *New York Times* and the

Washington Post print editorials complaining that public journalism eliminates the professional's authority to decide what is important. Doctors insist that it takes too much of their own time to apportion care to floor nurses. To let go of power or to relinquish authority in their own areas of expertise just sounds wrong. *They* are the trained specialists after all; *they* know what needs to be controlled or reported. If any of those professionals hope to regain consumer confidence in the years ahead, they must first relinquish their belief that they "know what's best."

Public journalism started when subscribers grew weary of journalists telling them what was important and commenting on what was wrong. The hopelessness (and even helplessness) that the journalistic enterprise instilled in its readers impeded the ability of the community to deal with its problems. Some newspapers, like the Charlotte (North Carolina) *Observer,* asked citizens to set an agenda for national elections, and then turned that agenda into questions they put to all the candidates. If the candidates did not address those specific questions and chose instead to dodge the issues, the *Observer* left the candidate's allotted space blank. In essence, the public pushed the agenda, and the newspaper forced the candidate's response to that agenda.

The Maine study circles cited in the chapter on communities of meaning emerged from local newspaper publishers' realizing that they had a duty to enliven civic involvement in solving the region's problems. Likewise, the local newspaper supported and nurtured Chattanooga's efforts to reset its civic agenda and establish a new course of action. Also, the Tallahassee (Florida) *Democrat* has sustained a community-based project to reform and better the city. The result has been the lowering of crime and greater civic involvement. In fact, the project became so popular that Knight-Ridder, the parent company, agreed to fund future projects, rather than force the local paper to raise money.

Public journalism opens the institution's doors to the subscriber/citizen. That restructures everything that happens inside the company as well, as professional journalists are forced to let go of excessive professionalism and learn what the new relationship is between press and citizen. That lesson was hard but in the end necessary for fashion designers, who thought they would always "lead" the fashion world. It has also been hard on traditional criminologists, who still insist that a policeman's job is arresting criminals and enforcing the peace.

Community policing offers an approach to law enforcement that is closer to where society is headed than was the old law-enforcement model. According to George Kelling, who has studied policing methods as well as worked for the chief of police in New York City (and with other urban police forces), "All police lore . . . said that you had to have police in cars. It was a matter of professional ideology. Powerful cars augmented their sense of authority. If you had police in cars," Kelling concluded, "they would move swiftly through city streets and create the feeling of omnipresence."

Under the community policing system, individual officers are responsible for the specific areas they patrol. Day in and day out, they study their own territory; officers are not moved around to different routes and unfamiliar constituencies. That is, they are not interchangeable. Under the old "professional" model, which insisted, "any officer, anywhere," each part was to be the same as every other part of "the force." With the community policing model, officers become part of only the community they patrol. They thereby get to know who they can trust and who they cannot, who most needs their help, who feels most vulnerable, who owns which apartments and businesses, and so on. They know their neighborhood as a functioning culture. "I discovered," Kelling admitted about his own conversion to community policing, "that the police on foot patrol were involved in the enforcement of laws against low-level offenses, such as public drinking, such as panhandling. And they negotiated, in a sense, the rules of the street."

Street-level officers have the power to help citizens redress grievances against the city, and they have sufficient connections throughout the bureaucracy to make things happen when changes are needed. They can order lights replaced in street lamps, or call in repair people to take care of faulty drainage systems or any other city service. They can help get kids into drug-rehabilitation programs and can address the courts in order to secure trespass orders so as to empower residents to control local troublemakers.

The ultimate resolution to many problems that communities face daily has moved from the bureaucracy to the street-level police officer. In places like Houston and St. Petersburg, Florida, community policing had trouble because those cities did not take the time to train the officers to make sure they were heeding their new area-policing plan's initial principles or following up with community leaders. In short, they announced a program but did not implement it fully. Yet, community policing worked in Portland, Oregon, specifically because the bureaucracy was *already* interested in responding to neighborhood concerns. City workers had earlier sought input from outside their own institutions. Taken together, public journalism and community policing offer solid examples of strategic restructuring that can help an institution let go of past practices and move on.

Primary nursing developed at Beth Israel Hospital in Boston because several nurses, most importantly Joyce Clifford, realized that the old way of doing things was ineffective. "The nursing aides, who had the least preparation, had the most contact with the patients. But they had no authority of any kind. They had to go to their supervisor to ask if a patient could have an aspirin. The supervisor would then ask the head nurse, who would then have to ask the doctor. The doctor would ask how long the patient had been in pain. Of course, the head nurse had absolutely no idea, so she'd have to track down the aide to ask her, and then relay that information back to the doctor. . . . The system was hierarchical, fragmented and impersonal, and overly administered."

What Mitchell Rabkin, a hospital administrator, realized was that "The nurses are the ones who care for the patients. They are who patients see every day, and they form the largest group of a hospital's employees. In the last analysis, a hospital is a nursing institution more than anything else. The rest of us function as support staff for the nurses." That changed context for viewing the hospital changed the institution's way of running things. Nurses became the center of hospital work. At preparatory meetings, nurses assumed responsibility for individual patients and gathered a team of assistants to care for them. As with community policing, nurses did not move around from wing to wing. Rather, they stayed with their patients, becoming familiar with everything about them—and thus becoming the local authorities with whom the doctor conversed about care issues. The new system distributed authority down to the person who met with the customer (patient), and then all operations, from doctor to linen service, had to respond to the new primary-care giver.

Journalists, police officers and nurses were simply the bottom rung of the old hierarchical-management ladder. However, in the new environment, they have become the center of power because they maintained direct contact with those being served. The new systems reverse old power arrangements because sustaining loyalty has become essential to success. For institutions hoping to sustain customer loyalty, ongoing contact with steady interaction is necessary. Because that can be time-consuming, some institutions reach dire circumstances before they accept strategic restructuring as necessary. Vermont's Bennington College reached that point. Enrollment at the once-vaunted liberal-arts college had declined from a lively 600 in the mid-1980s to under 400, and nearly a quarter of each year's freshman class was leaving before the sophomore year. Tuition increases had only made the situation worse, actually resulting in a decline in revenues that upped the annual operating deficit to $2 million. Also, faculty had become hardened in their expectations of what the institution should deliver.

Most colleges and universities facing reduced financing from tuition, state subsidies and endowment declines have reverted to the same tactics that companies typically use in tight situations. Administrators first turn their attention to issues of efficiency and productivity—raising classroom size, increasing teaching hours, and adding satellite and computer distance-learning programs. Next, they raise additional revenues by increasing tuition. Then, they make across-the-board budget cuts, hurting successful programs as well as weaker ones. Finally, they retreat to core competencies, eliminating some extraneous departments and focusing only on preselected areas of expertise. After all of these efforts, however, many still resort to selling advertising space in their facilities, renaming facilities for commercial donors and sticking logos on athletic fields.

Bennington College chose another path. When the college hired a new president, Elizabeth Coleman, *real* change started to happen. She closed all academic divisions (departments), released a third of the faculty and abandoned the school's limited-tenure policy. She also lowered tuition costs as well as room-and-board prices. But most important, she restructured the curriculum to address the genuine concerns and interests of students. Disciplines and academic specialists gave way to interdisciplinary courses across the curriculum, and the college charged individual faculty members with the responsibility of completely educating a small group of students. This was not a college counselor system. It was a full mentoring system.

The next year's incoming class sent enrollment down even further, but the college stayed with its programs. Strategic restructuring is a multiyear task that requires staying the course, even when a weakness surfaces. New faculty expressed excitement about the new responsibilities, and performing artists (a feature the college had lost over time) returned in greater numbers to the faculty. Private foundations and private donors supported the strategic restructuring, offering nearly $5.2 million to see the institution through its transition period—the largest yearly amount raised in the school's history. One year later, the college received 8,000 student requests for information (another high). John Barr, the investment banker and poet who headed the college's Board of Trustees, explained his excitement about the entire venture: "Bennington now stands in a field of dreams. Build it, and they will come."

Microsoft and Bill Gates made just such a turnaround, though the software giant made what could be called its "corporate pivot" within just a few short months. Historically, the company had focused its energy and resources on developing a "closed architecture" system. Operating systems handled only the company's own software, and the Microsoft Network (MSN) and Windows 95 were intended to force users to refer to Microsoft as their interface with the computer, their link to MSN's programming and services and their connection to the Internet. The company's ostensible goal was to take proprietary control of the user, and not let go until he or she turned off the computer.

In December 1995, however, Bill Gates surprised his employees when he announced that every bit of energy, ingenuity and money that

Microsoft had available would henceforth be put at the service of making Microsoft compatible with the Internet. Rather than control the user, Microsoft would facilitate the user's connection to the Internet. This more-open-architecture approach (meaning that all systems were now perceived as equally important and equally accessible) made the work at Microsoft fun again—at least Bill Gates said it was more enjoyable. Proprietary systems closed off the company from its customers, as more and more of them migrated to the open-access Internet. Recognizing that the old style of control was simply no longer possible, Gates moved quickly to become a facilitator.

Liz Claiborne also reached just such a turning point. Like Bennington College and Microsoft, Claiborne faced a changed business environment. In the 1980s, Claiborne was one of the most profitable and successful apparel companies, but because of market changes beyond its control (consumer changes), earnings declined steadily from 1990 to 1995. When Saks Fifth Avenue, an important client, finally dropped the line, the action sent a clear wakeup message to top Claiborne management. In the past, the company had targeted repeat customers who would return to freshen their wardrobes, thereby creating a steady business. The new consumer, however, put an end to that steady business.

Fortunately, Claiborne executives needed only to look to Dana Buchman, a division of Claiborne, for a model of how to change. Buchman had created a huge sensation in the bridge clothing market (that category of price that spread between mass and designer markets) by spending more time asking customers what they thought of the clothes and little or no time marketing and selling the styles. Buchman personnel actually went into the dressing rooms with potential customers, to ask them what they thought of the apparel—and then the company took that input and revised the line, constantly. Buchman actually halted a factory production line when store contacts learned that customers thought a blouse neckline was too low.

Claiborne initiated just such an open link with its customers, letting go of its past practices of creating styles and forcing them on the market. While the company did pass through a period of cost reductions, it quickly moved into a customer-feedback mode, collecting comments on apparel from roughly 6,000 individuals in the first year of the turn-around. The messages gleaned from these discussions led to a reworking of the entire line and the introduction of new features. Profits started to rise, as did the company's stock value—which grew from the mid-teens in 1995 to over $42 by the end of 1996.

Direct consumer involvement in brand creation creates sustainable relationships which lower marketing costs and expand profit margins. According to Thomas A. Stewart, author of *Intellectual Capital* (1997), "thinking and invention" represent the most important part of any knowledge company. Moreover, "Employees, companies and customers share joint and several ownership of the assets and output of knowledge work. . . . This change upsets the nature and governance of corporations." Thinking about institutions from this shared ownership perspective can help a company undergo its strategic restructuring.

For some, that process has already happened. Buckman Laboratories International, based in Memphis, offers a good example of a company moving on, specifically in terms of customer relations. When Bob Buckman's father died of a heart attack on his office couch and left the labs to his son, the young owner had a moment of insight. Looking around at the way his father had managed the company, Bob knew something needed changing. Every decision, process and venture passed through his father's office. "I thought, this is too much work," the young owner explained. Even before delving into the leadership role, he had reached his turning point and had decided to let go of the company's past practices.

During a conversation with Jan Carlzon, the former head of Scandinavian Airlines, one comment stuck in Buckman's head: "An individual without information cannot take responsibility; an individual who is given information cannot but help take responsibility." After thinking about Carlzon's experiences, said Buckman later, "I realized that if I can give everybody complete access to information about the company, then I don't have to tell them what to do all the time. The organization," he insisted, "starts moving forward on its own initiative." He also realized that this type of change would require a complete cultural over-haul—an inversion of typical company operations.

In March 1992, Buckman created a Knowledge Transfer Department to enable and guide this organizational transformation. The company eventually put its entire communications network on CompuServe, an on-line service. Four years after that undertaking, Buckman said that the experience had taught him four things: the necessity for customer involvement; the techniques for sharing knowledge; the importance of basic values (he printed company "values" on a laminated card and gave them to everyone); and how to rethink the concept of measurement ("There are no absolutes"). In other words, that four-year period allowed the company to move through its grounding-points reassessment and establish the basic important elements of the organization's compass points.

The key change involved a shift toward engaging the consumer. Distributed knowledge within the company was just a first step. Buckman suggested a formula concerning customer contact: "The number of people in the organization working on the relationship with the customer relative to the total organization will determine the momentum of the organization." He acted upon that thought, creating an electronic communications system, called K'Netix, which placed the company's entire work force and knowledge base at the customer's service. Restructuring access to knowledge (not through the company but directly to the customer) changed the way the company worked. In 1979, when Buckman's father died, just 16 percent of the company's employees engaged customers directly. By 1996, that figure had risen to 50 percent, and Buckman set a turn-of-the-century goal of 80 percent. "If an employee is not effectively engaged with the customer," demands Buckman, "why are they employed?"

To Buckman, the purpose of knowledge-sharing is to become a source for that knowledge in the customer's mind. Because so many services and products can be duplicated elsewhere, he understands that connecting with the client for other reasons creates a relationship that precedes any transaction. It creates a sustainable relationship. "Over the years," Buckman summarizes, "people have taught themselves to hoard knowledge to achieve power. We have to reverse that: The most powerful people are those who become a source of knowledge by *sharing* what they know."

Buckman also changed the compensation system within the company to reinforce the importance of connecting with the customer. The K'Netix system allows employees anywhere in the world to place a question on the bulletin board, and any other employee in the world to respond. The idea is that any client has access to the company's entire wealth of knowledge. One employee exclaimed: "If you are a global company, there's somebody awake and working all the time. Having K'Netix gives us the capability to respond. We wake up, they go to sleep—when they wake up, the answer is on the screen. It's unbelievable." Also, any employee with a special insight about a service, a product or a special-client solution can post that on the system for all to learn.

To make that system work, however, the leader had to add his personal involvement in the system (Buckman, too, answers questions on the system), and he had to establish that the structural changes were important. Buckman told his employees: "Those of you who have something intelligent to say now have a forum in which to say it. Those of you who will not or cannot contribute also become obvious. If you are not willing to contribute or participate, then you should understand that the many opportunities offered to you in the past will no longer be available." He knew that making changes without changing the measurement and compensation systems would be ineffective.

What the Buckman Labs example reveals is that changed relationships with customers require changed relationships with employees. To single out one area and focus on just that without reconsidering the entire range of relationships that constitute a company is merely another project under the old mentality: divide, analyze, break down into segments, incrementally manage the tiniest unit. The whole set of connections between customers and employees, and among employees, becomes open and flowing both ways. Hierarchical and categorical barriers come down, and information and knowledge flow freely.

Buckman's primary purpose was to engage clients in a sustainable

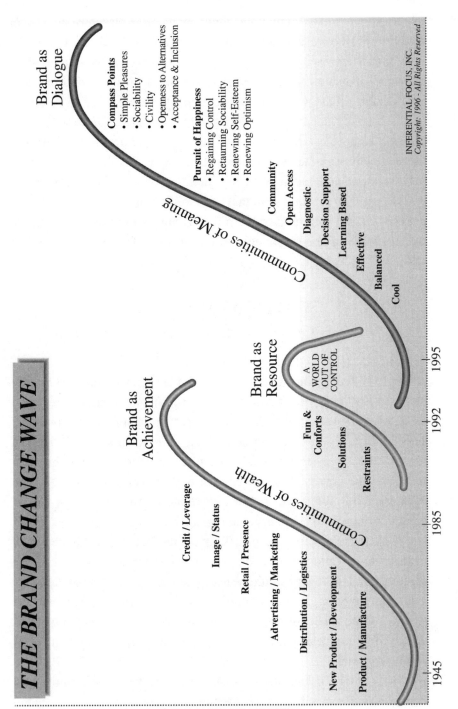

THE BRAND CHANGE WAVE

Brand as Dialogue

Compass Points
- Simple Pleasures
- Sociability
- Civility
- Openness to Alternatives
- Acceptance & Inclusion

Pursuit of Happiness
- Regaining Control
- Returning Sociability
- Renewing Self-Esteem
- Renewing Optimism

Community
Open Access
Diagnostic
Decision Support
Learning Based
Effective
Balanced
Cool

Communities of Meaning

Brand as Achievement

Credit / Leverage
Image / Status
Retail / Presence
Advertising / Marketing
Distribution / Logistics
New Product / Development
Product / Manufacture

Communities of Wealth

Brand as Resource

A WORLD OUT OF CONTROL

Fun & Comforts
Solutions
Restraints

MARKET SHARE / MARGINS

1945   1985   1992   1995

relationship—and to do that, the company had to restructure the way in which employees related among themselves and with clients. Everyone, including Buckman, is on K'Netix, and to everyone, including Buckman, the dedication and focus of resources means commitment and involvement all the way through the company. That level of involvement tells everyone, including the clients, that the transfer of knowledge is critically important, and it makes the organizational transformation more thorough and sustainable. Assessing the company's strategic restructuring, Buckman concluded: "The first year, [employees and clients] think you're crazy. The second year, they start to see; and in the third year, you get buy-in." He summarized the process, suggesting the right perspective for undertaking a strategic restructuring: "The whole thing is a journey."

CRITICAL INSIGHT:
Context Learning and Context Retailing

At the 1997 Technology, Entertainment and Design Conference (TED7), historian Daniel Boorstin described the two things that most threatened the vitality of American technology: bureaucrats and professionalism. The first are afraid of doing something "for the first time," and the second seeks to establish standards and controls to arrogate unto professionals the power that knowledge brings. He could just as well have been speaking about the troubles encountered by public journalism, community policing, primary nursing and any large institution seeking to make a strategic restructuring. Boorstin suggested that "amateurism" made Silicon Valley successful, and that the amateur's sense of play, creativity and discovery would be necessary for the success of the Internet, technology in general, and indeed society, in the years ahead. The crowd, composed of software designers and others involved with developing computer-related interactivity, rose to their feet clapping and yelling approval.

What Boorstin had done was give a context for the tensions and struggles under way in the area of technology. His explanation placed in perspective most everything from why some technology companies have their moment and then fade, to why censorship arises, and further to why the U.S. has raced ahead in Internet technologies. He had placed the entire range of social events in an historical perspective and had suggested a way out for those seeking to understand the situation.

Context has become absolutely essential to grasping what is taking place in society, no matter what the area of examination. Seeing the whole range of actions in a set pattern—the thing the Magic Eye requires of its enthusiasts—is essential to understanding the specifics of what needs to be done. That is why companies which become resources of knowledge create important and lasting connections with their customers. But an even closer look at this resource transfer could prove helpful.

Data, information and knowledge are levels of awareness along a continuous scale. Data are facts in isolation—the specific number of this, or the particular color of that. In common language, "Do you have the data?" means do you have specific, unconnected facts. Information emerges when data are combined to make a point about a topic. Again in common language, "information retrieval" means to acquire data within a specific category, or to piece together data in one category. Knowledge is information *in context.* In common language, "she's knowledgeable" means she has accumulated information within a larger context of theory or experience and has that learning at her disposal. All of these differ from wisdom, which would be knowledge in perspective.

These levels of awareness depend upon the mind for the ideas that make them make sense. Ideas, according to Theodore Roszak in *The Cult of Information,* create information. The phrase "mindless statistics" has some validity because data have yet to have the mind's ideas give them shape. Developing a context involves using the mind to create links between units of information in order to make connections and draw that information into a usable and comprehensible pattern.

"Information overload" is simply the lack of context for what temporarily appears to be too much data. The problem really is not a surplus of information; rather, it is too little context, the absence of a framework in which to assemble and order that information. As a result, people have often turned away from newspapers, with 17 of the 25 city news-papers losing subscribers over the past three years—too much infor-mation, too little context. Similarly, the evening news on the three networks has steadily lost viewers, down by nearly one-third in the three years ending in 1996. Many journalists and politicians confuse opinion with context, a mistake they make at their peril. Meanwhile, connec-tions to the Internet, where individuals can access (and assess) informa-tion they have contexts for, or discuss information in an interactive format, continues to attract more and more users. The entire "get smart" movement within the grounding-points phase involves not the accumu-lation of information but the development of knowledge—and, many people hope, movement toward wisdom.

Companies have been slow to recognize this quest for context in their employees and in consumers alike. Likewise, politicians continue to speak in generalities at their audiences that are not only devoid of relevant information but curiously lacking in a real context—ideology hardly substitutes for knowledge. Yet, some businesses have pieced together a context for their customers, managing to create a "world" in which purchasing decisions can take place within a larger context. As a result, these stores solve consumer gift-giving problems and also address their own interest in focusing on a specific area of knowledge.

No Kidding, for example, is a toy store in Brookline, Massachu-setts, that has embedded itself in the local community, creating con-sumer loyalty that surprises even the store's owner. The key to the business's success is not its merchandise—it does not stock Barbies, Nintendos, toy guns or violent video games. Rather, its success derives from the context change the owner made before opening No Kidding. Judy Cockerton explains: "I'm taken aback when people ask me if I'm an entrepreneur. No, I say, I'm a teacher." This context shift created opportunities for her to exploit and suggested unique pathways forward in her business. She hires retired or moonlighting teachers and graduate students studying to be teachers and works to develop the educational thrust to everything in her store. She trains personnel to answer ques-tions that go well beyond product-based issues. For example, the store's teachers know how to handle a parent's request for what to get a hyperactive child and how to guide the parents' effective development of that child. She is teaching in a store-based classroom.

This store also creates closer ties to the customers by offering special services. It wraps gifts at no extra charge, accepts returns without receipts, makes sizable contributions to local schools and grants discounts to teachers, grandparents and donors to public television. The shop has storytellers visit and holds contests to encourage kids to write. Its success is not because of low prices—some products sell for $10 more at No Kidding than at nearby Toys "R" Us. Nonetheless, while megastore Toys "R" Us was cutting back its outlets because of poor sales, No Kidding was expanding to meet demand, launching new stores elsewhere in the Boston area.

Rethinking the context under which an institution operates offers insight into the direction in which a strategic restructuring might best go. The San Diego Zoo, when it restructured its displays to present animals in their natural habitat, made a context change. They shifted from the analytical, scientific presentation to the life-science approach. They presented systems interacting with systems, rather than separate specific creatures displaying their behavior in isolation. The High Museum of Art in Atlanta rearranged much of its permanent collection around themes that recur over time, across cultures and via different media. Unlike the typical museum, which organizes works of art by historical time-period, culture of origin and art history styles (i.e., the intellectual categories of professional scholars), the new presentation offers a different perspective on what art is and why humans create it. An African chief's stool sits next to a contemporary American artist's chair and ottoman to link the thought that furniture is an extension of the human form. The context is not about intellectual structures but about human interaction with forms. Paintings from different parts of the world from different time periods, all focusing on the power of natural forces, hang in the same room. Ronni Baer, curator of European art for the museum, conceded that the new thematic structure "radically altered the way I think about the collection."

These context shifts prompt innovative thoughts, helping the viewer to understand in a different way the objects on display. Companies can sustain idea- or context-based connections with the customer better than they can with product- or price-based connections. Furthermore, stronger connections create steadier, more sustainable market behavior. In retailing, this same kind of shift can bring a positive response from consumers. The key to the shift, however, is a contextual shift in the institution and its leaders.

Customers do not shop simply for price. They are looking for a link, something that connects with their new point of view and makes them feel comfortable with their new set of values. Old retailing models do not work as well because they push a point of view and a mind-set that consumers are slowly leaving behind. Opening up to the new consumer means recognizing the need for a community-of-meaning context for marketing. When customers enter a fully stocked Urban Outfitters, for example, they enter a retail space constructed around a subculture's mind-set. Within a relatively small space, items as diverse as candles, condiments, clothes, dishes and greeting cards are available. The stores do not have a wide variety of these items—only those that match the attitudes and perspectives of their chosen market: young people, roughly under 30 years of age.

Unlike large department stores, Urban Outfitters units do not offer something for everyone, and they do not stock goods with only the cheapest prices. Instead, the company surrounds the browsers with choices consistent with those customers' personal perspectives on life and the world. Browsing through the store, the customer encounters a physical embodiment of an entire perspective on the world, made material through a variety of products. Like-minded individuals who shop at Urban Outfitters are part of a community of individuals who live similar lives and view events around them with the same emotional detachment. As mentioned earlier, the store's owner gathered this information by hiring employees from the targeted market and letting them choose the merchandise and design the individual stores.

Creating a context for retailing is not always generation-based, but context retailers do bridge many categories of merchandising for the sake of a unified perspective. Their appeal has affected mainstream retailers. Between 1991 and 1996, traditional bookstores (chains and independents) watched their market share decline from 54 percent to 45 percent. While some of that loss went to on-line bookstores, much of it, according to *Publishers Weekly,* went to context retailers. Williams Sonoma, which sells everything pertaining to cooking, displays a Kitchen Library. Smith & Hawkin, which offers everything related to gardening, carries books on the subject as well. Likewise, Crate & Barrel, Rand McNally's, F.A.O. Schwarz, museum shops and others carry books as part of their overall focus on a certain context.

Lower and lower prices have marked the retail environment for most of this decade, despite a steadily expanding economy. Outlet malls, discount stores and category killers lowered prices and won a market because reassessed individuals thought less of clothing. However, consumers quickly converted those new lower prices to the products' new market prices. Once they made that mental connection, then the connection between them and retailers dwindled, and any place that had a best price could win. In the Santa Monica pedestrian mall, shoppers can enter the Virtual Emporium, use the store's computers to browse through every store in the mall and to select items by price. "You can only look into so many stores," explained one happy Emporium shopper. The result of this meta-store (i.e., a store about stores) is that shoppers can locate the cheapest price in the area before buying. This process immediately converted the other stores in the mall into waiting corporations. One response to this hardened shopping edge is the creation of an environment that brings shoppers into the "feel" of a particular point of view and that also builds upon the community of like-minded individuals.

For the past three decades, regional malls supplied an expansive variety of merchandise that allowed shoppers to look and look until they found exactly what they wanted. Reassessed consumers have neither the time nor the inclination to follow that model any longer. As a result, context retailers offer a shopping advantage to time-pressed consumers, and consumers pay more for that convenience and lifestyle connection. Offering a context is a way out of the margin squeeze that typifies the modern consumer market. Knowledge about consumers, about society and about employees builds that context.

CHAPTER 9

LEADERSHIP AND
SUSTAINABLE RELATIONSHIPS

A lbert Einstein noted that the consciousness responsible for creating a problem cannot also solve the problem. That thought goes to the heart of America's leadership problems. Too many leaders see the world through old eyes and cannot see the problems that the old frame of mind has actually created. The 1990s launched a growth industry via leadership books, each trying in its own way to outline a set of behaviors and methods that would convert society's troubled institutions into viable and dynamic organizations. The essence of the leadership issue, however, is that although individuals are changing, leaders are still clinging to what went before. In short, they are operating with the old frame of mind, when a new frame of mind is needed.

One of the central differences between the old and new frames of mind revolves around the old analogy of organizations as lean machines and the new analogy of organizations as vital organisms. Machines respond to control but organisms develop their own order. Control cannot bring order to organisms, and control cannot force their growth. One of the principal misinterpretations of contemporary leadership is to confuse control with order. Firing workers, cutting expenses, reducing bureaucracy and other hierarchical commands are examples of trying to gain control.

Vital organisms find their own order, which arises from internal knowledge applied to direct, ongoing contact with elements outside the entity. The dynamism between what lies outside the organism and the knowledge contained within it allows it to evolve as the environment changes. Erich Jantsch, a systems scientist, has written: "To live in an evolutionary spirit means to engage with full ambition and without reserve in the structure of the present, and yet to let go and flow into a new structure when the right time has come." Many leaders are spirited in their participation in the contemporary world, but they resist movement toward a new structure that they cannot control. Jantsch added: "The more freedom in self-organization, the more order." Leaders want control, but vital organisms require freedom to create their own order.

"Communities of practice" express this self-organizing principle. The Institute for Research on Learning, founded in 1987 as a spinoff of Xerox's Palo Alto Research Center, studies communities of practice closely. Researchers there learned that these communities emerge from a common interest—that is, leaders and institutions cannot create them. Moreover, they work best when left to their own best interests—that is, managers can easily destroy them just by trying to direct them. They work without an agenda because knowledge, not management, guides them; yet they still develop a way of operating and of dealing with the problems that confront them. They are responsible only to themselves; they have no bosses, gather members voluntarily through shared interests and needs and do not respond to management. Most important, they are the baseline source of human capital within every institution. That is, even if a corporation creates a strong organizational structure, these communities of practice will pop up anyway because individuals want them and feel comfortable with them. Said another way, even when the organization tries to impose control, participants will still create their own order. If leaders try to lead them, they come apart or dwindle in effectiveness. In essence, letting go of control nurtures their strengths. They are self-organizing organizations.

Many of America's business leaders cling tightly to the old frame of mind, hoping that its retention will return past successes. This mistaken point of view led Kellogg's chairman and CEO, Arnold Langbo, to insist that nothing fundamental had changed in the marketplace, even though his company's market share had slipped two points after a 19-percent price drop in the sixth year of a cyclical recovery. Larry McKean, Boeing Corporation's head of human resources, admitted that the company's approach was harsh: "We monitored them, supervised them, told them when to go to the bathroom. We didn't trust our own people." Likewise, the board of Scott Paper Company thought that hiring "Chainsaw" Al Dunlap would prove that hard, cold actions could save an organization. In fact, his presence proved only that gut-wrenching tactical maneuvers merely prepare a company to be sold to another company that thinks the same way. His presence did not prove anything about sustainable relationships with customers, although it definitely drove home the point that it could sever all sustainable relationships with employees.

The life expectancy of organizations that continue to operate under this mind-set is decreasing. Like any machine that is overused and undermaintained, these institutions will eventually break down. The key piece of advice for the old-frame-of-mind leader who does not want to change is, of course, to be gone before then.

In *The Loyalty Effect,* Frederick Reichheld outlined the problem that modern businesses face: "In a typical company today, customers are defecting at the rate of 10 to 30 percent per year; employee turnover rates of 15 to 25 percent are common; and average annual investor churn now exceeds 50 percent per year." More specifically, Reichheld added that "Human capital, unlike other assets, does not depreciate over time. Like good wine, it actually improves with age." He further noted that retaining current customers can affect net present value by figures like 95 percent for advertising agencies, 90 percent for life insurance, 45 percent for industrial distribution, and 35 percent for software. The old frame of mind that Langbo and Dunlap represent cannot deal with these new realities in the same way it dealt with the world that formerly existed.

Many American leaders are wedded to managerial control without understanding organizational order. The old frame of mind cannot grasp that order arises from within, while control descends down upon. The first encourages dynamism and innovation, while the second restrains growth and retards development. The first nurtures change and growth, while the second struggles to get more out of an entropic system. The first fits a vital organism, while the second fits a machine. The first elicits the new terms of engagement, while the second leads to a disconnect.

The dissonance between where individuals within and around institutions are headed and where institutional leaders want to go fosters disorder in contemporary organizations. This dissonance causes the massive disconnect between individuals and the old communities of wealth, and it confuses American leaders and makes them seem out of step. Political leaders retreat to ideological name-calling, some business leaders resort to mergers and acquisitions, other managers turn to massive layoffs, and still others depend on tactical maneuvers like price cuts, increased ad budgets and new products to boost the bottom line.

The world outside has changed, and control as a management tool is losing its effectiveness. Order is emerging from within. The former "followers" are now leading society's evolutionary change, and leaders are now becoming followers. All of this disorients leaders who hold on to the old frame of mind: They have entered a world they can no longer control in the ways they once did. Quite simply, those who led the communities of wealth without reaching their own personal and professional turning points cannot lead the communities of meaning. They cannot carry the old frame of mind into the years ahead. Following Einstein's thought that the consciousness that created a problem is unable to solve it, to lead the communities of meaning (the *solution* to the problems created by the communities of wealth), leaders must undergo a process of personal reassessment *themselves*. More specifically: Personal transformation precedes organizational transformation.

LEADERSHIP DISCONNECT

The new terms of engagement have emerged at this time because of the confluence of technology and personal changes. The old terms of engagement depended upon a one-way system of communication—topdown within the organization and inside-out for marketing to customers. "Tell people and they will follow" seemed like the working model. Advances in communications technology have reversed that communication and power flow. At one time, network television programmers controlled the viewer throughout the evening, but the remote channel-changer ("zapper") placed that authority, literally, in the viewer's hands. The former leaders are now followers of changing consumers' tastes and needs.

The rapid advance of the Internet has likewise reversed old power flows. The user now owns the system's operation. Software providers must have a "user-friendly" interface or lose customers; and content providers, as one observer noted, must be either "extremely useful or highly entertaining" or else they are just taking up room. Microsoft thought it could control its customers—get hold of them at machine startup and hold on to them until they turned the computer off. Bill Gates soon learned that this thinking was misguided: *No one* controls the Internet user in an open architectural environment.

The Internet has altered all relationships in the electronic market-place. While the impacts have received considerable attention, a few specific *consequences* deserve listing here: Disintermediation has become common, chaotic interaction has evolved as a market norm, brand names have lost their impact, the price of market entry has dropped, territorial control has lost its power, and margin squeezes are the rule. All of these market realities have emerged because individuals (users) now have gained control of the terms of engagement. Old approaches from the communities of wealth, such as advertising, physical retail control, distribution power and imagery, cannot force a reaction if a user "points and clicks" the computer mouse on something else more useful or entertaining. The power to attract has diminished.

These are the realities of consumer contact on the Internet, but they are exemplary of the new terms of engagement throughout the business environment. In essence, the personal-reassessment process has led individuals to develop attitudes about outside influence and control in their personal lives that match the TV "zapper" and computer "point and click" capabilities: They are edgy and disloyal, immune to the "pitch" and interested in taking control of their own environment.

In the 1980s, a "new industrial revolution," the inversion of power away from the manufacturer (designer) and to the distributor, affected all business relationships. The person dealing directly with the customer became more powerful, and others faced ongoing competition from anyone who could produce something cheaper, faster and better. At the end of the decade, a "disposable-income squeeze" forced consumers to reapportion their financial resources, and that resulted in a massive revaluation of goods and services across the board. The combination of excess capacity and squeezed consumer budgets altered all marketplace dynamics. In essence, the brands that once commanded a premium price lost that privileged position, and, like Microsoft on the Internet, became players in the price-solutions market dynamic.

Eventually, individuals entered a reassessment process to rethink what they considered important and vital. Everything from personal health to professional time, and from food to consumer goods, came under this personal scrutiny. As a result, a massive juggling of personal priorities ensued. What seemed important at one time (e.g., shopping) now seemed wasteful, and what once seemed boundless (e.g., time) now seemed precious. Anything that encouraged wasteful activities (e.g., credit eating away at salaries) or stole what was precious (e.g., work stealing valuable time) lost value.

This massive reassessment process brought citizens, consumers and employees back to the center of society's operations. Like the former television viewer who suddenly had hold of the channel-changer, individuals in the marketplace, workplace and voting booth regained the powerful center of institutional life. Women were at the core of this change and became the avant garde of the personal revolution.

The huge reversal of social authority played havoc with traditional theories of leadership. Some of the treasured shibboleths of American management were—and continue to be—less and less effective. For example, followers no longer perceive leaders as being above them or beyond contact. Technology not only reversed power between leaders and followers, it also brought leaders closer to followers. Leaders no longer enjoy the psychological distance that made their roles so comfortable in the past. The technological shift in psychological distance has now become embedded in individual response to leadership in general. In 1997 Michael Eisner, head of Disney, announced to stockholders that he had dismissed his recent hiree Michael Ovitz, after paying nearly $100 million for a failed experiment in marketing synergism. At the meeting, a stockholder rose and suggested that since Eisner had made the hiring blunder, perhaps he should take the $97 million from his own bank account and pay the departing Ovitz. The suggestion that a leader has managerial responsibility and fiduciary accountability for decisions made as head of an organization matches an emerging view that leaders are, in the end, no more than hired help.

That leaders can manage favorable outcomes is another favorite (but now increasingly discredited) managerial value from the old frame of mind. This goes to the heart of the control–order dynamic. Leaders can still assert control, but firing people en masse is a sign that control is all that leaders have left. Because followers no longer follow, and because the tools available (i.e., advertising, marketing, public relations, authority expressed through hierarchical-management charts) no longer have as much influence as they once did, managers have trouble forcing positive outcomes. As a result, leaders focus on internal cost-cutting, the one area where the illusion of an old model of control still lingers.

Management's past dependence upon loyalty as a stabilizer has also come apart. Whether it be party loyalty, brand loyalty, worker loyalty or fan loyalty, the new environment does not favor predictable responses from followers. Everything is up for grabs, and the structure of the new terms of engagement suggests that *they* will remain up for grabs at each point of contact. This lack of loyalty also undermines another management fundamental—top-down hierarchies as effective management models. Without loyalty, without a passive follower and without control over information flowing freely through electronic systems, the whole top-down management model can no longer sustain the impact it once did.

Taken all together, the leadership models that worked so well no longer match the new environment. Furthermore, efforts to reassert control only inhibit an organization's ability to address that environment. Letting go of the control mentality will help an institution's leader to start the necessary process of changing in order to be in harmony with new realities.

RECONNECTING IN A DISCONNECTED WORLD

Ever since World War II, Americans and their public and private institutions have successfully expanded the country's wealth, increasing
standards of living as well as the number of individuals participating in
the communities of wealth. However, the wealth-generating institutions
ran headlong into a world out of control, which triggered a process
of personal change that broke the link between individuals and the
communities of wealth. The extensive personal-reassessment process
resulted in new priorities, values and attitudes among individuals. To
reconnect with these individuals, institutions must become communities of meaning.

Leaders have responded to the recent personal revolution by dou-
bling their effort to sustain the old institutional model. They have held
tightly to the old frame of mind, and to the recession-proven methods
that worked so well in the past. Their massive tactical restructuring
efforts focused on productivity and efficiency (both pieces of internal
operations), thereby ignoring or misreading the widespread structural
changes under way in the larger society. They responded to the secular
changes with cyclical tactics. Repeated studies have shown the ineffectiveness of various business tactics used to make American institutions
competitive in the new global business environment. This type of restructuring assumes a constant market (i.e., consumers want the same
things), plus a constant (or at least interchangeable) work force (i.e.,
employees remain personally motivated, as before). These types of
efforts are starting to wear thin as events reveal the assumptions to be
less and less valid. For most leaders, the time has come to face the reality that Americans are in the process of making changes that will *not*
end with a return to the way it was. Now, institutions must undergo the
strategic restructuring process that will lead to new connections with
reassessed consumers and employees.

Strategic restructuring rethinks the organization's purpose, objectives and methods; reworks the priorities; and resets operations and
activities to fit the new model. This type of restructuring recognizes that
the market has permanently changed and must be addressed on its own

terms. It also recognizes that employees have likewise changed and that institutions must engage them "where they are." Strategic restructuring requires that institutional leaders think of the customer and the employee as the same person in different roles. Doing one thing for customers and something else for employees ultimately dooms any effort to change to the new communities of meaning. Also, strategic restructuring is a dynamic process between and among all participants in the organization's life—customers, employees, investors. In that list, *any* organization has the intellectual and financial resources to move through a strategic restructuring.

In utilizing its own resources, both outside and inside, an organization is borrowing an organism's technique. That is, a vital organism uses its own resources. Margaret Wheatley explained that this ability to use an organization's own resources facilitates "orderly change in turbulent environments." Buying another consulting theory that has a complete answer for a company's restructuring merely wastes resources and time and ultimately interferes with a company's own order. Strategic restructuring brings the outside (customers) and the inside (employees) into contact. *They* create a dialogue.

Employing the organization's own resources does not mean that institutional leaders can learn nothing from others' successful restructuring efforts. Indeed, some successful examples share features which could help an institution to initiate a strategic restructuring. Becoming a community of meaning involves rethinking the "payoff" for both the individual and the social dynamic that integrates the individual's new priorities with the institution's new approach. The old context—profit and the expanding standard of living—is losing its impact on individuals. Successful examples of strategic restructuring have created new organizational attributes that facilitate the new terms of engagement— and they are Transparency, Openness, Knowledge and Context.

TRANSPARENCY

A strategically restructured company is outside-in, bottom-up. That is, the central resource for thinking about what needs to change involves understanding what has changed among individuals outside the organization. The environment has changed, so what are the essential aspects of that change, and how are those changes impacting this organization? Peter Drucker argued that "the customers own the business," a sentiment quite removed from the old frame of mind which argued that business decisions should only keep shareholders in mind. Using Drucker's perspective, an organization must interact with its environment to evolve successfully. A company looking only to its stockholders is looking in the wrong direction. Dana Buchman, for example, doubled its sales every year by going into fitting rooms and listening to customer comments about its clothes. Transparent organizations eventually bring down old managerial categories, push useful information throughout and develop new relationships across old categories. At that point, the organization moves toward *openness.*

OPENNESS

Open-book management changes dynamics throughout the company. It encourages across-the-board participation and responsibility, a dynamic change from past internal operations. Open access to information and resources, open scheduling and agendaless meetings all reinforce participation and responsibility. Bob Argabright, CEO at Chesapeake Packaging in Baltimore, turned the company's different divisions into "intracompanies" and had them each elect presidents. Each intracompany had control over the way it operated. It could make mistakes and learn from those mistakes. Each divisional enterprise elected new presidents from its ranks every six months, thereby slowly educating everyone about the way the company worked, and the role of leadership in that enterprise. "Until we learned to learn from our mistakes and not be afraid of them," explained one Chesapeake manager, "we had no idea how fast we could go. This place is humming now." That learning component moved Chesapeake toward another feature of successful restructurings: *knowledge.*

KNOWLEDGE

With information flowing outside-in and circulating throughout all parts of the organization, a new institutional learning curve comes into being. Whether the organization makes newspapers, creates designs or sells housewares, learning institutions work to bring their customers into the operations because that is where the dynamism lives. This new input moves the learning process toward meaningful change. From there, the organization becomes a community of inquirers and learners, individual and institution together on a quest to develop and grow. Learning companies like ASA software and Buckman Labs encourage information flow throughout their organizations in order to facilitate the ability of everyone both to make effective choices and to fulfill the needs of those actually being served. Transparency and openness distribute authority throughout the organization, allowing order to emerge. Knowledge moves easiest through a system that has successfully distributed authority. Information becomes knowledge when the organization creates an overall *context*.

CONTEXT

Jack Stack, CEO of Springfield Remanufacturing, explained: "The best, most efficient, most profitable way to operate a business is to give everybody a voice in saying how it is run and a stake in the financial outcome, good or bad." With that in mind, he established a cultural context inside of which his company operated. St. Luke's advertising agency explained that profit was like health—the company needs it, but it is not the reason why the company exists (that was another context). When Judy Cockerton founded her toy store, No Kidding, and established her role as that of a teacher, not a businesswoman, she set the context for the entire company's operation. All of the outside-in information flow, all of the open-management policies, all of the knowledge flowing freely through the company, must have a reason. Whereas the communities of wealth and their members thought profit was a context for action, communities of meaning do not find that context quite enough. It may be necessary, but it is not sufficient unto itself. Creating the new context is a key aspect to shifting from a community of wealth to a community of meaning—and *that* context is unique to *each* company.

CRITICAL INSIGHT:
Personal and Organizational Transformation

Conversion from a community of wealth to a community of meaning, or from a lean machine to a vital organism, requires leadership, even though the force pushing these changes originates elsewhere. Learning how to lead without control requires letting go of past certainties and models and initiating the institutional-reassessment process. Strategic restructuring cannot go forward unless individual leaders themselves reach their turning points and move toward their own grounding-points reassessment. Jack Stack of Springfield Remanufacturing, James Goodnight of SAS Institute, Mort Meyerson of Perot Systems and Bob Buckman of Buckman Labs, all went through a personal transformation that allowed them to see the world and their place in it differently. From that personal transformation came the organizational reassessment that energized the institutions they led. Without those personal turning points, their companies could not have undergone such thorough strategic restructurings. Perhaps leaders should consider whether or not they as individuals can pass through a personal reassessment when deciding whether to stay and take on the restructuring challenge, or leave and let someone else start the process.

When George Gilder realized that the so-called information age was displacing the industrial age, he reckoned that valuable commodities from the former era would lose value in the newer era. Specifically, he noted that knowledge was displacing physical commodities as key valued elements of society. "What used to be called 'precious natural resources,' " he proclaimed, are returning "to their previous natural conditions as dirt, rocks, and gunk." The automobile, cigarette, cereal and advertising industries (and others) are learning the cost of becoming their own industries' versions of "dirt, rocks, and gunk." That reality steadily eats away at the loyalty, influence and viability of the old communities of wealth.

In their old form, institutions cannot exhibit the new terms of engagement, and so they must change in significant ways. Playing around with more tactics to sustain short-term profit and quarterly upticks of the stock has run its course. Before the institution can change, however, individual leaders must reach their own turning points, move into their own reassessment periods and recognize in which direction to head their institutions. Some may never "get it," and in the interest of their own companies may choose to move on personally, leaving the task of strategic restructuring to those with a temporal interest in sustaining the institution into the distant future. The task for the wizened leader prepared to address the current malaise involves restructuring the old community of wealth into a community of meaning, in order both to create sustainable relationships with customers and employees, and to make the company viable in the new business environment.

TAKING INTELLIGENCE
SERIOUSLY

ANOMALIES AND INFERENCES

*T*he *Tao Jones Averages* (1983), by our late partner, Bennett W. Goodspeed, introduced the reader to Inferential Focus and its methodology. That methodology guided the work for this book—and, for that reason, we feel the need to share with you the way we discover the types of intelligence reported herein.

Reading is the core of the discipline. We divide nearly 300 diverse publications from around the world among the four principals (Charlie Hess, Joe Kelly and the two of us), the distribution based on neither subject specialization nor professional training. Everyone reads something in the sciences, arts and social sciences, as well as traditional business journals and mainstream newspapers—dailies, weeklies, monthlies *and* quarterlies. Such a spread in readings avoids "hardening of the categories," the tendency of people within specialties to see every event in terms of their own expertise and thereby to miss subtle changes because they have "special knowledge" that explains away such altered conditions. Our widespread reading creates what Ben Goodspeed called a "horizontal expertise," an ability to cross traditional categories of knowledge and to integrate seemingly disparate areas of study.

As we read, we eliminate the story line that the writer had created from the facts gathered. In putting his or her various pieces of information together, the writer needs to glue them into a seemingly consistent narrative, even if that story ends without resolution, and so we remove the narrative. We eliminate opinions, too—whether expressed by the journalist or by experts whom the journalist has questioned. We also eliminate the results of surveys and opinion polls, focus groups and market research. Those bits of information may be added at the other end of the process as additional evidence, but we do not allow them to color the basic discovery process which requires direct observation.

Often, after discovering significant changes, we look back at a survey or study and realize that the results, when viewed from our new perspective, can have a meaning quite different from what the research concluded. These new discoveries reorient our perspectives, altering the way in which even old information is assimilated. For example, in 1997 many experts were baffled by the fact that consumer-confidence polls were skyrocketing, but consumer spending (a number which had historically tracked the confidence number) remained stagnant. After understanding the meaning of the personal transformation that individuals—Mort Meyerson, for example—had made, and which we discuss in Part II of the book, the confidence numbers made sense. The reason why consumers were not spending was that they were preserving and reallocating their financial reserves. Their confidence rose as they gained control over those personal budgetary restraints. In other words: contrary to historical models, consumers were confident precisely because they were *not* spending.

Our massive, widespread reading gives us a feeling for the normal flow of events—the kinds of activities and behaviors that come to be expected in any given situation. For example, they might suggest to us what types of business decisions typically emerge from a specific set of market conditions. Overall, these expected events outline a picture of the flow of events.

We do not seek to catch that flow of events in an analytical bucket. Rather, we look for anomalies in those events, small contradictions in the expected flow. These anomalies draw our attention and tell us to *focus* closer. For example, when oil-industry specialists insisted that OPEC would reduce its production, and when OPEC officials confirmed such a course of action at their meetings, a small item in the foreign press noted that Saudi Arabia had started leasing huge oil tankers.

Focus. Why were they doing this—and would their actions affect the price of oil, and then affect inflation in this country? When the FBI arrested a suspect in the World Trade Center bombing, suggesting that expert detective work had brought results, two lines in one article noted that a woman who had rented the apartment that a suspect used was seemingly allowed to slip out of the country. *Focus.* Why would the authorities allow that to happen, and what does that action say about the relationship between intelligence organizations and citizen safety? When some articles mentioned that the number of credit-card delinquencies had steadily risen, other articles noted that the number of people paying off monthly credit-card balances (a contrary economic indicator) also steadily rose. *Focus.* Why were numbers that historically moved in opposite directions moving in parallel, and what does that change say about the business environment? While California voters (1996) passed a traditionally conservative antiaffirmative action referendum by a wide margin, we noted that they also passed by a wide margin a traditionally liberal pro-marijuana referendum (medical use). *Focus.* What had changed in the way that citizens thought about government and leadership, and what do leaders need to learn about why this change had occurred?

These types of anomalies catch our attention, and each of us gathers these types of observations into packets of materials. Then, twice each month, we meet for two days to discuss the strength of these observations, to make connections with other observations and to work our way to a deeper understanding of what is taking place. We look for a group of anomalies, because these are early signals of change—a shift in the ongoing flow of events. We move by inference and intuition from the anomalies to the new situation. In our discipline, inference takes place at two levels. First, we assemble the anomalies and infer what has changed, and second, we infer what the implications of this change are.

Peter Drucker in "Planning for Uncertainty," an article published in the *Wall Street Journal,* noted that traditional planning asks the question "What is most likely to happen?" That is, traditional planning uses a statistical mind-set that tries to assess the future based upon probable scenarios which are essentially extensions of past behavior into the future.

They assume that *nothing* will change—a highly dubious assumption in the contemporary world. Drucker adds, however, that planning in what he calls the "age of uncertainty" requires a more forceful question: "What has already happened that will create the future?" In other words, what sort of events have already taken place which, as we go forward, will determine future events?

Our two levels of inference bring Drucker's question into play. The first level of inference, the *deductive* inference, involves examining the collected facts and anomalies, and diagnosing what has taken place. Like a veterinarian who looks at symptoms (with a patient who cannot talk) and infers what has happened to the animal, we look at the anomalous events to infer from them what has taken place that has not been discussed or reported. What has changed so that what appears to be an anomaly at first glance is actually the beginning of a new pattern or flow?

This highly creative phase in the process requires several controls. First, we must eliminate our own biases. To do this, we depend upon partner interaction. Our meetings are raucous, stimulating and fun—and they must be *all* of those things to shake loose personal opinions. Second, we need to avoid theory. The inference must be based upon the specific examples before us, and not on some extraneous model or theory about how people should, might or could act. Third, we have to ignore all outside interpretations, whether they come from the reading sources themselves or are commentaries from sources not directly involved with the specific examples before us. Finally, we cannot allow possible impacts on clients, friends or ourselves to affect the process. Whether the inference is extremely negative or positive for a client cannot affect the discovery itself. With these safeguards against tainted inferences, we proceed into our lively and protracted discussions.

In the anomalies cited above, we inferred that the Saudis were bucking OPEC and, further, that they were making a market-share play. In the bombing example, we inferred that the FBI had been following the suspects for some time, well in advance of the bombing, and we further suggested that perhaps an entrapment plot had gone awry. In the economy, we noted that two types of economies were developing, one for those with position and education and another for those outside that privileged circle. In the California voters instance, we inferred that voters had very different parameters for voting than those explained by the old conservative–liberal dichotomy, and that commentators and politicians alike had yet to understand what was taking place in America.

This first level of inference involves deduction, in that it diagnoses a change from specific events and anomalies assembled. The second inference leads us to implications and involves *induction*. Having identified the change, we assay what that change will do to an existing technological, political, economic, social, market or policy dynamic. That is, we seek to know what impact the change will have as it spreads and becomes more obvious to everyone else. We still maintain our disciplinary restrictions against personal bias, current theory, popular interpretations and private implications. This time, we are looking for "actionable" implications.

As examples of the second level of inference, look again at the above anomalies. In the oil example, we suggested that its price (contrary to the prognostications of industry analysts) would turn downward—which it did, easing inflation and positively affecting companies that depend on it (e.g., airlines). For the World Trade Center bombing, we noted that more people were involved than the ones originally arrested (many more were arrested one year later on charges of planning to bomb several New York City sites) and that a speedy and successful trial could ease public anxiety about the ability of public institutions to solve society's problems. For the economy, we noted that different types of investments, services and products with different objectives and approaches would be needed to address the two radically different economic realities. With these kinds of insights into consumer economic and political changes, our clients—corporations like Bankers Trust, GE Capital, Fidelity Investments and Leo Burnett—have been able to take advantage of change, rather than be its victim. Looking at the California voters, we suggested that "fairness" and "balance" were now guiding citizen decisions in the political sphere despite the fact that politicians had moved to other priorities.

Our process of discovery (events, anomalies, inferences, implications) leads to places, ideas and contexts not anticipated at the beginning—and that generates excitement in our work. This discovery process creates intelligence, which, unlike pure information, brings context to events and distills mountains of data down to essential elements. Unlike vertical or analytical expertise, which eliminates information by category in order to go "deeper" into one narrow area of study, intelligence seeks to focus on events that signal changes, wherever on the horizontal expanse of information they may come. Categories of study become irrelevant, and change becomes the central focus. By the time we have finished, we have identified changes that have political, technological, market, managerial and personal implications.

INTELLIGENCE AND DECISION-MAKING

Delivering the intelligence, however, leads nowhere unless that intelligence becomes an integral part of an organization's own decision-making processes. Oddly enough, we have confronted a wide range of reactions when we have brought significant, yet difficult, changes to the table. When presented with an outline of how to deal with personal changes in the values and priorities of employees and consumers (the main subject of this book), some business leaders have responded "Not on *my* watch." Approaching retirement age, having enjoyed a reasonably comfortable ride to the corporate top, some leaders look at the half-open retirement door, their anxious board members, and edgy staff, and conclude that they want to keep the ship on the same course until they retire. They have lost the will to drive significant change through the organization.

At the same time, we have received some positive responses as well. "Bring it on!" some have insisted. These clients cherish the opportunity to lead their institutions in new and challenging directions. For them, staying ahead of the economic, technological, personnel and market curves is more important than staying comfortably in the middle of the pack.

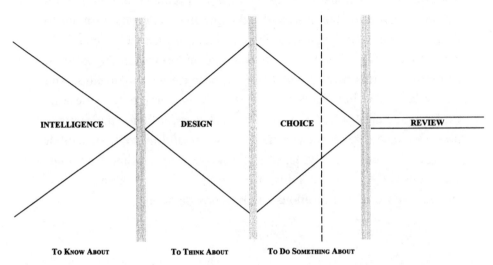

INTELLIGENCE IN CORPORATE DECISION MAKING

Programmed activity tends to crowd out non-programmed activity

INTELLIGENCE   DESIGN   CHOICE   REVIEW

To Know About   To Think About   To Do Something About

Using intelligence requires assimilating it smoothly into the flow of decision-making. But how can we do that? The Intelligence in Corporate Decision Making chart depicts a use model.

The process of intelligence looks across a broad array of resources and then narrows that down to the actual changes taking place. That is, information overload becomes less of a problem because the essential change leads to a context which organizes that information into a comprehensible whole. But at that point the organization must *act*.

The first transfer point within an organization moves that intelligence to the *design* stage, which encourages those with the responsibility for formulating corporate strategies first to be aware of the intelligence and then to start watching the new dynamics on their own. This early warning gives senior executives time to think about the changes and to work through an effective response. As the change spreads, the organizational overseer has valuable lead time to build up the kind of conviction needed within the right constituencies to see the selected responses through to completion.

The choice and review stages represent an organization's initiative and assessment actions. *Intelligence* brings an issue before the organization, *design* starts the process of adopting the organization's plans to deal with that issue, *choice* involves deciding on a specific course of action and *review* involves reconsidering and revising the adopted action. All of this takes place, however, because the organization and its leaders take intelligence seriously. "It is commonly believed," explained Peter Drucker in a *Wall Street Journal* article, "that innovations create changes—but very few do. Successful innovations exploit changes that have already happened. They exploit the time lag." Integrating over-the-horizon intelligence into the decision-making process embeds "successful innovations" into the organization.

BIBLIOGRAPHY

Abraham, Marilyn J., and Sandy MacGregor. *First We Quit Our Jobs: How One Driven Couple Got on the Road to a New Life.* New York: Dell Publishing Co., Inc., 1997.

Baritz, Loren. *The Good Life: The Meaning of Success for the American Middle Class.* New York: Alfred A. Knopf, 1989.

Barlett, Donald L., and James B. Steele. *America: What Went Wrong?* Kansas City: Andrews and McMeel, 1992.

Beardstown Ladies Investment Club, and Leslie Whitaker. *The Beardstown Ladies' Commonsense Investment Guide: How We Beat the Stock Market—and How You Can Too,* vol. 1. New York: Hyperion, 1995.

Bennett, Michael J. *When Dreams Came True: The G.I. Bill and the Making of Modern America.* Washington: Brassey's, 1996.

Borst, Arno. *The Ordering of Time: From the Ancient Computus to the Modern Computer.* Chicago: University of Chicago Press, 1993.

Brown, Richard M. *No Duty to Retreat: Violence and Values in American History and Society.* New York: Oxford University Press, 1991.

Canfield, Jack, Mark V. Vansen, and Martin Rutte. *Chicken Soup for the Soul at Work: 101 Stories of Courage, Compassion, and Creativity in the Workplace.* New York: Health Communications, Inc., 1996.

Cantor, Norman F. *The American Century: Varieties of Culture in Modern Times.* New York: HarperCollins Publishers, 1997.

Capra, Fritjof. *The Web of Life: A New Scientific Understanding of Living Systems.* New York: Doubleday, 1996.

Carroll, Peter N. *It Seemed Like Nothing Happened: The Tragedy and Promise of America in the 1970s.* New York: Holt, Rinehart and Winston, 1982.

Carter, Paul A. *Revolt Against Destiny: An Intellectual History of the United States.* New York: Columbia University Press, 1989.

Chafe, William H. *The Unfinished Journey: America Since World War II*. New York: Oxford University Press, 1986.

Champy, James. *Reengineering Management: The Mandate for New Leadership*. New York: Harper Business, 1994.

Clecak, Peter. *America's Quest for the Ideal Self: Dissent and Fulfillment in the 60s and 70s*. New York: Oxford University Press, 1983.

Cos, Allan, and Julie Liesse. *Redefining Corporate Soul: Linking Purpose & People*. Burr Ridge, Ill.: Irwin Professional Publishing, 1996.

DeGeus, Arie. *The Living Company: Habits for Survival in a Turbulent Business Environment*. Boston: Harvard Business School Press, 1997.

De Santis, Hugh. *Beyond Progress: An Interpretive Odyssey to the Future*. Chicago: University of Chicago Press, 1996.

Dominguez, Joe, and Vicky Robin. *Your Money or Your Life: Transforming Your Relationship with Money and Achieving Financial Independence*. New York: Viking Penguin, 1993.

Dorrance, Tom. *True Unity: Willing Communication Between Horse & Human*. Fresno: Word Dancer Press, 1996.

Drucker, Peter. *The New Realities: In Government and Politics/In Economics and Business/In Society and World View*. New York: Harper & Row, 1989.

Edvinsson, Leif, and Michael S. Malone. *Intellectual Capital: Realizing Your Company's True Value by Finding Its Hidden Brain Power*. New York: Harper Business, 1997.

Forester, Tom. *High-Tech Society: The Story of the Information Technology Revolution*. Cambridge: The MIT Press, 1988.

Gardner, John W. *Self-Renewal: The Individual and the Innovative Society*. New York: W. W. Norton & Company, 1981.

Gleick, James. *Chaos: Making a New Science*. New York: Penguin Group, 1987.

Goleman, Daniel. *Emotional Intelligence: Why It Can Matter More Than IQ*. New York: Bantam Books, 1995.

Goodich, Michael E. *Violence and Miracle in the Fourteenth Century: Private Grief and Public Salvation*. Chicago: University of Chicago Press, 1995.

Goodspeed, Bennett W. *The Tao Jones Averages: A Guide to Whole-Brained Investing.* New York: Penguin Books, 1983.

Grove, Andrew S. *Only the Paranoid Survive: How to Exploit the Crisis Points That Challenge Every Company and Career.* New York: Currency Doubleday, 1996.

Hammer, Michael, and James Champy. *Reengineering the Corporation: A Manifesto for Business Revolution.* New York: HarperCollins, 1994.

Handy, Charles. *The Age of Paradox.* Boston: Harvard Business School Press, 1994.

———. *The Age of Unreason.* Boston: Harvard Business School Press, 1990.

———. *Beyond Certainty.* Boston: Harvard Business School Press, 1996.

Heilbroner, Robert. *Visions of the Future: The Distant Past, Yesterday, Today, Tomorrow.* New York: Oxford University Press, 1995.

Helgeson, Sally. *The Female Advantage: Women's Ways of Leadership.* New York: Currency Doubleday, 1990.

———. *The Web of Inclusion: A New Architecture for Building Great Organizations.* New York: Doubleday, 1995.

Hillman, James. *The Soul's Code: In Search of Character and Calling.* New York: Random House, 1996.

James, Jennifer. *Thinking in the Future Tense: Leadership Skills for a New Age.* New York: Simon & Schuster, 1996.

Johnson, George. *Fire in the Mind: Science, Faith, and the Search for Order.* New York: Alfred A. Knopf, 1996.

Jones, Howard M. *The Pursuit of Happiness.* Ithaca: Cornell University Press, 1953.

Kauffman, Stuart. *At Home in the Universe: The Search for Laws of Self-Organization and Complexity.* New York: Oxford University Press, 1995.

Korda, Michael. *Success.* New York: Ballantine Books, 1977.

Lears, T. J. Jackson, *No Place of Grace: Antimodernism and the Transformation of American Culture 1880–1920.* Chicago: University of Chicago Press, 1994.

Maclean, Norman. *A River Runs Through It and Other Stories.* Chicago: University of Chicago Press, 1976.

Mandel, Michael. *The High-Risk Society: Peril and Promise in the New Economy.* New York: Random House, 1996.

Martin, Steve. *Picasso at the Lapin Agile and Other Plays.* New York: Grove Press, 1996.

Marty, Martin E. *The One and the Many: America's Struggle for the Common Good.* Cambridge: Harvard University Press, 1997.

Micklethwait, John, and Adrian Wooldridge. *The Witch Doctors: Making Sense of the Management Gurus.* New York: Random House, 1996.

Mitroff, Ian I., and Harold A. Linstone. *The Unbounded Mind: Breaking the Chains of Traditional Business Thinking.* New York: Oxford University Press, 1993.

Moore, Thomas. *Care of the Soul: A Guide for Cultivating Depth and Sacredness in Everyday Life.* New York: HarperCollins Publishers, Inc., 1993.

Negroponte, Nicholas. *Being Digital.* New York: Random House, 1995.

Neruda, Pablo. *Love: Ten Poems.* New York: Hyperion, 1995.

Nye, David E. *American Technological Sublime.* Cambridge: The MIT Press, 1994.

Oldenburg, Ray. *The Great Good Place.* New York: Marlowe & Company, 1989.

O'Neill, William L. *American High: The Years of Confidence, 1945–1960.* New York: Macmillan, Inc., 1986.

Pais, Abraham. *Inward Bound: Of Matter and Forces in the Physical World.* New York: Oxford University Press, 1986.

———. *"Subtle Is the Lord . . .": The Science and the Life of Albert Einstein.* New York: Oxford University Press, 1982.

Peters, Tom, and Robert H. Waterman. *In Search of Excellence: Lessons from America's Best-Run Companies.* Old Tappan, N.J.: Mac Libe Re, 1997.

Potter, David M. *People of Plenty: Economic Abundance and the American Character.* Chicago: University of Chicago Press, 1954.

Pugh, Emerson W. *Building IBM: Shaping an Industry and Its Technology.* Cambridge: The MIT Press, 1995.

Raines, Howell. *Fly-Fishing Through the Midlife Crisis.* New York: Doubleday, 1993.

Redfield, James. *The Celestine Prophecy: An Adventure.* New York: Warner Books, 1993.

Reichheld, Frederick F. *The Loyalty Effect: The Hidden Force Behind Growth, Profits, and Lasting Value.* Boston: Harvard Business School Press, 1996.

Rifkin, Jeremy. *The End of Work: The Decline of the Global Labor Force and the Dawn of the Post-Market Era.* New York: G. P. Putnam's Sons, 1995.

Sampson, Anthony. *Company Man: The Rise and Fall of Corporate Life.* New York: Random House, 1995.

Samuelson, Robert J. *The Good Life and Its Discontents: The American Dream in the Age of Entitlement, 1945–1995.* New York: Random House, 1995.

Schlesinger, Jr., Arthur M. *The Cycles of American History.* Boston: Houghton Mifflin Co., 1986.

Schuster, John P., Jill Carpenter, and M. Patricia Kane. *The Power of Open-Book Management: Releasing the True Potential of People's Minds, Hearts, and Hands.* New York: John Wiley & Sons, Inc., 1996.

Segil, Larraine. *Intelligence Business Alliances: How to Profit Using Today's Most Important Strategic Tool.* New York: Random House, 1996.

Shear, Claudia. *Blown Sideways Through Life.* New York: Bantam Doubleday Dell Publishing Group, 1995.

Shi, David E. *The Simple Life: Plain Living and High Thinking in American Culture.* New York: Oxford University Press, 1985.

Stewart, Thomas A. *Intellectual Capital: The New Wealth of Organizations.* New York: Currency Doubleday, 1997.

Strauss, William, and Neil Howe. *The Fourth Turning.* New York: Broadway Books, 1998.

Tannen, Deborah. *You Just Don't Understand: Women and Men in Conversation.* New York: Ballantine Books, Inc., 1991.

Wacker, Watts, Howard Means, and Jim Taylor. *The Five Hundred Year Delta: What Happens After What Comes Next.* New York: HarperCollins, 1994.

Wheatley, Margaret J. *Leadership and the New Science: Learning about Organization from an Orderly Universe.* San Francisco: Berrett-Koehler Publishers, 1994.

White, Donald W. *The American Century: The Rise and Decline of the United States as a World Power.* New Haven: Yale University Press, 1996.

Whiteley, Richard, and Diane Hessan. *Customer-Centered Growth: Five Proven Strategies for Building Competitive Advantage.* Reading: Addison-Wesley Publishing Co., 1996.

Whyte, David. *The Heart Aroused: Poetry and the Preservation of the Soul in Corporate America.* New York: Doubleday, 1994.

Wilson, William J. *When Work Disappears: The World of the New Urban Poor.* New York: Alfred A. Knopf, 1996.

Wurman, Richard S. *Information Anxiety: What to Do When Information Doesn't Tell You What You Need to Know.* New York: Bantam Doubleday Publishing Group, 1989.

Zunz, Olivier. *Making America Corporate, 1870–1920.* Chicago: University of Chicago Press, 1990.

INDEX